THE EVERYTHING

START YOUR OWN BUSINESS BOOK
3RD EDITION

Dear Reader,

If you have been thinking about starting a business but are not certain you have all the information necessary to get going, this book will show you the way. Whether you're ready to move a favorite pastime or hobby into a profit-making venture or have a concept for an e-commerce business, you'll find the fundamental information you need to get started.

One of the trickiest parts of business planning is financial forecasting: predicting when a business will become profitable. This book shows you how to prepare a break-even analysis so you can plot your own path to profitability.

There is no reason your idea or dream cannot become a reality. As long as you go into your new venture with your eyes wide open and understand the risks and responsibilities, you should be able to bring your idea into being. Taking the time to research what is involved in starting and running a business can save a lot of pain and heartache later. There are many resources available to help you along the way, from government agencies such as the Small Business Administration, to websites such as Allbusiness.com, to entrepreneurial publications and the expertise of established entrepreneurs you may already know. Take advantage of all of them and you will soon be on the road to your own successful venture.

Judy Harrington

Welcome to the EVERYTHING® Series!

These handy, accessible books give you all you need to tackle a difficult project, gain a new hobby, comprehend a fascinating topic, prepare for an exam, or even brush up on something you learned back in school but have since forgotten.

You can choose to read an *Everything*® book from cover to cover or just pick out the information you want from our four useful boxes: e-questions, e-facts, e-alerts, and e-ssentials.

We give you everything you need to know on the subject, but throw in a lot of fun stuff along the way, too.

We now have more than 400 *Everything*® books in print, spanning such wide-ranging categories as weddings, pregnancy, cooking, music instruction, foreign language, crafts, pets, New Age, and so much more. When you're done reading them all, you can finally say you know *Everything*®!

QUESTION

Answers to
common questions

FACT

Important snippets
of information

ALERT

Urgent
warnings

ESSENTIAL

Quick
handy tips

PUBLISHER Karen Cooper

DIRECTOR OF ACQUISITIONS AND INNOVATION Paula Munier

MANAGING EDITOR, EVERYTHING® SERIES Lisa Laing

COPY CHIEF Casey Ebert

ACQUISITIONS EDITOR Lisa Laing

EDITORIAL ASSISTANT Ross Weisman

EVERYTHING® SERIES COVER DESIGNER Erin Alexander

LAYOUT DESIGNERS Colleen Cunningham, Michelle Roy Kelly,

Elisabeth Lariviere, Ashley Vierra, Denise Wallace

THE EVERYTHING®
START YOUR OWN
BUSINESS
BOOK

3RD EDITION WITH CD

A step-by-step guide to starting, managing,
and building a profitable business

Judith B. Harrington

Avon, Massachusetts

This book is dedicated to my father,
John Quinn Birmingham, Jr.

An Everything® Series Book.
Everything® and everything.com® are registered trademarks of F+W Media, Inc.

Published by Adams Media, a division of F+W Media, Inc.
57 Littlefield Street, Avon, MA 02322 U.S.A.
www.adamsmedia.com

The accompanying CD contains material adapted and abridged from *The Everything® Start Your Own Business Book, 2nd Edition,* by Judith B. Harrington, copyright © 2006, 2002 by F+W Media, Inc., ISBN 10: 1-59337-661-8, ISBN 13: 978-1-59337-661-1; *The Everything® Accounting Book,* by Michele Cagan, CPA, copyright © 2007 by F+W Media, Inc., ISBN 10: 1-59337-718-5, ISBN 13: 978-1-59337-718-2; *Streetwise Sales Letters with CD,* by Sue Reynard and David Weiss, copyright © 2001 by F+W Media, Inc., ISBN 10: 1-58062-440-5, ISBN 13: 978-1-58062-440-4; and *Streetwise Incorporating Your Business,* by Michele Cagan, CPA, copyright © 2007 by F+W Media, Inc., ISBN 10: 1-59869-094-9, ISBN 13: 978-1-59869-094-1.

ISBN 10: 1-4405-0407-5
ISBN 13: 978-1-4405-0407-5
eISBN 10: 1-4405-0408-3
eISBN 13: 978-1-4405-0408-2

Printed in the United States of America.

10 9 8 7 6 5 4 3 2 1

Library of Congress Cataloging-in-Publication Data
is available from the publisher.

This publication is designed to provide accurate and authoritative information with regard to the subject matter covered. It is sold with the understanding that the publisher is not engaged in rendering legal, accounting, or other professional advice. If legal advice or other expert assistance is required, the services of a competent professional person should be sought.
—From a *Declaration of Principles* jointly adopted by a Committee of the American Bar Association and a Committee of Publishers and Associations

Many of the designations used by manufacturers and sellers to distinguish their products are claimed as trademarks. Where those designations appear in this book and Adams Media was aware of a trademark claim, the designations have been printed with initial capital letters.

This book is available at quantity discounts for bulk purchases.
For information, please call 1-800-289-0963.

Contents

Acknowledgments

A special shout-out to Lisa Laing of Adams Media for her wisdom and coaching. Again, thanks to my family of stalwart troupers through this, my fourth book, in one fashion or another: Wes, Heather, Teddy, Kyle, and now the addition of Quinn.

Top 10 Things You'll Learn from This Book

1. How to avoid the usual pitfalls of a young business.

2. How to determine when your business idea will become profitable.

3. Ways to assess risk and, even better, how to manage it.

4. How to put together a business plan.

5. Ideas on how to finance your start-up.

6. Discover resources you already have that you might not have realized.

7. How to make the most of any business online.

8. How to turn adversity into opportunity.

9. Tips for keeping your business in the winner's circle after it's up and going.

10. The best ways to sensibly incorporate green planning into any business idea.

Introduction

IT ALL STARTS WITH an idea. A really great idea—yours. Your eureka moment comes when you realize you have the capacity to take that idea, hobby, or part-time activity and turn it into a full-time profitable business. You feel in your gut you have the ability to take control of your professional destiny and achieve financial success. But are you aware of the risks and challenges of owning a business? In this book you will find the key aspects of owning a business that can make or break you.

Most entrepreneurial ideas come from one of two types of folks. The first are those who have a passion for a particular field, an activity, product, or service and want to bring it to market. A fly fishing aficionado may want to open a tackle shop. A corporate sales trainer may want to go out on her own and provide training on a contractual basis.

Another group of entrepreneurs are people who are captivated by the dynamics of owning a business. These are business school majors or capitalists who are seeking profitable businesses to open and run. For these individuals the running of a business is their passion, as opposed to a particular field.

Either approach can lead to great success. Whether you're thinking about the advantages of working for yourself rather than others, or seeking various business alternatives, this book is for you.

Starting and running a business requires a great deal of knowledge. Setting realistic goals for yourself and your business—weekly, monthly, quarterly, and annually—is critical to success. Build step by step, and focus on getting the business off the ground rather than getting lost in dreams of a lavish lifestyle that might come with huge financial success down the road. You won't be able to own the best hardware store in Albuquerque if you don't have a retail location and the paint, tools, and other supplies your customers will be seeking. Once you have launched your business, continue to set reachable goals, and make new plans often, checking to make sure they're realistic. Don't let the business become mundane. If you lose interest, why would your customers be interested? Longevity may come from reinventing yourself from time to time with an updated look or image, or new products or services.

Become familiar with who your customers are—their likes and dislikes. Reading trade publications (every industry has them), networking with others in the business community, joining organizations, reading or even writing blogs about your field, and communicating with your clientele are ways to stay in touch with those people who will make or break your business—your customers. Good customer relations are critical to any successful business.

To start and run a successful business you'll need a lot of information, but the basics are simple. Maintain a positive attitude, stay current with the times and market, stay focused and motivated, plan step by step, get to know your customers, and keep a close eye on all monetary transactions.

In this book you will find important information for each stage of starting and running a business. The book takes a general approach that you can apply to your individual business concept. You will find specifics on tasks such as writing a business plan, calculating the break-even point where your business becomes profitable, and using the Internet to grow your business. You may find yourself looking back at different chapters as you build your business, first as a concept, and then for real. The most important function of this book, and of all the resources you use when starting and running a business, is to answer your questions. By reading this book, you're already off to a great start!

CHAPTER 1

Ready, Set, Go!

Making your start in a new business, even if it is only new to you, can be one of the most thrilling and rewarding experiences in the world. No one sets off expecting to fail, nor should you. Success will not rain down on your head, however, without a lot of preparation, diligence, guts, risk taking, and perseverance. Before you can have a happy ending, you must begin at the beginning. Read on to see if you are ready to launch your idea.

Self-Evaluation

While it is true that starting and running a business is difficult, it's done all the time, and done very successfully, by many individuals who have built empires large and small. It's done by Wall Streeters and by everyday people who simply want to be their own bosses. Business takes many forms and, thanks to the capitalist system, a business can flourish if it's run well.

Before you even consider starting your own business, you need to determine whether you're the right person for the job. Would you hire you? The position in question involves being your own boss and running the show, which includes bookkeeping, short- and long-term organizing, marketing, providing customer service, possibly maintaining an inventory, supervising other employees, and establishing investor relations. Most importantly, the job hinges on your ability to make many key decisions, some on short notice, and the effectiveness of your people skills, since nearly every business involves interaction with others. You may be skilled in all of these key areas, but if you aren't, you'll have to find other people who can assist you by providing strengths in areas where you aren't as well versed.

Here's a list of traits and characteristics that will help you to run a business successfully:

- The ability to gather facts and make important decisions
- The ability to stay motivated, even when the business starts off slowly, as most businesses do
- Good organizational skills
- Good communication skills
- Stick-to-it drive that keeps you working long hours to get the job done
- Physical stamina to weather the long hours and lack of sleep that may be part of the job, especially in the early stages of the business
- The ability to get along well with many different types of personalities
- A diplomatic manner of harnessing or managing anger and frustration
- Confidence in your skills, knowledge, and abilities to run a specific type of business
- Confidence in your ability to find the answers to questions you don't yet know

- The ability to be firm or flexible, as required, so you can make adjustments or changes in your plans
- The ability to successfully balance a business life and a personal life

The last item on this list is the toughest one for many people who find that their business eats into their family, social, and leisure time. There are twenty-four hours in a day. You need to know from the outset that you can't work all of them, or even most of them, and remain sane. While running a business takes many hours and extreme dedication, if you sacrifice everything else in your life, you will eventually have regrets and even jeopardize your own well-being, as well as the business itself. A business is not worth building if you can't stick around to see it prosper. It's important to be able to enjoy the fruits of your labor.

ESSENTIAL

You will need to know every aspect of your business, not just the areas that involve your particular interests or strengths. Even if you delegate some tasks, such as bookkeeping or inventory management, you will need to be aware of how things stand at all times. Sometimes small mistakes can tank an otherwise worthwhile business. Don't get blindsided.

Be honest with yourself and determine how many of the previously listed skills and talents you possess. How many do you see yourself learning? How many indicate the need for a business partner (or partners) to fill the void? How many simply do not describe you? If it's more than 40 percent, then you may not be ready right now to go into your own business. It's better to make that determination early on. After all, if you conclude that you aren't ready to start a business, all you've invested thus far is the price of this book.

Pros of Starting Your Own Business

While nonprofit organizations deploy their resources to serve the needs of others, most commercial businesses are built on someone's desire to chase the American Dream. If you aren't looking to reach a goal by opening up a business, then why go through all the trouble? As it turns out, there are quite a lot of pros associated with this great endeavor. Here are just a few:

- You are your own boss. No longer are you working for someone else. You only have to answer to yourself (and your investors, the bank, the IRS, and regulatory agencies). You get to make the big decisions for a change. You may also be the boss of other people, which will let you display your leadership abilities.
- The sky's the limit. Hoorah for capitalism! You can become the next Bill Gates or Meg Whitman, or at least enjoy financial independence. Working for yourself may afford you the opportunity to make more money than working for somebody else. The risks are greater, but the potential rewards are greater as well.
- You can prove yourself. You have the opportunity to use your skills, abilities, and creativity to do things your way. You can fully utilize your attributes, including ones that may have been stifled in your former workplace.
- You'll have a hand in all aspects of the business. Unlike working for someone else's business where you're only responsible for your area of expertise, you'll be involved in all areas of the business—from funding and finance to many of the smaller daily details.
- You'll take pride in promoting and marketing your own company. While many sales and marketing people take great pride in the work they do and the company they work for, there is a special feeling you get when touting your own business.
- You decide where to locate your business. Tired of commuting an hour or more every day in slow-moving traffic to get to the office? Now you can set up the office closer to home or open up a store just ten minutes away. You might even work from home.

From the design of the website and company logo to the sales strategy and marketing plan, it's your call, your ball game, and your business. There's something exciting and invigorating, yet scary, about going into business for yourself. Like a roller-coaster ride, starting a business has the proverbial ups and downs. For all the parts of your business plan that work, there will be a few parts that won't work at first and will need revising.

Good ideas will compete with bad ones, and all the positives of going into business have a flip side, reasons for not going into business.

ALERT

You'll see many tempting ads for how to earn money with little effort. Don't believe them. Avoid anything that smacks of a pyramid scheme in which you recruit people who in turn recruit others and somehow everyone gets a piece of everyone's sales.

Cons of Starting Your Own Business

Whenever there are pros, there are offsetting cons. In the previous section, you saw some of the positive aspects of starting your own business. It's important also to be aware of some of the negatives:

- No guaranteed salary or paycheck. There is always a financial risk involved in starting a business. Not only may you not make money for some period of time, you very likely will have to put your own money into the business. It may be some time before you're in a position to pay yourself. Depending on the type of business, it often takes three to five years to show a net profit after all expenses, and sometimes even longer.
- It's all on your shoulders. While it's good to be the king during times of prosperity, you will also occupy the throne during lean times. In other words, along with making the exciting and fun decisions, like where to hold the grand-opening party, you'll have some tough decisions to make, such as choosing which of two valued employees to let go because you can't afford to keep them both on the payroll.
- You can't please everyone. When you work for someone else, you may be able to excel in the art of making your boss happy, or even thrilled, with your performance. As the boss, however, there will be occasions when you won't be able to make everyone or even anyone happy, and will have to make some hard choices in the best interests of the business. Keeping customers satisfied, employees feeling valued, and investors happy can be a dicey balancing act.

- The 168-hour week. There are 168 hours in a seven-day week. You may find yourself sacrificing other aspects of your life to work a good portion of those hours. Starting a business can take away from a lot of other aspects of your life. There are numerous responsibilities and plenty of administrative details that are not the fun part of being a business owner. If finances allow, you can hire people to handle much of this work. However, you will need to train people, review their work, and maintain some control over all areas of the business. No one has the same vested interest in the overall success of an enterprise as the owner.
- Growing pains. Some businesses grow smoothly while (most) others experience growing pains. These are the times when there may be a drop-off in progress because the market, industry, or economy slows down, or because competition heats up. You will need to be ready to ride out the storm each time your business hits a rough patch.

Before You Start

Plenty of business owners, for better or worse, don't sit down and thoroughly develop their goals before starting out. Some of the most successful entrepreneurs will tell you that if they had realized what they were getting into, they probably would have lost the nerve to start a business in the first place. Other business owners say that they wish they had thought it all through more carefully and been able to foresee some of the pitfalls they had to deal with once the business was off and running. To get a basic feel for the road that lies ahead, it's important to ask yourself three basic questions.

What Are Your Goals?

Yes, you want to make money, but how much and how fast? Do you see yourself running a mom-and-pop store, or do you hope to own a national chain in several years? Is this a business you hope your children will run for years after you retire, or do you hope to build a successful business over the next ten years, sell it, and retire in some exotic locale with plenty of cash? Are you looking at altruistic goals? After all, people don't open recycling centers or even thrift shops without a sense of responsibility to the community. There are many goals beyond the obvious one of making money. You may also ask yourself how much money is enough? How will you know if you have created a successful business if you have nothing by which to gauge success?

As crazy as it sounds, it's possible to bring a product to market too soon, before customers know they need it. You also don't want to be too late coming to market. The last thing you want to do is invest in launching a product or service if there is no ready market for it. Investigate the market to find if it is the right time and place for your idea before investing too much time and money in your plan.

How Well Do You Understand Business?

You don't need to be an astute reader of the Wall Street Journal to open a business. Eight-year-olds who can barely read the famed financial paper can set up a lemonade stand and rake in some cash on a hot day. However, it's important that you understand business principles as they pertain to your business concept. Do you have a good idea of all that is involved in running a business? This includes bookkeeping, paying taxes, paying employees and vendors, signing contracts, making deals, marketing, and operating in accordance with state, local, and county rules, laws, and regulations. You don't have to know how to do all of this before you start out, but you will have to be ready to research what you don't know and learn as you proceed.

How Will Running a Business Impact Your Life?

Can you emotionally and financially roll with the uncertainty a business faces until it shows a profit? Can your family handle it? Will you be able to maintain a life outside of the business? How motivated are you? How well do you deal with adversity? If running a business is going to turn your hair gray before you reach thirty-five and give you an ulcer, then perhaps the comfort and security of working for someone else isn't so bad after all.

You need to assess how well you can balance the many demands of a business, emotionally and physically, with the rest of your life. You need to be able to have a life away from your business; otherwise, you'll lose all perspective. If you neglect other areas of your life, such as family and health, in the end the business will also suffer as a result. It's important to nourish yourself by maintaining interests and activities that refresh you. Down time away from the business actually let's your mind sift through ideas and issues, enabling you to bring fresh thinking to your challenges.

Know What You Don't Know

Often, the best way to get a feel for what to do is by being aware of what not to do. Instead of making mistakes and learning the hard way, you can learn from the mistakes of others. In the following sections, you'll find some advice to help you avoid the pitfalls and common mistakes that often go along with starting your own business.

Determine Your Target Audience

Too often, when asked whom their business will appeal to, people starting a business say "everybody." Unfortunately, while you would like everyone to be a customer, huge variations in demographics, and other factors will make it virtually impossible to attract everyone. Most businesses cater to a particular segment of the population. If you're lucky, there will be some crossover audience, but for the most part, you'll need to set your sights on a specific target audience of potential customers, whether it's baby boomers, seniors, investors, athletes, or kids.

Don't Act Impulsively

Not doing the proper research is a big no-no. You need to know all about the business you're entering. Learn all the details. Spend time checking out locations, competitors, banks, places to find resources, and so forth. Know what permits and licenses you need to obtain. Save yourself headaches later by being prepared up front.

Have a Marketing Plan

There are plenty of ways to spread the word that you're in business. However, all of these methods take planning. You may have the best product or service in the world, but if you don't market it, no one will know about it. You will need to allocate funds for your marketing.

Don't Ignore the Competition

How will you know if your prices are competitive if you don't know what your competitors are up to? You'll need to thoroughly check out your competition before you open your doors for business. Find out who's selling the same products or offering similar services. Get a feel for what the competition is doing, how successful they are, and what you can do differently to carve a niche in the market. It's also a good idea, if possible, to figure out who else may be considering coming into the market. If you get wind of a major national company planning on moving into your field, you might feel like David vs. Goliath. You might still have the edge with local connections, but it's always best to know where you stand in relation to others in your field.

FACT

Keeping an eye on your competition should be an ongoing exercise. You should always be looking for that little something extra to set you apart from the crowd. It might be lower prices or deluxe service. However you do it, you need to distinguish yourself from others offering the same goods or services.

Don't Underestimate Your Time Frame to Profitability

Having a sound business plan, being aware of the competition, meeting the needs of your customers, and executing a solid marketing strategy can make your business successful sooner rather than later. However, it takes time to build a reputation and gain steady customers. During that time, you will exhaust a great deal of funding. Don't ignore the numbers. If they tell you that it should take three years to show a profit, then don't start spending "profits" in the first six months before you have any. Too many businesses (particularly those that are web-based) have made the mistake of spending paper profits. At first, this system worked, as everyone went along with high hopes. Then reality set in as banks and venture capitalists looked at profit-and-loss statements and said to web entrepreneurs, "Show me the real money."

Don't Cut the Wrong Corners

While you don't want to spend money foolishly, you need to carefully determine where to save and where to spend money. Spending a fortune to create a product, then saving money by not having an advertising or marketing campaign is a colossal waste of your efforts. Cutting the sales force may save you money, but cripple your revenues. Find appropriate places to save money.

Focus on People, Not Just Technology

While technology can do wonders, it will not substitute for good relationships with your customers and employees. Don't let yourself become so consumed by technology, or anything else for that matter, that you neglect to train, motivate, and appreciate your staff. And always practice good customer relations. Technology by itself cannot forge strong bonds between people. Use it as a tool to reach your objectives.

Don't Bite Off More Than You Can Chew

Many businesses are built in phases, and for good reason. If you plan to stock your brick-and-mortar location while building a website, starting up a mail-order division, and maybe putting together a catalog to coincide with your grand opening, you may be trying to do too much at once. Even major companies roll out new products and open new divisions in a carefully planned manner. This allows them to focus on each step of the process. Start small, and let the business grow. This works best from a financial standpoint, and safeguards your time and resources, as well.

Thinking Like a Businessperson

If you're going to be an entrepreneur, you'll need to think like one. So, before you determine which business is best for you, take a moment to make sure you've mastered Business Think.

First, you need to see yourself as a people person. You need to be able to establish and maintain many relationships in a professional business manner, including those with suppliers, customers, investors, and the bank. You must be confident in yourself in a leadership role, being able to successfully motivate and manage employees. You need to be able to communicate effectively with a variety of personality types. Present yourself professionally, offer the short version of what your business is all about, and listen and learn from others. You need to conduct yourself maturely without letting your emotions take control. You also need to hone your networking skills. Collect business cards and practice matching names to faces so that you remember who's who.

Next, you need to be both driven and confident in your ability to stay focused and not lose sight of, or give up on, your goal. Initially, your business will seem like a 24/7 proposition. Even during non-business hours, you will focus on aspects of the business and constantly be thinking of ways it can be improved. You need to be able to act and react when necessary. For example, you may be on vacation in Tahiti when you get a message that your supplier has gone out of business. You instantly need to find another supplier to make delivery deadlines. In other words, you're never completely away from a business, if it's yours.

And finally, you need to think like a successful entrepreneur by continually looking for new opportunities and figuring out how you can use them to your advantage. Your mindset must include business radar, which involves looking at products and services in a whole new way. Look for what is being done well, what can be improved upon, and what is lacking or missing. You will become much more critical of other goods and services and may find yourself thinking as a consumer advocate. A shrewd business thinker can assess the positives and negatives of products, services, and of other businesses and evaluate the effectiveness of the competition's every move.

ESSENTIAL

It's important to realize your strengths and weaknesses so that you can hire people accordingly to handle various areas for you. A craftsperson might want to run an Internet retail business selling his crafts over the web. He may not be versed in the technical aspects of the Internet, however, and should bring in someone who is able to set up and maintain the website.

Once you're secure in your leadership abilities, have the drive and determination to see your business ideas through to fruition, and learn to look at the business world as a strategist seeing new opportunities, you will have mastered Business Think. Here's a list of questions to ask yourself to measure your progress:

- How well can you formulate new business strategies and research them? Can you open your eyes and ears to draw new ideas for your business from other areas of your life?
- Can you present your business to others in an enticing, succinct, and compelling manner?
- Are you able to establish and maintain relationships that benefit your business?
- Do you have ways to regularly keep in touch with people?
- Can you take feedback and criticism constructively?
- Are you able to present a positive image of your business and get your employees or staff to do the same?
- Can you earn the respect of your employees or staff?
- Are you able to make customers or clients feel special?
- Can you motivate yourself to stay focused even when things go wrong?
- Can you motivate others and rally employees, family, neighbors, and friends around your business venture?
- Can you handle the risks that come with starting your own business and remain focused on the long-term goal of turning a profit?
- How well can you spot potential opportunities to enhance your business?
- How good are you at staying abreast of new developments in your chosen industry?

- Do you know how to keep accurate records?
- Can you gauge how much your products or services are worth?
- Do you have the skills for maintaining a budget?
- Can you find ways to maximize profits through modifications of the business?

These are just some of the questions that you should ponder while teaching yourself Business Think. Each of these areas will become part of your mindset as you explore business possibilities. The areas in which you're strongest may be those that point you toward one type of business as opposed to another. For example, a people person will be more likely to open a retail business or service business that deals with the public than someone who is a skilled craftsperson and is not interested in dealing directly with customers.

Talk to the Experts

It's very hard to build a business in a vacuum. The feedback, suggestions, and opinions of others can be extremely valuable in getting a business off the ground. In fact, companies pay large sums of money for studies and focus groups that answer a lot of their key business questions before they present goods or services to the public.

QUESTION

What are small business development centers (SBDCs), and how can they help?
Small business development centers are quasi-government agencies located across the country. Usually based in college or university settings, their mission is to coach business owners and teach them how to solve specific problems. Classes and workshops are offered and individual counseling can be scheduled.

Advisors need not be successful businesspeople. They can be friends or even relatives who simply promise to provide objective opinions. You might even put together an advisory board to discuss ideas with as they arise. However, someone who has already opened a business and knows how to get from the idea phase to turning a profit can be a valuable mentor.

Whomever you choose, be ready to ask your advisor many questions. Keep thinking of new angles to approaching your business, and bounce them off other people. Ask others to play devil's advocate. They used to say that you could pan thousands of pieces of rock before coming up with just one piece of gold, but in the end it was worth the search. The same holds true with ideas. The more alternatives you consider, the more likely you'll be to find the ones that are best for your business.

Plan Your Exit Strategy Now

Thinking about leaving your business before it has even been hatched may seem counterintuitive. Yet, it is one of the most important planning steps you will make. You may have a vision of taking your company public after a few years of rapid growth. You may have a dream of taking care of future generations by providing employment and income through your enterprise. Or perhaps you don't want your surviving spouse and heirs to have to worry about the business at all. So you plan to strike a buy/sell agreement with a worthy competitor who will have right of first refusal to buy the business at a fair market price. Whatever the scenario, eventually you will no longer be involved in the business; whether you are savoring your newly fattened bank account or are pushing up daisies, an end will come. Now is the time to set forth a plan that covers a number of contingencies. As time goes on, you will want to revisit your exit strategy and make adjustments accordingly. Be ready for your harvest.

CHAPTER 2

Choosing a Business

Business dreams come in all shapes and sizes, and making one come true is an experience that can take many forms. You might be stepping into a family firm, buying a franchise, launching an e-commerce business, or hanging out your shingle. In any case, you'll need to understand what you are in for. This chapter covers various business options, as well as ways to help you judge what's right for you.

All You Need Is One Great Idea

Starting up a business requires some levelheaded thinking about risks and rewards, in addition to a lot of careful planning. For just a moment, put aside all the research that you'll need to do to determine whether your business venture appears worthwhile. Dream about a perfect world in which your business is sure to be a success. Ask yourself the following questions:

- What is it that you really enjoy doing?
- What would give you a sense of satisfaction?
- What type of business would make you proud?
- What type of business could you immerse yourself in for fifty, sixty, or seventy hours a week?
- Do you want to run a full-time business or a sideline, part-time business?
- Do you see yourself in an office? Online only? In a storefront location? Working from home?

Once you've painted a mental picture of your perfect world, the next step is to start applying it to real market conditions and your personal situation. Questions to ask yourself at this stage include:

- What would you enjoy doing every day that could be profitable?
- Will people pay for this service or the products you want to sell?
- How much financial backing do you think you can get?
- How much of your money can you afford to invest?
- What resources can you gather to run a business?
- How much time and effort can you put into a business without sacrificing other aspects of your life?

Design the perfect business scenario for yourself. No, you probably won't end up with that exact picture, but at least you'll have an idea of what it is you're looking to achieve. If, after five years, you find yourself in a situation that's close to what you pictured, then you've done very well indeed. After all, since we aren't living in a perfect world, you can't expect the scenario to play out precisely as you envisioned.

ALERT

People who've become successful in business often forget to look back at their initial dream and realize how close they are. They focus on the 30 percent they haven't accomplished and neglect to see the 70 percent they have. Always remember that most successful big businesses grow step by step.

For some people, the right business is centered around a practical skill, such as sewing, carpentry, or cooking, while for others it is based on knowledge or expertise in a technical area. If you are headed in this direction, surround yourself with people, articles, books, blogs, magazines, and anything else you can find to support your area of interest. Take classes to hone your skills and enhance your knowledge. Join an organization or association. The idea is to get yourself immersed in this area of interest and determine whether it is a hobby or something you really want to pour your heart, soul, and money into. Meanwhile, you also need to be looking to see if the marketplace supports your desires. Unfortunately, you may love to do something that is either too narrow in scope to make money at, or so popular that other people with the same interests and skills have already gained too strong a hold on the market.

Not All Good Ideas Are Profitable

The sad truth is that your dream venture may in fact not be financially viable. Before going too far down the primrose path, you need to answer some hard questions to determine whether your idea can succeed as a business enterprise. As part of your preparation, take the time to write a solid business plan to test the economic soundness of your concept. Find out how big the market is for the product or service you are envisioning. Be sure to look at comparable products and try to learn all you can about the costs for producing, promoting, and delivering them to the marketplace. Try to learn what kind of net profit margins exist in that industry.

When you are determining if your undertaking can make a profit, you will want to figure out your overall strategy. Will you be a low-cost merchandiser? Years ago there was a store in Massachusetts called Spags, which was a forerunner of the big-box discount outlets. Their famous tagline was "No bags at Spags," which conveyed their cost-saving strategy to consumers. As with the big discounters today—Costco, BJ's, Sam's Club, and the like—customers had to carry their purchases out of the store without bags.

Conversely, you may opt to aim for the high end of service and quality, which justifies correspondingly higher pricing. In either case, selling budget or deluxe, you need to clarify your objective and then do the research to decide if you can make a profit before you commit to a doomed undertaking.

Buying a Proven Winner

Sometimes the fastest way to get going in business is to buy a business that is already going. However, you will need to do your due diligence before signing on the dotted line. As you weigh this option, consider the following pros and cons:

PROS

- No start-up phase
- Possibly big savings in start-up costs
- Existing client base
- Going concern in marketplace
- Good will already established
- May be able to purchase only the assets you want and not assume liabilities
- Immediate cash flow
- Easier financing opportunities as an existing business

CONS

- Old receivables may be hard to collect
- Customers may not be loyal to business
- May be more costly than starting from scratch
- Takes time and money to research opportunities of good value
- Relocation may be necessary for you and your family
- May be difficult to change established reputation—good or bad—in the market

Franchises—Thumbs Up or Down

Just as there are many advantages to buying an existing business, there are also specific pluses to buying a franchise. First, the product or service is established and may already have a national reputation. Marketing is structured and supported by the overall corporation. Training and guidance for success is provided.

Challenges to consider in buying a franchise may include finding a suitable location, a very high financial bar for the initial investment, ongoing financial obligations, and lack of flexibility in how to present, price, and promote the product or service. It also may be difficult to get solid information on the expected profitability of the franchise you are considering.

ALERT

As you ponder buying a franchise, you will want to do an honest assessment. Do you relish the structure that operating within a franchise framework will provide, or will you chafe at it? Is there a market for this product in your area?

Not all franchisers offer the same degree of expertise and support. How will you know if the one you are interested in suits your goals? One way to find out is by studying the franchiser's disclosure document, known as the "uniform franchise offering circular" (UFOC). Here you will find key facts about initial and recurring fees. The document will include the amount of your initial investment, as well as a list of references you can call—folks who own or have owned franchises. Call them and discuss their experience with this franchiser. If you are looking at a publicly traded franchise outfit, read their SEC filings, annual reports, and other public records to learn their financial track record.

Services

From dog walkers to financial consultants, people all over the world sell their expertise by performing services for others. Clowning at parties, window washing, computer repair, catering, childcare, hairstyling, public relations, graphic design, and business consulting are just some of the countless services that you may be able to provide.

Having the ability is only part of the plan. Like sales, starting a service business requires contacts, contacts, and more contacts. That means finding ways to spread the word and let people know that you're ready to perform your service for a fee. You'll need to investigate the going rate for your service, based on what others with your background and knowledge are getting. Rates will also be influenced by the part of the country where you're planning to provide the service.

ESSENTIAL

In addition to setting fees at a profitable, yet competitive, level, you should be aware of out-of-pocket expenses your service may require, and be properly reimbursed for them. Don't be shy about explaining that you will be charging the customer for postage for a marketing campaign or for purchasing diapers for your day care.

The more you specialize, the less competition you'll have. However, the more you specialize, the smaller the potential market will be. A public relations firm for medical and pharmaceutical companies, for example, will not be in competition with PR firms that serve the entertainment industry. However, you will have to market yourself that much more carefully to your defined target audience. On the positive side, finding a niche or specialty can make you highly sought after if you're good at what you do, and thus the word of your expertise can easily spread.

Sometimes, the market is in need of businesses providing your service (or has room for more). For example, an entertainment PR firm might still be able to find a market in Los Angeles, even though there is stiff competition, because the entertainment industry is so large in that area. However, the new firm may need to focus on a niche, such as child actors, and provide services or contacts that the competition cannot provide. This can make a new company valuable.

Billable hours are the key to making profits in the service industry. Your overhead may be low, but time is money, and you will need to keep precise records of how many hours you put into a project. Many skilled individuals fail when going into business for themselves because they don't keep careful track of their hours and end up spending way too much time on a project without being fairly compensated. Flat fees can spell trouble unless you do the math ahead of time and calculate how much you're actually getting hourly. A good service provider charges a competitive but fair rate and offers first-rate service with extras, while not compromising professionalism or wasting valuable time.

You can also set up and run a service-oriented business without providing the service yourself. You may decide to open a catering business because you know several excellent cooks and own a van. You would approach the business as the coordinator and manager, making sure that all the pieces fit together. Building a service business means finding the right mix of talented people who possess the necessary skills, the ability to work well with clients, and the ability to follow direction—both yours and the clients'.

The key to a service-oriented business is providing services that earn you a strong reputation. As a service provider, you can build your business through satisfied customers telling other potential customers how wonderful you are. Word-of-mouth promotion can save you a bundle on paid advertising and make or break a service business.

If you're thinking of opening up a service business, consider that you will:

- Perhaps need proper licensing
- Need promotion and marketing
- Have to handle the bookkeeping and record keeping—or hire someone to do it
- Need to provide good customer service

Retail

Whether you're selling tubas or T-shirts, the principle is the same: You're trying to get people to buy your product. The sales approach, venue, and products are quite different, but the idea is to make your customers see why your product is right for them.

Retailing is a special entity unto itself. It involves selling to the public, which most often includes drawing customers to your store or sales location, even if it a virtual location online. Then you need to present your merchandise in an appealing manner. You must have strategically placed displays, a well-stocked inventory, and a store layout designed so that customers will easily find what they're looking for as well as discover new items they'll find appealing.

A traditional retail business comes with numerous specific responsibilities beyond the business plan, need for capital, and other aspects of business in general. You need to:

- Determine which products your customers want that will also provide best profit margins
- Find the best possible location
- Determine which items are more popular than others and, hence, more marketable
- Locate suppliers, wholesalers, or distributors
- Buy display cases, equipment, and all the necessary accoutrements
- Hire employees whom you can trust
- Stock the store and maintain the stock
- Establish pricing and store policies
- Purchase insurance
- Set up an alarm system, and possibly include cameras and a security guard
- Offer amenities, such as free parking or gift-wrapping
- Market, promote, and advertise
- Keep tabs on your competition
- Set business hours that are convenient for your customers

And that's just the beginning. While you may know a wealth of information about antiques and want to open an antique shop, there's much more than knowledge of the product that goes into a retail business. Besides all that it takes to open the store, you'll have to market your store and establish your presence in the community. There's also the issue of customer relations to consider. It's important that you find ways to make the customer feel special. Some stores today go to great lengths to enhance the shopping experience and build customer loyalty. Many have adapted the airlines' frequent flyer model by using frequent purchase cards rewarding customers with a discount or free product after certain conditions have been met. The more you offer and the better the customer experience, the lower the likelihood that your customers will be drawn to the competition.

Once your retail business is off and running, you'll need to focus on maintaining inventory and adding new products. This provides you with an opportunity to get creative with new displays, promotions, and ideas to attract customers.

Many people thrive on the busy, round-the-clock effort it takes to open and build a successful retail business. In addition to this great amount of time and effort, it requires a good location, organizational skills, and retail know-how (which often comes from being in business awhile). It also takes a keen awareness of the industry. Ask someone in the clothing business a question about two different fabrics. If she's been in business for several years, chances are she'll be able to talk for five minutes on the virtues of each fabric.

Business-to-Business (B2B)

While a store has the benefit of walk-in business, and a good location can make all the difference in the world, B2B sales are very much built around contacts, networking, and creating a list of potential customers. In business-to-business selling, the product or service is tailored to commercial customers, not individual consumers. An example would be a business travel agency that caters to corporate travelers who want the best rate at hotels convenient to airports or major business centers, rather than palm trees and piña coladas. Another might be a security service that offers night guards for office buildings or stores. Business-to-business selling is also based on maintaining satisfied customers; relationships and repeat business are key. The more specific your product or service, the more you will need to rely on steady clients.

To build the business, you may attend meetings of the local chamber of commerce, link to websites of colleagues, or mail a CD-ROM to prospective customers. In whatever manner you do it, you need to find new clients and stay in touch with your current clients to make sure they're satisfied. Let your regular customers know about new products and special deals, or offers that only they can enjoy.

A knack for selling successfully includes having the right look (polished and professional) and sufficient knowledge to present yourself and your products or services in a confident, self-assured (not cocky) manner. Presentation is very important, so you'll need to hone your sales skills. You'll need to demonstrate to potential clients why they should establish a working relationship with your company. You'll also need to make sure they clearly see the benefits of your products or services.

Top salespeople learn that fine line between selling and overselling. They are able to hear what their customers' needs are and immediately direct them to the right product or service. Boilerplate, one-size-fits-all selling is almost nonexistent in a day and age of detailed technology and customized services. If you need training, numerous sales courses are offered at universities and through business schools. Finding a successful salesperson as a mentor is also advantageous because he will know the tricks of the trade in the area of sales you're looking to enter.

Manufacturing the Products You Sell

Opening a manufacturing business definitely requires significant capital. Plus, like all other aspects of running your own business, manufacturing takes ingenuity. If you can create a product that isn't on the market, then produce and sell it cost-effectively, you're on your way. The old supply-and-demand theory is never clearer than when you take a year to design your latest and best concept, only to find there is absolutely no demand for glow-in-the-dark toilet seats. Therefore, unless you simply enjoy a hobby and hope only to sell a few of your embroidered tea cozies to the local country store, don't dive headfirst into manufacturing anything until you have proof that people will want what you make.

FACT

Getting into manufacturing requires studying up on the details that make up the product. People who think about starting a manufacturing business should have both a thorough knowledge of and a strong interest in whatever it is they are about to manufacture.

Often manufacturing businesses start small. They may consist of two people making clocks in a basement on weekends and selling them to local stores or at flea markets. If you enjoy making something, and can make it profitably in a reasonable amount of time, you can start a small manufacturing business. Such businesses grow as the product gains in popularity. There are numerous stories of individuals who sold an item to a local store and eventually the product went national.

Creating the product is only half the battle, however. There's marketing, sales, and delivery involved, as well as keeping track of costs and overhead. One positive aspect of manufacturing is that there is often less competition because a limited number of people have the skills and resources to make a particular product.

Growing a Manufacturing Business

Consider expanding your manufacturing business not only by adding more products, but by offering repair service and by designing tools or parts that will help others use the products more efficiently. For example, if you're manufacturing eyeglass frames, you might also manufacture, or at least sell, the tools used to repair them. In addition, if you provide training in care of eyeglasses, you can make additional income. Manufacturing today often starts with making a product, and branches out to maintaining it, fixing it, and developing new ways to use it. Then the product line expands into your new lemon-scented version, low-fat version, and so forth.

Bringing Your Product to Market

Whether you're making jewelry yourself or have a small factory manufacturing handbags or sweaters by machine, you need to test market your goods. You may ask friends and neighbors what they think or bring in focus groups, but either way, you'll want good, honest appraisals on the positives and negatives of the product you're manufacturing. It's also very important that you keep up with sales trends, particularly if you're entering the fashion or technical arenas, where change is a daily occurrence.

How you introduce your line of products is also significant. Golf equipment manufacturing companies, as one example, constantly try to come up with new innovative clubs designed to hit the ball harder and straighter, balls that will travel farther, and the perfect golf shoe. They boast about the strengths of their products and the inner workings of the club or ball and compete heavily for their share of the market. It's very important that they meet the demand for new products at the major golf trade shows that take place twice a year. They then market their wares at other golf trade shows and at tournaments around the country.

As in all business, marketing is key to your success. Good salespeople are also very important. If you're running a small manufacturing business in which you're the person behind the handmade goods, you may do your own marketing and sales. You will need to reach out to the people in your industry who represent, sell, and market the types of products that you create. As the business grows, you'll seek out help in these key areas so that you can concentrate on creating the best product possible.

CHAPTER 3

When Opportunity Knocks

Sometimes a business opportunity thunders into your life when you're not expecting it. Circumstances such as a corporate downsizing that leaves you jobless may place you in the position to consider starting a business. Or perhaps you have created a unique and exciting product and want to find a way to bring it to market. Maybe a close friend or colleague taps you on the shoulder and asks you to join her in a business endeavor. Sometimes all the planning in the world yields nothing, and then when you least expect it, opportunity knocks.

The Upside to Downsizing

Young people entering the workforce today can expect a career that takes them through many different phases and employers. This experience is in sharp contrast to their grandparents, who may have had the stability of joining a firm right out of school and retiring from the same place with a tidy pension forty years later.

Then along came the technological revolution of the late twentieth century, and the norms for how business is conducted got turned upside down. The basic principles of operating profitably while offering quality products and services continue, but the manner in which these are carried out has evolved with stunning speed, in some cases leaving workers who were highly skilled, but in specific or limited areas, on the sideline.

With the advent of technological efficiencies, large companies began reducing their workforce with rapid and severe slashes in payroll. Soon thereafter, corporations began to compete globally, seeking ways to extend their reach through mergers and acquisitions. These mergers, which continue today, naturally result in duplication of certain functions, necessitating more layoffs to reduce redundancy.

One thing's for sure, there is no shame in being laid off due to a corporate downsizing or merger. So many people have gone through this mill that it is commonly accepted as not being a poor reflection on you or your performance. Sometimes it is just bad luck.

So what to do if you are one of the thousands of people who find themselves the star of an unplanned farewell party? There are two broad answers to this question: Try to keep doing what you were doing, or try something new.

Option 1: Stick with It

After being laid off, you will probably consider looking for another job in your field. But to get something at the same level or better may require relocating. If you are not currently burdened with real estate, kids in school, or other major commitments, this may be just the excuse you have needed to see another part of the country—or the world, for that matter.

Perhaps you want to continue in your field but cannot, or do not want to, make a major move to a different area. This could be a great time to review your skills and experiences and transform yourself into an independent provider of services. You may even be able to get hired as a subcontractor by the very firm that turned you out. Assuming some of the old team of managers is still there, they certainly know your talents. They would probably even be willing to pay you a higher fee than your prior salary because they are no longer carrying the overhead of your paid vacation, health benefits, 401(k) contributions, and more.

Most likely you would start off by offering your own services. Say you had been a marketing manager for a consumer products company. You have gained knowledge and experience over the years in sales promotions, developing marketing materials, and buying different types of media for advertising. You may have been involved in organizing and running trade shows for your company. Throughout all that time you were building relationships with advertising agencies, members of the media, printers, convention centers, travel agents, and hotels. You have found sources for promotional items. You have negotiated contracts. So, without missing a beat, you have a full Rolodex of talented and reliable vendors you can put to work immediately for your own customers. It may even make sense to join forces with some of these vendors and create a new, more compelling marketing firm.

Option 2: Radical Change

Have you ever found yourself driving upcountry on a beautiful fall day thinking, wouldn't it be great to chuck it all and run a charming bed and breakfast? Or maybe the secret chemist side of you has been watching the aging baby boomers drop serious money on youth-restoring creams and you are thinking, "I could do that." Well, the "woulda, coulda, shoulda" may all converge in the form of a pink slip freeing you to get started on what has only been a niggling idea until now. One of the best homemade ice-cream stores in the Northeast was started by a fellow after his high-tech company was acquired by an out-of-state corporation.

Making a big change is scary, especially when you didn't plan the change. However, you may be ready to stop working eighty hours a week for someone else and do it for yourself. When you are the boss you only need to look in the mirror to see if it is okay to leave for a few hours to watch a child's performance.

ESSENTIAL

If you're planning to make a radical shift with your new venture, perhaps trying out a field you have always thought would be fun but is unfamiliar to you, fear not. In our information-rich world, you will be able to get whatever information you need to start your new undertaking and make it flourish.

Your Idea, Someone Else's Know-How

If you perform a specialized task day in and day out, whether it's kidney surgery or installing copper gutters, you are naturally going to find ways to improve your efficiency. You may even have designed an adaptive device that improves your work and could help others carry out the task as well. If you are a medical professional or a contractor, you may not have the time or resources to organize all the steps necessary to convert your idea to a marketable product. However, there are folks out there who are seeking ideas to manufacture and bring to market.

Your widget may seem like a small miracle to you, but you will need to conduct a market analysis to determine whether enough customers would buy it to make commercialization a viable undertaking. In time, you may find a company related to your field that will purchase your design and pay you a royalty for it. Who knows—you may find you have many marketable ideas based on your real-world experience. Keep in mind that in addition to finding a manufacturer, you may also need patent protection.

It's great to have a service idea that can relieve a business owner of part of the administration duties of running a company. Getting another group to help sell your idea is better. Say you have a payroll service that small businesses can use instead of hiring a full-time bookkeeper. You can market directly to the 50,000 or so small businesses in America. Or you can let someone else do the work by targeting accounting firms who want to perform tax preparation but not bookkeeping, and would refer these duties to you.

Taking the Family Business Reins

It's possible your future career was settled before you were born. However, not all children of business owners can expect to take over a multibillion-dollar enterprise. Some folks will have to look hard at taking over the local gas station that has been in the same family for three generations or joining a law practice with one or both parents. The process of shouldering the mantle of a family enterprise can be fraught with emotional and intra-family dynamics absent in other such entrepreneurial endeavors. Such an inheritance is not all bad, though. Consider some of the advantages:

- It is an established business.
- It has an established clientele.
- It is known and valued in the community.
- There can be tax advantages as opposed to selling and distributing proceeds.
- Family members should be more naturally vested in the success of the business.
- It is possible to learn all aspects of the business before committing to take over.

The goal of passing a business on to the next generation is to preserve wealth, and possibly to provide employment for family members. To ensure minimum difficulties and challenges later, you must plan carefully in advance. An estate planner, an accountant, and an attorney all need to be involved.

You never want to make big life decisions in the throes of a crisis. The choice to take over a family business should be unhurried and dispassionate, rather than in the immediate aftermath of a death.

Before deciding to join a family business, ask the following questions:

- How will equity be determined?
- Will family members who work in the business have the same stake as those who do not?
- To what degree, if any, will the older generation remain involved?
- When and how will transition take place?
- Is there an escape clause if a sibling wants to sell shares?

- Are in-laws factored into shares of the business—how about after divorce?
- What will the decision-making process be as the company goes forward?

When children are too young to begin working in a business, the owner may want to protect his family by having a buy/sell agreement in place with a worthy competitor. This acts as a right of first refusal and establishes a fair market value so the surviving family members don't engage in pipe dreams about the true worth of the company. Conversely, it keeps predators from coming in and stealing it at a bargain price.

ALERT

Fresh ideas will enrich any business. For this reason, offspring who contemplate entering the family business should work at other companies for a few years in order to obtain a different perspective on the field or industry. Once they've gained broader knowledge of the field and some general business and financial savvy, they can return home and put their new skills to work for the family.

Should You Try a Business Broker?

Although there are professional business brokers, a banker, attorney, or other party can just as easily put buyers and sellers together informally. Perhaps you have had your eye on a shoe store in town that has served generations, but you have some ideas of how to jazz it up. Being involved with your local chamber of commerce can help you gently get the word to the owner that you'd like to talk with him when he is ready to sell.

On the other hand, if you have a dream of owning an elite sports car dealership that would necessitate relocation, a broker can help do the research for you, and be involved with negotiating a fair deal. Finally, investment banks are hired to facilitate sales of very large, usually publicly traded firms. They command correspondingly gargantuan fees. Be prepared to provide some form of compensation for someone who aids a transaction between you and a seller.

Know What's Hot

Many entrepreneurs want to bring the newest ideas to market—whether it's a lifestyle gadget or life-saving equipment. The difference between the long-term winners and losers has less to do with what is hot at the moment than what will serve a continuing need in the marketplace.

You know your business—have you noticed any new or growing segments of your audience? Are customers asking for something new? Check out the competition to see what new services or products they're offering. Read industry blogs and magazines. Identifying an emerging trend that has staying power can be your best bet for a new business in a crowded field.

How Green Can You Be?

One trend that seems to be here for the long term is sensitivity to the environment. This is driving decisions across all industries and sectors for both new and established businesses. Younger workers in particular seem to resonate with the urgency of saving the planet from global warming by making intelligent choices on a personal, local, and global basis.

No matter what your business, you can take steps to make your company greener:

- Replace all incandescent light bulbs with compact fluorescent bulbs.
- Use alternative energy supplies if available.
- If you're building a new space, look into nontoxic dry walls or reclaimed building materials.
- Choose paints with low volatile organic compounds (VOC) ratings.
- Use bamboo for wood floors.
- Choose recycled paper and soy inks for printed materials, stationery, and business cards.
- Reduce the amount of paper used for hard copies and use digital filing methods.
- If all employees don't need to be in the same place every day, consider an all-telecommuting office.

Being green is smart on many levels. As you consider your new business, going green will color decisions from the type of light bulbs you use, to the kind of car you drive, to where your products are manufactured. From a marketing perspective you will want to assure your customers, and more importantly prospective customers, of your commitment and sensitivity to environmental issues. For now this will be a differentiating factor for your company. Over time it is hoped that common sense choices about using resources prudently will be so pervasive as to be universal. For now, during a time of cultural transition, smart business people will jump on the green bandwagon and promote their commitment to an environmentally safer, shared world.

In addition to committing to green business practices, consider starting a green business. You don't even have to learn a completely new business—just think about your field of expertise in a new way. Most businesses can be adapted to an environmentally conscious business model. And your marketing materials can highlight your company's commitment to making the world a better place.

Here are a few ideas for adding a green twist to a traditional business.

- **Green Workout Studio/Gym:** Use green heating and cooling systems and natural, sustainable wood floors. Sell organic-fiber workout clothes, along with natural health supplements. Equip showers with low-flow shower heads.
- **Green Florist:** An ecology-friendly florist uses organically grown flowers and creates arrangements using potted plants instead of cut flowers.
- **Green Maid Service:** Use non-toxic cleaning products and reusable or recycled cloths and dusters.
- **Green Hair Salon:** There are lots of non-toxic, biodegradable hair care products available, and many are made from organic materials. You can use eco-friendly tools, like bamboo brushes and combs instead of plastic ones.
- **Recycled Clothing or Furniture Store:** If you're comfortable with sewing and clothing design, you can buy used clothing and create new retro-trendy pieces. Similarly, old furniture can be refurbished and given new life.
- **Green Wedding Planner:** Eco-friendly wedding planning is growing in popularity. You can promote the use of plants instead of flowers for centerpieces and other arrangements, develop contacts with eco-travel agents and organic caterers, and start a recycled dress exchange.

CHAPTER 4

Meet the Expert: You

How credentialed do you need to be to prove you can do the job? Perhaps you only need to be a graduate of the "university of hard knocks," where your life experiences give you the knowledge you need. Yet, if a person is going to do business with you, there cannot be a shred of doubt in his mind, or yours, that you have the skill to deliver the goods. Bringing your experience, energy, and drive to your new endeavor will move you toward your goal, but you may also need degrees or certifications to demonstrate your expertise.

Highlight Your Track Record

If you are starting a business that is a direct offshoot of an industry you have worked in for some time, you will be strengthened by the experience you have gained talking the talk and walking the walk in that field. Perhaps you are coming from a corporate environment where you were a staff person or even a department head. No matter what level of responsibility you have had, you have been exposed to the issues of your particular company in the context of that industry. All of that experience is logged in your brain, ready for you to tap into with your new business.

Begin an organized inventory of your experience. As you make an honest assessment of what you know, you need to acknowledge your weak spots, and then begin the task of filling in the gaps. Try to engage someone who is older and wiser, or at least with loads of experience in your field, as a mentor. Any number of folks can furnish you with different perspectives, and many of them will also offer a more extensive knowledge base.

ESSENTIAL

When looking for a mentor, try to find a person who is not only knowledgeable in her field but who also knows you. This person should be able to give you credible feedback on your plans and your suitability to undertake the business you've chosen.

Most likely you will discover that you already possess tremendous resources to draw upon. Your confidence will soar once you identify and organize these resources. When you begin to market yourself or your product, this confidence will go a long way in assuring your customers they are receiving the services of a pro. Don't panic if gaps appear in this discovery process. There are endless ways to fill them. Part of the excitement of undertaking a new endeavor is the thrill of trying something different.

The key to success is to not hold back. Stop dreaming, and get going with the preparations that will launch you into your next career as an entrepreneur. There are many facets to starting and running any successful business. The knowledge, expertise, and experience that you bring to the table as an individual business owner is the yeast in the dough. If you do not already have it, you will gain it with a combination of planning, hard work, and realistic goals.

Licenses and Certifications

Various types of professionals—from doctors and lawyers to electricians and plumbers—are regulated by their own professions, as well as the government and municipalities. If you are in one of these professions, you absolutely must have the licenses required. In many others, the type of specialized education or training you bring to your work is up to you. These credentials do not come free, however. Whether you are looking into a degree or a certification program, you will need to invest both time and money.

Before committing to such an investment, research what these credentials will do for you. In some cases you may want to complete a training program or earn a college or advanced degree for your own self-esteem. This is great, and it very often does the trick. But take a look at the cold hard facts to see if a few more years of work in the field will achieve just as easily the same economic impact.

How Many Letters Do You Need after Your Name?

There are a number of reasons to consider pursuing individual certification or industry accreditation. At the very minimum, it is a reflection of your willingness to make the effort to prepare for and be tested on your industry's objective standards for competency. It is important to note that, in most cases, the standards measured reflect the minimum required. Certification usually requires a combination of having worked in an industry for a minimum number of years (usually three to five), and passing an exam.

There are many advantages to being accredited or certified. When weighing whether to pursue certification for you or accreditation for your company, consider the following things these qualifications will allow you to do:

- Create a competitive marketing advantage by differentiating yourself or your company from competitors.

- Deliver services more efficiently and profitably to your customers.
- Increase your professionalism within the industry.
- Stay current with industry trends and requirements.
- Evaluate your own core competencies against nationally recognized standards and best practices.
- Enhance and motivate individual performance.
- Participate in extensive peer-level communication and networking opportunities.

The opportunity to associate with other certified individuals gets heavily promoted by organizations that grant certifications. They want you to demonstrate your professionalism by networking with others holding the same certification.

QUESTION

What is the difference between certification and accreditation?
Certification applies to individuals. Accreditation applies to organizations. You can be certified in your field, while your company can be accredited. Certification validates you as holding the threshold of experience and knowledge to perform competently. Your company is measured for its structural competencies in how it delivers goods and services to the market.

Advanced Degrees

Since you are preparing to start a business you may have considered getting a master's in business administration (MBA), if you do not already have one. Once considered a most distinctive and career-advancing degree, the almighty MBA has become somewhat ubiquitous. Higher education itself has truly become a big business. Colleges and universities are competing for students and, in trying to distinguish themselves, are coming up with all sorts of specialized twists on the basic business degree. This can be great, and may in fact be an important step in improving your standing as an expert in your field, giving you an edge over your competition. Shop around and see where a program might be best suited to you.

If you are a development professional for nonprofit organizations, there are specialized MBA programs that target this field. If you are planning to become an independent development professional you may decide this is an important credential to support your expertise. Similarly, other industry-specific programs abound. Check them out.

One way to determine the value of such a degree is to study the job postings in your field and see what experience and credentials employers are seeking. Whatever industry you choose to set your stake in, know the landscape. Even though you are not looking for a job because you plan to be self-employed, it is useful to know the industry norms.

Whether you are in the early years and looking ahead to a dream career for the future, or you are ready to shift career directions, you can find a wealth of programs, with and without degrees, to get you on your way. Many community and junior colleges offer programs in everything from interior design to running a funeral home. There is no fluff here, only the concrete, specific topics needed to get you going. Plus, many colleges can assist you in getting internships in your field of choice, which may lead you to clients over time. The financial investment at a community college will be a lot easier to swallow than at an elite private college. It is up to you to weigh the relative advantages of any educational option.

No matter what your particular combination of education, training, and life experiences may be, when all of these experiences are stitched together, you may find that they have prepared you for your new independent venture. However, be sure to look critically at your saleable experience, and where you need to fill in the gaps. You may not need a university or even a community college setting to fill out your resume for your new business.

Get on the Speaker Circuit

Some folks would rather die than stand up and speak in front of a group of people. Even seasoned actors admit to experiencing stage fright. It can be intimidating, if not downright scary, to stand before a sea of faces—

even a very small sea of ten to fifteen of your colleagues—and hope that what comes out of your mouth is at least in your native language, much less coherent and relevant. It may be worth getting over the anxiety of this type of experience. When you can address a group about a topic in which you have extensive knowledge, you join that all-important group of people known as experts.

FACT

Public speaking is a skill that can be acquired through practice. Organizations such as Toastmasters International and the National Speakers Association can provide speaker training opportunities.

The fact that you are talking to a group does not make you smarter; it makes them smarter. And the smarter they get about what you know, the more valuable you become. Some people actually morph into paid professional speakers in their area of expertise. Perhaps that is your aspiration, or perhaps it may evolve for you. Until that day, though, look at opportunities to speak publicly about what you know as another way of solidifying your credentials as an expert in your field, making your services worthy of compensation.

It is not enough to have a solid knowledge base. You have to be able to get information across in an appealing way. Unfortunately, not everyone stood in the charisma line when gifts were being doled out through their DNA. That doesn't mean you can't be a credible presenter with a bit of training and a lot of practice, however. Once you get out there, you will become more sought after. The more folks see and hear you, the more your business reputation will be enhanced, and at the end of the day, this should bring you more customers.

Blog Your Way to the Head of the Pack

Tooting your own horn is always a good thing to do when you're spreading the word about your new business. Today millions of people are reading and writing opinions via web logs, or blogs. Too often these are rants. But smart folks write well, make coherent points, and bring a perspective others are eager to read. This may be an excellent way for you to make a name for yourself in your field. There are even websites that show you how to establish your own blog.

If you write about your observations of trends in your field, whether you're concerned with new uses of technology, buying habits of certain age groups, or even a particular color that keeps appearing, you will get people thinking. While they are thinking about your observations, they will become familiar with your name and your business. You will have established yourself as an authority in your field. This can only help draw customers. It can also give you something tangible to offer when you are pitching new business.

Submit Unsolicited Articles

Every imaginable activity, profession, or endeavor has an association that nurtures the interests of that group. Within all of these special interests will be newsletters, both in traditional ink and paper as well as online formats. Most have regular staff writing for them, but there is always an interest in editorials, or even guest columnist submissions. Whether you are launching a jewelry line on the Internet or starting a local auto parts supply store, you have something to say about it.

It might seem like a distraction from your core mission to begin writing articles that may or may not be accepted, yet consider the possibilities. If a publication thinks enough of your point of view to publish or post it, then certainly a prospective customer will be assured of your reliability as a good source for whatever goods or services you are selling.

ALERT

When publicizing a new business, people often forget to include media outlets with the closest links to them. Don't make this mistake! Community newsletters or other specialized publications are always looking for new material. And don't forget your alma mater. Alumni magazines make it their job to highlight the success of their graduates.

Writing articles can be an especially useful tool if your budding enterprise is something new, either for you or others. Perhaps you are the victim of downsizing and are setting up shop to sell your talents independently. Not only do you have the specific skills to bring to the marketplace, you actually have perspective on the factors that caused the downsizing. By articulating these in written form, you may strike a chord with other parties that would be most interested in communicating with you further.

CHAPTER 5

Researching the Market

A great idea is a very exciting thing indeed. But without a market for the service or product you'd like to center your business on, your idea could be dead in the water. Before going too far with your new venture, it is key to do a little reality checking to make sure there will be clients for your new business. This should include such tasks as staying current with the particular industry you're considering, and scouting out the competition.

Conducting Market Research

So, how do you begin to do the research you need? A competitive market analysis by an expert would be terrific. However, you may not want to spend that kind of money to start a small business, although it wouldn't hurt to check with some market research firms and get quotes. Specifically, you need to measure if there is a ready market for your product or service in the area you want to serve. This can be in your neighborhood, city, state, or the vast reach of the Internet. Naturally, the larger and more comprehensive the analysis, the more money you'll need to spend on it.

Believe it or not, you can do your own market research. Some places to find vital information include:

- Your local library, or any good business library, where there are numerous research volumes that will provide you with up-to-date data on companies, demographics, and market research.
- Business periodicals including Forbes, the Wall Street Journal, and numerous others.
- Trade publications, including newsletters for the industry of your choice, so you can get to know exactly what is going on in the industry before you jump in.
- Your local chamber of commerce or city hall records office or bureau, which can provide you with data on competitive businesses.
- Annual reports from other companies, which help you get an idea of what your own expenditures, income, and overall cash flow might look like.
- The Internet, where you can get your hands on numerous facts and figures.
- Individual company websites, where you can find out what's going on with similar businesses.
- The Small Business Administration (SBA) at *www.sba.gov*. This site will give you tips on a range of topics from writing a business plan to securing low-interest loans.
- Other business owners, who can tell you what it's like on the inside.
- Associations that have members in the same industry who can offer you advice.

Some people assume that their business concept has to be completely original in order to be successful. Think about it. How many pizza parlors are in your town? How many auto dealers? You certainly do not need to possess an original business concept to succeed in the marketplace. If you are going to take on an existing business concept, however, you will need to differentiate yours in some way to entice customers. In New Orleans, a city famous for the chicory in its coffee, PJ's Coffee Shops are springing up all over town, promising customers that their cup of joe offers a change of pace without the chicory.

Assessing Your Potential Market

One of the first things to do is get an idea of the size of your potential market. Will you be catering to a specific market by selling a specialized service like home health care for seniors, or will you be reaching a mass audience with a product like breath mints?

It's important to gauge the overall industry and where it's headed. Opening a business in an industry that's headed for a fall is an invitation to disaster. Conversely, you may find the hottest growing industry. Can you tailor your skills and passion to fit into an up-and-coming industry?

You also want to gauge your overall competition. How many competitors are there? What companies are capturing the lion's share of the market? Is the field oversaturated? Can you carve a niche market from a larger one? What can you do to differentiate yourself from the competition? Study how well your potential competitors are already doing in the marketplace. Do you see how you might catch them napping and grab some of their customers? Is there a way to learn from their mistakes—or successes?

As you conduct your research, you should be looking for substantial information that supports your idea and your business plan. If you find the right supporting information, then you can proceed. However, if all signs are negative, you may just save yourself from a potential disaster. In essence, you're doing a feasibility study to see if your plan can fly, based on the current market and economic climate, and on the prospects for the future.

Industry Trends

Besides looking at the dollar figures and competition within a certain industry, you should look at trends, both in business and in lifestyle. For example, if more people in your neighborhood own dogs than ever before, there may be a need for pet care or pet accessories. If people also are traveling more frequently, then there may be a need in your area for an innovative kennel, perhaps featuring doggie vacations. You could start your own doggie resort or fancy kennel with some nice amenities that dog owners would find appealing for their pets.

You may find that there have been a great number of layoffs from major nearby companies. There may be a greater need for outsourcing, because these companies still have tasks that need to get done. You might open a placement service for freelancers and contractors. You could also open up a resume-writing service or even start career coaching for people who are having interviews. Perhaps there are companies that need your manufacturing skills because they can't afford to keep full-time in-house people to manufacture goods.

If you look at the trends taking place around you, locally and nationally, you can start to think about specific market needs. Trends may illustrate needs in specific areas and point to voids that you might fill. The next step is to determine if the need is great enough that a business could profit by filling that void.

Also look at the overall economic climate to determine if the time is right for your business. A town experiencing layoffs and going through hard times will not be the best place for selling luxury items or extravagant services. Give thought to this type of timing issue as you conduct your research.

ESSENTIAL

Be aware of the present but focus on the future. It's to your advantage to be able to foresee demographic shifts and changes in the economic climate. If you can continue to structure and restructure your business in accordance with events in the world around you, you'll be able to stay on the cutting edge—or at least be keeping pace with the competition.

You can also use your own awareness as a consumer to find voids in the marketplace. If you're unhappy about having to drive ten miles to find a stationery store, then perhaps other people in your area are experiencing the same needs for greeting cards and paper products. Conduct your own survey. Hand out 100 short questionnaires asking people where they buy greeting cards, stationery, and other such products, and whether they would shop at a store in their community if one opened. If 60 percent say they would, then you know there's a need for such a store. However, if 60 percent indicate they order cards and stationery goods online, then there may not be sufficient demand for a new store.

You also may see products and services that you feel you could improve. You need to be careful, however, to determine whether the product actually needs to be improved. One gentleman commented, upon seeing a garage door opener that opens a door from 100 feet away, that he could devise such a product that could open a garage door from a distance of 500 to 1,000 feet. The question he was asked was simply, "Why would anyone need to open a garage door from 1,000 feet away?" Making something more powerful or potent is only marketable if it's worthwhile. Battery-powered dice, for example, did not catch on.

Here are some key questions to ask yourself when you're looking at your industry trends:

- What is your target market group?
- What does your research indicate that this group needs?
- How much will people pay for these goods or services?
- Will there be enough profit to make for a successful business venture?
- What trend or trends will be prevalent in the near future?
- What impact will these trends have on your target market group?
- Who is your competition and what are they offering or not offering?
- Based on current needs, upcoming trends, and the competition, what can you do to gain a competitive edge in the marketplace?

Several years ago, companies needed to better manage their data by moving it to computers. More recently, companies needed to add modern communications systems, and retail outlets needed to add price scanners to stay competitive. The next phase may be smart card technology, replacing credit cards. These cards are already gaining in popularity on a global level and in closed environments like military bases and universities. These examples are broad-based. Each industry has specific new technologies, styles, or manners of handling business that are becoming the norm.

But trends reveal more than industry developments. They also represent changes in society. Are there more single-parent families that may need your services? Are more seniors buying certain holistic medicines and vitamin products? Are more teens able to travel abroad than ever before? Look at rising numbers in demographic groupings.

Scouting Out the Competition

To be competitive in the marketplace, you need to know exactly what the competition is doing. Therefore, if you're going to have the best pizza in town, you'd better see what the most popular pizzerias are offering and figure out what you can offer to draw customers to your establishment.

One pizzeria owner realized that the number of families was increasing in his neighborhood and that many of the trendy new pizza restaurants were oriented toward young professionals in their attempt to woo a business clientele. He noticed parents with restless kids waiting to be served and decided to do something a little different. Well aware of how much kids love pizza, he decided to go after the family market with a special selection of children's pizzas, sized for smaller appetites and including a soda and Italian ice (which are incredibly inexpensive). He priced this combination less than the competition. He then enhanced the child-friendly appearance of his restaurant and put crayons and entertaining placemats on the tables. He soon drew the families with kids. The pizzeria found a way to entice a neglected share of an existing marketplace without taking away from its regular walk-in business of all ages.

Gaining a competitive advantage can mean changing a particular style, image, packaging, or service; adding new selections; changing the pricing structure; or trying a whole new look. Whatever the competition isn't doing well to draw customers is what you need to implement. Change for the sake of change, however, doesn't work, so research what you think is a viable plan of action. When Coke switched to New Coke, Pepsi did not respond with New Pepsi. They waited to see what the effect would be on Coke's business. It wasn't very good and New Coke disappeared. You may need to wait to see if your competition's bright idea is a hit or a dud.

Finding Your Niche

Filling the right void in an industry can also make you an industry giant. Federal Express saw a need that either wasn't being addressed or aggressively marketed by another company: prompt overnight delivery. They stepped in, promoted overnight shipping, and have become industry giants. Naturally, you have to make good on your claims, but finding new ways to do something, make something, or sell something will put you in an advantageous position.

Once you find a competitive advantage or fill a void, you need to make sure to promote that fact. Federal Express made it clear from the start that overnight shipping was its specialty.

Customer service can be the difference between beating the competition and lagging behind. Provide service that makes people want to come back and do business with you again. Not surprisingly, surveys show that customer service is the leading concern among customers.

Filling a void and finding a niche are two different strategies for approaching your business and gaining a competitive edge. The former involves finding something that isn't readily done and stepping in and doing it. The latter means taking something that is being done and doing it better. For example, if a company came along that specialized in overnight animal transport, it would be finding a niche by moving into an area that is already being covered by delivery companies. However, it would be specializing in one small aspect of that business.

You might be able to corner an industry by becoming a specialist, as long as you make sure there is a large enough potential market for your specialty. City Bicycles, for example, is one of a few small bike shops in Manhattan. Sure, other stores may sell bikes, but this is a definitive place to go for them, because it has expertise in that one area and a wider selection—bikes are the cornerstone of its business. While such a store might not succeed where only 3 percent of the population cares about bikes, 3 percent of New York City is still a potential audience of nearly a quarter of a million people. Add to that the fact that biking is a great way to stay fit and the owners have a successful business.

Before you go into business, assess the competition carefully. While it's always advantageous to beat the competition's prices, you may not be able to do so and still turn a profit. However, you should certainly try to offer competitive prices. Meanwhile, see if you can offer more in the area of services. Can you offer any of the following?

- Free, or at least easily accessible, parking
- Warranties or service plans
- Free repairs
- Gift-wrapping
- Free shipping
- Overnight delivery
- Personalized attention
- Twenty-four-hour service
- A secure payment system online
- Customization of products

As your business grows, determine what you can do to improve service and customer relations. Keep track of what the competition is doing so that you can plan your own strategy. It's no coincidence that every time one fast food chain has a movie tie-in promotion, its competition ties in with another hot movie. You need not go so far as to attack the competition—leave that technique for politics—but always be ready to think of your next move. Remember, it's like a chess match. Company A makes a move, then Company B needs to make a countermove, and so forth.

The Name Game

Finding a name for your business isn't always as easy as it sounds. Often, you need to do a bit of research to see what name will work best. The right name can make the difference between success and mediocrity. It can make you stand out from the crowd or blend in. Most importantly it helps clients find you! It's important that your name be:

- Short
- Easy to remember

- Easy to spell
- Easy to pronounce
- Original
- Defining

The first five on the list are self-explanatory, but the last one—defining—is the important quality that indicates what your business is all about. The names of Aunt Peggy's Bakery or Mrs. Field's Cookies not only tell you who makes the product, but more importantly, what is in the package. A store named Just Kites not only tells you what it sells but what it doesn't (namely, anything else). However, "Jake's Corner Store" tells you nothing, except that the store is on the corner.

You can include a lot of information in a name, even a concise one. "Ace Overnight Delivery" clearly describes a delivery company that provides overnight service. If possible, it's advantageous to include a feature of your products or services in the name to give potential customers a heads-up on what you offer.

Of course, many companies have simply used a common name, such as Wendy's or Uncle Ben's. If you can heavily promote a person's name that's easy to remember, you can also grab attention. People relate to the personal feeling that a name exudes.

More often than not, the best business name is something that sounds right to you. You'll probably consider numerous possibilities before coming up with the one you like best. Perhaps you'll include your own name, such as Arthur Murray's Dance Studios or Jack LaLanne Fitness Centers. For a legal practice, it's customary to be more formal and use last names of the partners, such as Steinman & Harris, Attorneys at Law, which sounds more professional than "Mark and Ted, Attorneys at Law," or "The Little Shop of Law." Keep in mind who your target audience is. Fun, trendy names may attract a young audience, while more formal names may be better suited for a conservative industry.

Sometimes using the name of your town or location draws attention and puts you one step ahead of your competitors. Yorktown Deli sounds like the official deli of the town, though it isn't. However, when looking for a deli in Yorktown, you may think of it first. Another tactic is to use the name associated with the town or city in which you're doing business. New York

City, the Big Apple, is home to the Big Apple Circus, and you will likely find a Big Apple Cleaners or Big Apple Diner. New York is also known as the Empire State. So you'll find business names there that include the word "Empire," just as you'll find Washington, DC businesses with "Capitol" in their name, or businesses in Texas using the words "Lone Star."

ESSENTIAL

> Names like Shoetown, Record World, and CD Universe are all the result of thinking big. The reality is that Auto World may be a larger store than Auto Universe, but either way, they both sound like they have a major inventory and can service the needs of any car owner.

Bounce names off of other people and get their knee-jerk reactions. If the name is throwing them off, then it may be misleading. The name "Monsterdaata.com," for example, may confuse people who focus on whether or not the word data is misspelled (or why it is spelled in such a manner), rather than on the services of the website. Also, if the name has people thinking of another, similar business, the similarity will be counterproductive as you try to drive customers to your business.

There are numerous ways to derive a name, so take your time, research the market, and in the end find one that makes you feel good. Like a comfortable shoe, the name should fit just right.

CHAPTER 6

Structuring Your Business

Once you've gotten over the hump of choosing an industry and focus for your business, it's time to work on the structure of your new venture. This is the point where more technical aspects come into play—things like control, liability, and taxes. You also need to decide what type of operation you prefer. Do you work better as a lone ranger, or with a buddy? These and other considerations will drive your decisions on how to organize your business.

Overview

Perhaps the most serious, grown-up aspect of launching your new business will be planning for the tax and legal structure of your entity. There are a number of organizational options to consider, primarily:

- Sole proprietorship
- C corporation
- S corporation
- Partnership—in a number of forms
- Limited liability company (LLC)

The people involved in establishing and later running your business will be a factor in deciding your legal structure. It is important to consider what liability protections are needed, and for whom. You need to weigh the tax consequences of your actions, from establishing your business, to operating it, and ultimately to ending it through a sale, dissolution, or even death. The information below is intended solely to give you a rough overview of the various organizational structures. Only a professional accountant and attorney can give you the best understanding of the consequences of various options and guide you in the decision-making process. You can find cookie-cutter legal documents, as well as government rules, on the Internet, but you will be doing yourself a disservice if you forgo the experience and wisdom of professionals in this important area of planning.

Partnerships

Once they were Sears and Roebuck, now they're just Sears. Whatever happened to Roebuck? Comics ponder this question, while business partners often wonder which one of them will be Sears and which will be Roebuck. Will you be the next Ben and Jerry? Will you be together for many years?

A partnership exists whenever two or more people work together in a single business and have not formed a "legal entity," such as a corporation, under state law. You can find business partners who have been in stride for twenty-five years, and others who split up shortly after the sign on the front door was put into place. It's all in how you approach the business and whether or not you have common goals. If one person sees the business as a friendly, local mom-and-pop operation, and the other is thinking about new locations, franchises, and four catalogs a year, the pairing may not be right for a long-term partnership.

It's imperative that everything be set up carefully and spelled out on paper, even among the closest of friends—especially among close friends, who may need that written agreement as a legal document at some point in their business future. Most significantly, people who team up to go into business need to be on the same page. It is usually a good idea for prospective partners to spend some time together, developing a common vision, mission, values, strategy, tactics, and overall game plan for a new business, before jumping headlong into getting the new business off the ground. They also need to:

- Recognize each other's strengths and weaknesses.
- Accept that one partner may put in more hours while the other may be highly visible and get name recognition.
- Divide up tasks fairly, based on their respective strengths.
- Have an open line of communication.
- Learn how to resolve conflicts and differences of opinion.
- Decide percentage of ownership and control of the business. A 50/50 split is never good.

General Partnerships

All types of business structures have certain legal implications. In a general partnership, each of the partners is jointly and severally liable for the debts and liabilities of the business. That means that both partners' personal assets are on the line for all of the business's liabilities. Between themselves, the partners can share the profits and losses any way they like. But to the outside world, they are equally responsible for the business. Unless there is a written or oral agreement that can be proved, partners will share profits and losses equally. Partners can and should determine in advance who is responsible for which aspects of the business, and contractual agreements should be carefully drawn up with good legal counsel.

FACT

From a tax standpoint, a partnership is not treated as a business. Instead, the partners are taxed individually. Each partner pays personal income tax. An IRS form (Form 1065) shows the pass-through of income and loss to each partner. Even if you run a business with someone without filing or creating an agreement as a partnership, you will likely be considered a partnership for legal purposes.

A general partnership can be advantageous because it allows you to pool resources and often makes it easier to gather funding. Partnerships enjoy a greater compendium of knowledge and skills. If partners share common goals and visions for the company, they can often complement one another by focusing on different functions. Any liabilities incurred, however, are shared among all the partners. This can be a disadvantage if one partner is clearly at fault or causes the business to go into debt. Each partner in a general partnership is responsible for the actions (and sometimes for the inactions or omissions) of the others, and for the overall business. So if your partner sends the company into debt and takes off for Rio, you are still held responsible. Less drastic, but more frequent, is the situation in which partners have different aspirations for the business. One partner may want to embrace technology while the other may want to do things the old-fashioned, tried-and-true way. This can present operational problems.

Limited Liability Partnerships

Limited liability partnerships are another option that can be advantageous. A limited partner, unlike a general partner, takes on limited risk and is only liable for her investment and not for the entire business. If, however, the limited partner is a manager, she can be liable for debt. Even in a limited partnership, a general partner is necessary to take on the overall company liabilities. However, the general partner can be a corporation so that no individual is personally liable for the business. Also, limited partners can be replaced, or leave the business, without having to dissolve the partnership, which reduces legal entanglements. To form a limited partnership you must file with your state and pay a filing fee and annual fees.

Sole Proprietorships

If you choose to go it alone, without incorporating or otherwise establishing a business entity, you are a sole proprietor. This is the easiest form of business to start because you don't need to draft partnership agreements or register to incorporate. You may need to obtain proper licensing in your state, county, town, or city to conduct your type of business, however, and you will need to file a "doing business as" (DBA) form.

Being a sole proprietor means that you are the boss, the head honcho, the top dog, the big cheese, whose name will appear on greeting cards and other congratulatory notes when you announce that you are officially open for business. As a sole proprietor, you'll be the one lonely soul reviewing the profit-and-loss statements. You'll be the one with the tough decisions to make, and no matter how much you delegate responsibilities, the overall accountability of the business will fall on your shoulders, for better or worse.

On the plus side, if and when the business takes off, you'll be the one reaping the rewards. You will have total ownership and control of the business. Of course, if the business fails, you'll be responsible for answering to the investors and the bank.

ALERT

One of the problems of being a sole proprietor is that you are responsible as an individual—so if your business goes into debt, even if you shut the doors and take down the sign, you can still be held liable. You can take out product insurance, insure your equipment, or take out other forms of insurance to try to cover yourself, but it may not be enough to protect you completely.

As a sole proprietor, you don't need approval to make changes and implement new ways of running the business. In fact, others need your approval. You don't have to worry about a partner being in agreement with your decisions. Even taxation is a simple process, as you pay taxes based on your income.

At the same time, it can be psychologically difficult to go it alone in business. Just as you have no one to answer to, you have no one to do half the work, raise half the money, and solve half the problems as you do when you have a partner. If you're confident in your abilities and can handle a wide range of responsibilities, calling in the right people at the right times for help, then this might be the best structure for your business.

Corporations

A corporation is a legal entity unto itself. In a corporation, you may have less liability exposure than as a sole proprietor, though it's not as simple as just teaming up with a few partners. Instead, a corporation is a legally formed business entity with laws, rules, and guidelines to follow.

The process of incorporating is done in accordance with state laws and can be completed by filing the proper paperwork and paying certain fees. You'll need an attorney to assist you in the process and to review the state requirements. Once filed, you will be incorporated in that state. Subsequently you may need to register as a "foreign corporation" in other states in which you plan to conduct business. For guidelines you can generally contact the secretary of state in the state where you are planning to incorporate or do business. You will pay a fee to the state for incorporating, file corporate certificates annually, and pay annual franchise taxes. It is also advisable to get a corporate seal in case documents require it.

Once you begin the process of incorporating, you will also need to determine if there is another business in your state with the name that you planned to use. You may need to change your name slightly. Conversely, you may think of several variations on the name you like and incorporate under a few of them to keep other companies from having similar names. However, remember the general trademark rule: If you don't use it you will lose it.

The most significant advantage of incorporating is that it allows your business and personal responsibilities to be handled separately. Therefore, you are protected to a much greater degree. Your corporation can be held responsible without you being held personally liable. This is very significant in the event of a lawsuit, because you can protect your personal assets. You can also leave a corporation without having to dissolve the business, since you and the corporation are separate entities.

It can also be easier to obtain funding as a corporation than as a sole proprietor or partnership. As corporations grow, they may sell shares in the business to stockholders who are not involved in the day-to-day activities of the corporation, but have a vote in its policies and share in the profits.

ESSENTIAL

Do everything possible to demonstrate that your corporation is not a sham by separating your personal world from your business world. Keep personal records separate from corporate records. If you need money from the business to pay a personal bill, do not pay it with a company check. Withdraw the money as salary, paying the appropriate taxes.

Once you incorporate, you pay yourself a salary or other compensation from the corporation. You also pay corporate taxes, as well as your own income taxes based on how much salary you receive. Unlike a sole proprietor, whose profits land on top of his taxable income, a corporation pays tax separately.

C and S Corporations

It should also be noted that from a tax perspective, there are different types of corporations. Most common is the C corporation (it has just been described and is taxed as a separate entity at corporate level tax rates). There is also an S corporation, which is a "small business corporation." By definition, it is a company that cannot have more than 100 shareholders, and it can only have one class of stock. An S corporation still provides personal liability protection. However, the profits and losses from the S corporation are not federally taxed but are passed through to your own personal income and taxed accordingly—just like a partnership.

Often, someone running a small business does not incorporate until the company is seeing significant profits because:

- There are franchise fees and attorney fees to pay.
- It will be necessary to file both corporate and personal tax returns, which can be time-consuming and costly if an accountant is required.

On the other hand, you may choose to incorporate if:

- You want to keep your business and personal assets separate to guard against lawsuits or paying higher personal income taxes.
- You suddenly see significant profits as a sole proprietor. (You're more likely to be audited if your personal income jumps dramatically because of your new business venture.)

Limited Liability Company

You can also form a limited liability company (LLC). This type of entity provides the limited personal liability benefits of a corporation and the tax treatment of a partnership. Profits are passed through to you and taxes are paid as part of your personal income tax. An LLC can, when you reach that point, have unlimited stockholders and corporate stockholders, like a C corporation. An S corporation, on the other hand, is limited in number of owners, and you cannot have entities as stockholders in most cases.

Making the Choice

You should weigh the pros and cons of incorporating, discuss the options with an accountant, and hire an attorney to guide you through the process. There is no set rule dictating who does and does not need to incorporate. It's a personal decision based on the size, structure, and type of business as well as your personal assets, tax status, and potential for liability.

ESSENTIAL

If there are other individuals involved in helping you start up your new business or investing in it, you may find the process of selecting and establishing a business entity to be helpful as you consider such issues as defining who has control over the new business, how you will raise capital, and others.

If you choose to incorporate, you will need to select a state in which to file. Generally it is the state in which you will have physical facilities.

You can, however, select another state and qualify to do business as a foreign corporation in your own state. Corporate laws, costs of incorporating, and the state's tax structure will usually be deciding factors. As it turns out, doing business in any state, whether you are incorporated or a "foreign corporation," makes you subject to that state's tax laws.

In most states, contact the secretary of state for information on registering your corporation. However, some states have different procedures. If you're not sure what to do in your state, contact your state's department of commerce.

Get Tax Advice Now!

When talking with your tax professional, ask for the particulars of how income is taxed in the various legal structures. In general, income can be taxed twice in a C corporation. The corporation's earnings are subject to federal income tax, and then the shareholders will be taxed on any after-tax income that is distributed to them as dividends. Corporations are taxed at increasing rates from 15 percent on taxable income under $50,000 to 35 percent on taxable income greater than $10 million. The monies that are distributed to shareholders are taxed at different rates, with a maximum cumulative rate of 44.75 percent. There are ways to avoid the double taxation in a C corporation, such as:

- Retaining earnings and not distributing them to shareholders
- Structuring payments in a deductible form such as interest, rent, or royalties
- Compensating shareholder-employees with payroll, reducing earnings subject to tax

S corporations and partnerships are not subject to federal tax. These structures allow profits and losses to be passed through to individuals.

It is possible to change your election and move from one legal structure to another, but there are restrictions and consequences for doing so. Again, seek the advice of professionals when considering a change.

Certain personal service businesses are not eligible for graduated income tax on earnings. A personal service business is defined as one in which an employee-owner performs the principal activity, such as hair cutting, dog walking, or private chef services. These businesses are subject to a flat 35 percent tax rate. Check with your attorney to see if your service falls into this category.

Deductibility of Losses

The way a loss is treated depends on how a business is organized. In general, with sole proprietorships, S corporations, and some partnerships, the loss passes through to the individual. With a C corporation, there are many more variables and much more flexibility in applying the loss backward and forward to different tax years. An S corporation does not have the flexibility of these forward or backward losses. Your tax advisor will be able to counsel you on your options based on the particular circumstances of a particular year.

Taxable Year

You will need to decide when you want your taxable year to start. You do not need to have your business taxable year be the calendar year in most instances. If you can demonstrate an accounting period in which you regularly wrap up your books and determine your annual profit and loss, you can use that time frame for your taxable year. In a partnership it can be a little tricky, but the decision would be determined by the taxable year of the one or more partners whose aggregate interest exceeds 50 percent. Most businesses follow a calendar year, but you may find reasons to organize your taxable year otherwise.

Choosing an Accounting Method

Before settling on your business structure, you will want to weigh the pros and cons of various accounting methods. The primary consideration is whether you would benefit from operating on a cash basis or an accrual basis. With a sole proprietorship, S corporation, or partnership you may make this choice. With a C corporation, you are prohibited from using a cash basis. This may be an important factor in deciding which direction to take. (Certain C corporations are eligible for cash-basis accounting, including some farming or qualified personal service businesses, and certain corporations with receipts under $5 million.)

Exiting the Business

As exciting as it is to start something new, it is necessary to keep a level head with a view toward the ultimate wrap-up of your venture. No one has a crystal ball to see exactly what shape the end will take. Nevertheless, you can think about the ultimate tax responsibilities associated with each business structure option and make an informed choice in the early stages. Selling the assets or shares of a company triggers either capital gain or ordinary income and its attendant tax liabilities. The details of how this would apply to your undertaking should be thoroughly reviewed with your tax professional. The rules are different for each option, and are further complicated by choices made along the way, such as opting for a different form of organization. The tax consequences of liquidating or dissolving your business has tax consequences dependent on how you are set up, but generally a gain realized by selling off assets winds up passing through to you as the owner.

FACT

Believe it or not, there are cases where your entity may suffer an inadvertent termination. An S corporation's election is revoked when it exceeds 100 shareholders, has more than one class of stock, or in a few other cases. If a partnership is no longer operating, or sells more than 50 percent of its interest, a termination of the partnership may be instigated.

Retirement or Death

The death of a sole proprietor does not generate any immediate business-related tax responsibilities. If a shareholder of a corporation passes away, the corporation may want to buy back the shareholder's stock. Most likely, the heirs or estate will want to redeem the stock. There are myriad rules surrounding how such a redemption gets executed and the corresponding tax fallout. Partnerships have quite a bit of flexibility in planning for the death or retirement of a partner, including everything from considering such an event to be the dissolution of the partnership to selling the partner's share to a third party.

Offering Employee Benefits

Generally speaking, tax code permits favorable tax treatment for benefits to employees only. The key here is that persons who are self-employed are not considered, in this tax view, as employees. A sole proprietor is usually treated as a self-employed person. Shareholders in S corporations as well as partners in a partnership are considered self-employed individuals and not employees. Shareholders who work for their own C corporation, however, may be treated as employees. The benefits people expect, such as health and accident insurance, pension plans, life insurance, and employer-paid meals or lodging may be a significant factor in deciding how to structure your business.

CHAPTER 7

Crafting a Business Plan

There's an old saying, "If you don't know where you're going, any road will get you there." But you do have an idea where you are going with your business concept. Now it is time to get it down on paper so you'll know how to make it real. Business plans are dynamic and you will want to revisit yours frequently as your business grows and changes shape. It may seem daunting at first, but think of it as a chance to demonstrate the validity of your concept.

How to Know if You Need a Business Plan?

In an ideal world, an entrepreneur would have all the planning for her business sorted out and neatly presented in a document worthy of review by investors ranging from family members to venture capital firms before opening the door for business. Some businesses start slowly and organically, growing out of a hobby. Examples include a baseball card collector who starts to sell via online auction sites or at flea markets, or someone whose expertise in a particular field gets tapped informally deciding to set up shop as a consultant. In these instances, a business may be going before a plan is put in place. Even so, the value of a business plan cannot be underestimated. It is never too soon to prepare one, but it can be too late. If you get too caught up in the excitement of starting something new, and a year or so into it realize you have not planned for cash flow properly, instead of growing your business you may find yourself bailing out of a sinking ship.

More than just a proposal to draw interest from investors, a business plan sets the foundation from which you will build your business. You will use it as an outline to guide you and help you make sure each area is covered and each goal is met. The plan will help you make sure you stay on track and don't lose your focus.

ESSENTIAL

There are many reasons to write a business plan, from defining a business at the outset to providing a chart for future growth. It can also be used to set a valuation on your business when you are getting ready to sell. The most common use, though, will be to support your application for a loan.

A good business plan will not only keep you on track, but like a good outline for a screenplay or novel, it will allow you to put your thoughts and ideas on paper, and manipulate them until they are just right. You can then expand upon them as the business takes shape. When it's completed, the business plan will answer all the pertinent questions and tie up all the loose ends, including the details that are part and parcel of running a successful business.

While business plans will vary depending on the structure and the type of business, many of the principles remain the same. The basic elements in a business plan are:

- Executive summary
- Description of the company
- Goals and objectives
- An overview of the industry
- Market analysis
- Products and services
- Marketing plans and strategies
- Financial plan
- Overview of key personnel

Business plans include additional information as necessary to tell the overall story of how the business will be formed and evolve into a profitable entity. Furthermore, the business plan will demonstrate how your business will move forward once you have opened your doors. You may begin with a fairly simple plan if your initial financial needs are not extensive. Over time, you may need to obtain more money and will have to show how it will be used for your expansion ideas. Projected sales figures, cash flow, and anticipated profit and loss for one, three, five, and ten years will help you illustrate the anticipated results of your plan.

Getting Ready

Writing a business plan may appear intimidating at first. However, if you take it step by step, you won't be defeated by the thought of creating this important document. You should realize before you begin that you will have to revise the plan as you incorporate new ideas. As you're developing the plan, be sure to show portions to other people for feedback, to assess what's missing or unclear. Then return to the plan and make the needed revisions. So don't sweat over every word you put on paper—numerous changes will be made down the road.

Since thousands, if not millions, of business plans have preceded yours, you don't need to reinvent the wheel. Look at sample business plans and get a general idea of how other plans have been put together. Focus on plans for businesses that are similar to yours so that you can get a general idea of what you're trying to accomplish in your business plan. These samples may be more or less detailed than what you will need, but they will give you an idea of the different types of information that can be included. Remember, the best plan is not the one with the most jargon, most pages, or most superlatives and keywords. The strongest business plan is one that clearly paints the picture of your business and demonstrates how and why it will be successful.

FACT

The best business plans are concrete. They define specific goals and decide who will be responsible for meeting them and when they will be met. For a plan to work, it must be practical, with more emphasis on implementation than on lofty strategies. Interim dates for review and course correction should be part of the plan from the beginning.

Neatness also counts. While it probably won't make or break a business deal, it is certainly to your advantage to have a professional-looking business plan, complete with cover page and binding. Make sure you have proofread and edited the document. Graphs, charts, and even illustrations or photos can enhance a presentation if you're looking for backers. Use them, however, only if they help significantly to make the case for your plan.

Organize the format so that a reader can skim through it and see the highlights before studying it. If you don't need to get investors, and the plan is for yourself and your partners, you may be less formal. Either way, don't cut corners. Include all the pertinent information. You'll be glad you did when you refer back to the plan.

A Step-by-Step Guide

The process of writing a business plan is easier if you take it one step at a time. In the following sections, you'll find all the information you need to write a plan that convincingly explains what your business is about and why it will succeed.

Title or Cover Page

Include all contact information for yourself and your partners, if any, on the cover page. This page doesn't need to contain much, but keep in mind that first impressions say a lot. With that in mind, you might use an elegant typeface for a more upscale business or a cutting-edge logo for a company appealing to a young audience.

Table of Contents

A table of contents (TOC) provides an easy way to find key information. In the TOC, you present an itemized overview of what's included within the business plan. It lets readers go back and find each subject without having to flip through the entire plan again and again.

ESSENTIAL

Although a business plan is structured in a particular order beginning with an executive summary, the summary is the last piece you should write. First, work on the business description, marketing plan, operations, financial plan, and management overview. When you have all these components completed it will be easy to extract the highlights for the executive summary.

There are no hard and fast rules on how to number your TOC topics. Simply using 1, 2, 3 is fine; or using subsets (1, 1A, 2, 2A, etc.) is also perfectly acceptable.

Executive Summary

The executive summary is the single most important section of the business plan. It appears up front, to provide the readers with a concise overview of the business.

In one or two pages, your executive summary should include a description of the products or services offered and the features that make your business distinctive. It's important that you present your target audience, costs, objectives, marketing plans, and financial projections. Your summary should express your confidence in the future success of the business and make potential investors want to read more. Don't hesitate to rewrite as many times as necessary to polish this important section.

Establish a foundation for your business. Point out the current climate and explain what it is that you will offer. For example, you could say, "Last year, residents in New England ate 9.2 ice-cream cones per capita," or "According to statistics from XYZ Source, the demand for frozen healthy prepared foods will rise 10 percent per year for the coming decade." Then explain how this fact or figure opens the door for your business to step in and solve a problem, provide a service, or simply make life simpler for these individuals, your target audience. For example, "Momfood will be available in two metropolitan markets in the coming year, rising to twenty in ten years."

Include your strongest selling point. You may have an ideal location. You may be the first to do something, or the first to do it in a specific way. You may provide a unique service. Whatever aspect you choose to highlight, be concise.

Business Overview

This section of your business plan is also known as the business description, company overview, company plan, or company summary. No matter what you decide to call it, this is the place where you can elaborate with a comprehensive description of your plans, being sure to stay within a few pages. Start off with the goals of the business. Explain the legal structure (sole proprietorship, partnership, corporation, etc.) and the status of the business. Is it a start-up or is it expanding?

FACT

Each business has its own systems that govern its operation. Guide the reader through the process, from preparing the food to stocking the shelves to client checkout. Will customers be billed in thirty days for their portrait photographs, or will they be required to place a 50 percent deposit at the time of the sitting? Perhaps you will offer both options for different levels of service. This is the place to explain your plan thoroughly, but simply.

If it is an existing business, describe its history to this point. List the existing and/or proposed services and products. Next, include the resources needed to run the business, the location, and the anticipated time until you will be open for customers. If it is a new concern, you should also include methods of record keeping and how the business will operate. It may be interesting to describe the genesis of your business concept. Most importantly, you need to explain why the business will be successful.

Business Operation

As part of your business overview, it is necessary to explain exactly how your products or services will be produced and sold. Explain your product in succinct, easy-to-understand language. This is not a place to dazzle the reader with high-tech lingo. Writing this section is very good practice for marketing the product or service. If you can explain it clearly in your business plan, you'll have a prototype for future marketing literature, which must be understandable to all potential customers.

Explain what it is your business will do, and outline the steps involved in the process. And, lastly, include all of your requirements for facilities, equipment, and personnel, as well as the supplies that will be needed, and the sources of these supplies.

Management Team

Here you will list the key players, with short bios and the value that each brings to the table. For businesses seeking capital, this is significant, since the potential venture capitalists want to know the recipient of their investment capital. They will be particularly interested in knowing if your key people have the goods to take the business to the next level.

One or two paragraphs should be sufficient to sum up the qualifications and overall background of each key person involved. Don't get into philosophies or include extraneous material. Include pictures if you like. You might also mention your board of directors or advisors and include their names and backgrounds, because they're definitely pertinent to this business endeavor.

Market Analysis

A major part of your business plan will address the market you are entering. The number one priority of this section is to buttress your assertion that there is enough of a market to support your business. Start by pinning down the unique characteristics of your product or service, or at least define the particular niche you will serve. In the popular area of fitness, as an example, there may be three health clubs in a five-mile radius of your planned location, but none of the others has child care and an on-site nutritionist, which you will be offering.

To show how your distinctive features matter, you will need to show the characteristics of your target market. Using the health club example, you might be able to show that 35 percent of the residents in your geographical area have spouses at home at least half of the time with children under school age, and have socioeconomic and educational backgrounds that suggest they value a healthy lifestyle. These statistics can be used to reinforce the value of offering child care at your facility. Explain how your club will make it easy for members to get in a quick workout and not have to worry about babysitting arrangements.

You will need to understand overall trends in the industry, look at your competition, do a market analysis, research prospective locations, and ultimately come up with a solid, but perhaps flexible, marketing strategy. Even in advance of concrete market research, you will have a gut feeling about the market and how your endeavor will fill a need. Try sketching out a rough outline of where your customers will come from, be it a mixture of government, consumer, small or large business. Put some percentages on each segment based on where you believe you will get the best response. Over time, you may need to undertake more formal research to identify the best areas for expansion.

Industry Analysis

In this section you present your business in the context of the overall industry. Here, you take a step back and look at the big picture: the industry as it currently stands and projected future developments. You will need to do your share of research before putting this part of the plan together. It is key to make note of the size and growth rate of the industry as a whole.

For example, if your business will be part of a $10 billion industry that in the next ten years is expected to grow to more than $50 billion, then include that information.

ESSENTIAL

Feel free to use charts, graphs, or simply text to explain the sales and profit trends culled from your research. Present changes in the industry and share news that will provide your business with an entry point into the market. Also, clearly delineate the market in your area or region. Then show the response of your business to the marketing demands and trends.

The end result of the industry analysis should be a demonstration of why your business will be able to grab a piece of the pie. It is important for you as a future entrepreneur to see this very clearly in order to advocate for your proposed enterprise. If you don't have a potential market share, no matter how great your idea may be, you'll have trouble convincing others that your company will be successful.

Marketing Strategy

Once you have examined the industry as a whole and worked out a market analysis showing where you fit into the big picture, the next challenge is getting into that market. In this section, you need to explain who your target market is. Describe this market and why they would pay for your product or services. The main components of your marketing strategy should include:

- Pricing
- Advertising
- Networking
- Promotion
- Sales strategies
- Sales tracking

Readers of your business plan will want to know how you came up with your pricing. If you are selling bagels, did you factor in the cost of your utilities and counter staff as well as the eggs and flour? Did you account for the need to discount a certain percentage that doesn't sell on the day they are made?

Most successful businesses are geared to reach a specific market. The size of the market will depend on the nature of the product. Explaining how you will reach your market is a very important part of supporting your business plan. Mass marketing to everyone is generally reserved only for major corporations with plenty of money and an established track record. Keep in mind that if you try to reach too large an audience, you may be unable to serve the customers you attract. If you can only accommodate twenty customers and fifty show up, you'll be at your peak capacity with the first twenty and you'll lose thirty potential customers as well. Likewise, you should also be careful about having such a specific, narrow target group that you don't have enough potential customers to make your business profitable.

There are a number of advertising and promotional avenues to consider. You will need to spell out which you are choosing and why. If you are opening a bicycle repair shop, you will want to be in the local yellow pages and the community publications. If you are seeking contract work for your management training seminars, you may need to advertise in in-flight magazines or seek speaking engagements at conferences.

However you expect to do it, you will need to explain how you intend to capture a portion of that market. Detail the methods and media you will utilize to promote your business. Will you use direct mail? A radio and television advertising campaign? The Internet? Are you seeking subscribers? Membership? You then need to spell out how much money you will spend on publicity and advertising. It's very important to justify your marketing strategy to show others (and remind yourself) you aren't throwing money away on a poorly planned marketing strategy.

If you have contacts or relationships with publicists or others who can help get your name in the media or give you discounts on advertising, this is the place to let it be known. Perhaps you have some barter opportunities that will preserve cash at the outset. Highlight these. If you have ideas, including any special promotional events, giveaways, special combination pricing or other discounts, contests, or anything else that will hype your business, include those plans here.

Show how you expect to be perceived in the marketplace, whether you will be the bargain haircut chain with no appointments necessary, or the elite concierge service for wealthy residents of luxury apartments in major metropolitan areas. Share your thoughts on how you plan to define your image right out of the box and over time.

Competitive Analysis

This is the section where you discuss the competition. Rather than a negative, your competition may be one of the best supporting arguments for the success of your business. First, if there are already other companies doing what you plan to do, it proves there is a demand for it. Naturally, you have ideas to serve this market better, with innovations, better quality, more competitive pricing, or all of the above. Prove it. You'll need to do some investigative research so that you can adequately describe your competitors. You want to present an overview of their business operation, their location, products, share of the market, and anything else you think is pertinent—all in a concise form. You may need to visit competitors' stores or sample products of competing manufacturers. Or you may have had discussions with clients of service providers who have revealed weaknesses in the services they have received.

Your next step is to make comparisons to your business and explain how you will improve upon the products and services offered by your competitors. Study what the market wants and show how you can provide solutions in a better way. If you can show that you will draw customers based on what you're offering (whether it's service, products, location, or anything else), then you can gain the upper hand.

You aren't trying to denigrate other businesses; you're simply trying to separate what you intend to do from what's being done by others. Let those who are reviewing your business plan know that you're prepared to carve out your own segment of the market and how you propose to do so.

Financial Plan

Everything in your business plan so far is a setup for the main event, which is the numbers. Show them the money. This is where you will need to include all key financial information, from start-up costs to balance sheets. Be clear about your total financial needs and how the funds will be used. This section demonstrates what will make your business profitable. It includes all the charts and graphs necessary to illustrate your points, but most significantly it follows a logical trend and tells your financial story, just as an annual report provides a compelling background for the numbers. There's nothing wrong with asking your accountant or any qualified financial expert to help you put this part of the plan together.

You'll want to clearly show how much money you're seeking and then explain exactly how you plan to spend it. Manufacturing facilities? Product acquisition or manufacturing? Marketing? Sales reps? Technology? Make sure it's all spelled out. All expenditures need to be justified, beginning with your start-up costs and continuing with your ongoing operations costs.

ALERT

You will probably finance your new business from a variety of sources. Don't hesitate to be forthcoming with the mix of resources as you write your business plan. Most importantly, you will want to show how much of your own assets you are putting into the venture.

You then need to explain where your profits will come from. Be conservative to a fault. Don't fantasize. Include the next three, five, seven, and possibly even ten years in a profit-and-loss income statement. Break it up by months at first to show how you plan to build the business, and then break it up by years. Include your:

- Break-even analysis
- Projected balance sheet
- Projected income statement
- Projected profit and loss statement
- Projected cash flow (you need to illustrate that you will not run out of cash)

Just as you want to show your projected expenses, assets, and liabilities when starting a new business, you should include financial statements from the previous three to five years if you're buying an existing business. No matter how brilliant your idea is, if the numbers don't add up, your business will not succeed. The bottom line is just that—the bottom line.

Reviewing and Tweaking Your Plan

Now that you have all of the key ingredients included in your plan, it's time to step back and look at it with fresh eyes. Can it work? If you are satisfied that your idea deserves to be funded, you will want to check over your document carefully. Make sure you've included all key points, the business plan flows clearly, all spelling and grammar is checked and edited, all graphs and charts are easy to read, and the plan is printed on high-quality paper and bound, and has a professional appearance.

A business plan usually runs from twenty to thirty-five or, at most, forty pages in length. Lines should be double-spaced and have enough white space around the margins so that it doesn't look too dense. Make sure pages are numbered. Go back to your table of contents and add the corresponding numbers (along with correct section names and subsections if you use them).

Attach any supporting documents that you have in an appendix. This could include any research material, articles, graphics, product illustrations, or other data you think are relevant. Keep these supporting documents to a few pages.

ESSENTIAL

Once you have filled in the rough business plan, start shaping it as you think through and plan out each dimension of your business. Remember, the business plan needs to be a realistic portrait of your business. If the pieces don't fit together or the numbers don't add up, not only will the plan fail, so will the business.

Business plans vary in their style and manner. Some have subsections throughout the plan, while others paint broader strokes. There are numerous variations on the main theme, but the business plan should include, in some form, the elements discussed in this chapter. Read the business plan in Appendix A, and then put together a rough outline of your own. Don't worry about the writing at first—just do your best to express your ideas and explain your business.

Once your plan is complete, continue to think of it as a living document. Revisit it, updating pertinent information and goals over time. It will help keep you on track and offer a benchmark against which to measure your progress. When you have a proven track record of setting and meeting goals you become more attractive to future investors. There are a number of various business plans you may want to prepare over time. This chapter has focused on preparing a plan for a start-up business. You may want to generate internal plans as you proceed in your business. Less formal than plans for funding proposals, these can be used for managers to set and measure goals. If you review them on at least an annual basis, you will know how you are doing. Once your initial plan is working and you have your legs under you, you may be ready to develop a growth plan for expansion or creation of a new subsidiary for your business.

CHAPTER 8

Get Your Capital Act Together

Businesses can do one of three things financially: make money, break even, or lose money. Often at the very beginning, it is necessary to operate in a deficit. At some point, however, you will want to crest right past the break-even point and begin to have something in the bank to show for all your hard work. Making money is a goal. Finding and using money to get you to that point is another story.

Finance Basics

No matter how terrific your idea may be or how ready the market is to buy it, nothing is going to happen without funds to get it off the ground. You may have some general ideas of what you will need to make your business go, but this is the period when you need to take off any rose-colored glasses and put on your accountant's green visor. Some would counsel you to have enough funds set aside to carry your day-to-day expenses for at least six months to a year. If you know you don't have to worry about which utility you are going to be able to pay, or be juggling multiple car payments, you will be free to give your idea your full attention. If making money instantly becomes the driving force, the flowering of your idea may be shortchanged. You don't want to be siphoning off funds to make a mortgage payment when the funds more appropriately need to be going into building the business.

In simplest terms, money for your business will come from one of two sources: you, or you and others. If yours is a service business, you may be able to comfortably fund your start-up costs yourself. If your overhead is low, your cash flow may become positive relatively quickly. But no business starts with zero cash infusion needs. In most cases you will need to find funding beyond your own capabilities. Depending on the nature of your business, you may need to go after money from a variety of sources. This is in itself a time-consuming undertaking. It is also one you may need to revisit as your company grows.

Typically your own savings and other financial resources such as a home equity loan are the beginning of your funding journey. Many entrepreneurs seek additional capital from private sources such as family members and friends. If this takes the form of a loan, it is often extended with very low or no interest. It could also come as an equity investment giving the party an ownership stake in your business. Relatively smaller, and shorter-term, funding comes from banks, savings and loans, or credit unions.

Angel investors or venture capitalists, usually high-net-worth individuals who would be buying a share of your company, are sources that should not be tapped until you are ready for significant and rapid growth and contemplate selling within the next few years.

Before you embark on the quest for dollars, take the time to do a thorough analysis of why you need money now. Here are some points the Small Business Administration suggests you consider:

- Are you able to work with your current cash flow?
- Are you looking for a cushion or funds to expand?
- How urgent is your need? Anticipate cash needs rather than try to borrow under pressure.
- How much are you willing to risk? These will determine available financing choices.
- At what stage of development is your business?
- How will be borrowed capital be used? Lenders will want to know.
- Overall, what is the state of your industry? Is it depressed, stable, or growing? Each drives different money sources and needs. Flourishing businesses will get better terms.
- Is your business seasonal or cyclical? Construction can be cyclical and require loans to survive depressed periods. Seasonal needs can be much shorter.
- How strong is your management team?
- How does your financing request dovetail with your business plan? If you don't have a business plan, writing one has to become a top priority.

How to Get Start-up Cash

When you are seeking money from outside sources, you have two broad paths to pursue. One is debt financing. The other is equity financing, which will be discussed in Chapter 9. Debt financing is money you borrow from a financial institution such as a bank or a savings and loan. These borrowed funds must be repaid over a period of time with interest. When you seek a business loan, the lending institution will ask how much of your own money you are staking to the business. Additionally, you can be asked to submit assets you have as collateral for the loan. A bank will never use the full value of the asset to back a loan. On the other hand, being light in assets cannot be the sole reason to deny you a loan. Assets that could be used to collateralize a loan include investments you have in real estate, stocks or bonds, or some other fairly liquid form.

There are formulas that apply to particular types of loans, but you should plan on demonstrating your ability to front anywhere from 10 to 30 percent of the equity in a start-up business. If that isn't scary enough, the bank is going to tell you next that you will have to personally guarantee the loan. This is not a step to be taken lightly. If the business fails, the debt obligation remains, and you will be making those payments with no income to support them. Sobering thought. Once the business has become viable with a track record of profits, or can prove profits are in the near future, different terms can be worked out.

ALERT

Keep in mind the premise that the asset you use as collateral will be sold if you default and do not repay the loan. The antique train sets you have lovingly restored may be worth something on eBay, but they are not going to carry the day with an ultraserious loan officer.

Looking for Equity Investors

Banks earn interest on loans. It is their obligation to be conservative in selecting how they write loans to keep their owners' risk of loss to a minimum. Other funding sources can be individuals or lenders who will trade their dollars for a share of equity in your company. Unlike a bank that gets paid back on a predictable schedule, investors do not realize any profit—or loss—until your business is sold.

Investors come in many sizes and shapes and sport many personalities. You may meet with numerous candidates before finding the right investor. Just like dating, you'll meet people who aren't interested in what you have to offer and others with whom you don't feel comfortable entering into an agreement. One of the biggest mistakes you can make is jumping at the first offer of money that comes along. On closer inspection, you may find other strings attached, such as control issues.

It's very important that both sides feel comfortable when entering this kind of business relationship. When meeting with investors, they're sizing you up, too. Are you someone they want to put their money behind? Does your plan sound feasible, and can you make it happen? Often more than 50 percent of their evaluation of the investment is their evaluation not of the idea but of the person sitting before them. Many people can come up with good ideas, but few can actually make them work. That's why so many businesses fail in the first few years.

Investors are looking for:

- A sound idea
- A good, comprehensive business plan
- Someone with the drive, determination, and skills to make that plan happen

You're looking for:

- Someone who understands your idea or shares the same vision
- Someone who will let you maintain control of your business
- An individual, or individuals, with the funding to help you make your idea happen

Before you start raising money, it's worth mentioning that financing is often tied closely to control issues. If you get a loan, then you need to pay back the money with interest, no ifs, ands, or buts. If you take on an investor, be it a friend, relative, or stranger, you may be giving up some degree of control over your business and some percentage of your profits. Therefore, determine specifically what people want for their investment. Are they seeking profits, control, or both? Try to reach an agreement that makes you feel comfortable—and get it in writing.

ESSENTIAL

At the very beginning you might need to rely on your training or past industry or entrepreneurial experience to demonstrate your readiness to head this new venture. As the business grows, you may need to bring in talented folks in specialized areas: sales and marketing, finance, inventory management, data management, and other facets of the company. Investing in this talent will offer proof of your commitment to success and to strategic planning for the continued growth of your business.

Personal Credit Scores Matter

You are not going to convince a bank or other lender to part with its money based on your good looks. You should have a personal financial track record that is squeaky clean and demonstrates prudent judgment and reliability. Even if you are incorporated, the bank will be reviewing your personal financial track record when you go for a loan. First and foremost, they want to be sure that you and your business, if it has been operating for a while, have a solid credit history. If you have a good history of meeting your personal loans—and this includes every credit card, school loan, mortgage, auto loan, or other loan you currently have or have paid off—you will be viewed as creditworthy. Likewise, if the business can prove it has consistently met its obligations for lease payments and the like, a record of dependability will have been established. You can order a credit report for a nominal fee from Equifax, Experian, or another credit bureau to see what your credit record looks like. If you find any irregularities, such as credit cards you thought were closed but remain open, you can clear them up. Or if there is a one-time blip in life that caused you to miss a payment, such as a medical emergency, it can and will need to be explained.

ESSENTIAL

Did you know that even if you have unused credit on credit cards, a lending institution will view that as debt obligation? That's because you could access or use that credit at any moment. If you did, you could exceed your loan capacity. If you do not use or need a particular credit card, even a store card, close the account now.

If you had filed for bankruptcy within the past seven years, you may not be able to secure a loan. Likewise, if you have a pattern of slow payments or collections against you, most lenders will not be eager to support your loan request. Lastly, banks and governments are closely tied, especially when the government is backing loans. A strong record of meeting all tax obligations is very important in establishing your creditworthiness. Even when taxes are not owed it is imperative to have a record of filing returns on time. This includes state and federal income taxes, or estimated taxes, if that is how you pay. All of these factors paint the picture of your creditworthiness.

Prove Your Business Is Loan-Worthy

When you approach a lender you are making the ultimate sales pitch for your company. You will need to be prepared with a fully developed loan proposal. If you do a sloppy job, there may not be another chance. A bank will look at a poorly prepared loan proposal and may decide it reflects on your professionalism. Remember, they are in the business of loaning money to make money. They want to be very sure you will be responsible in re-paying the loan.

You want to show not only that you fully understand your business but also that you know why your business is viable. From the bank's point of view, that means that it will make money. A loan officer will want to read a succinct summary first, in the form of either a cover letter or an executive summary. This will introduce you, including your business background, the nature of your company, what the money will be used for, and how it will benefit the business. You should spell out how much money you are looking for, the terms you desire, and when you will be able to repay the loan.

When you make your pitch, keep in mind that the person reading the application is a banker or other financial lender and may or may not be familiar with the ins and outs of your business and industry. Be sure to include a brief overview that includes not only the genesis of your individual endeavor, but a view of the market and how you see your company relative to the competition. Describe the type of organization you have and the proposed future operation you envision. List your products, services, customers, and suppliers. Include resumes of all the key players, including all the owners, managers, and any specialists who will add to the credibility of the business. All of these will flesh out the strength of your proposal.

Good Documents Are Gold

Important documents that should be included with your proposal might include copies of any licenses you hold, contracts, leases, franchise or partnership agreements, letters of reference, articles of incorporation, and plans and specifications. In other words, furnish every possible piece of paper that gives the loan officer a full understanding of your business's legal standing and obligations.

The financial statements you actually supply need to be recent, no more than ninety days old. In addition to the balance sheet, the bank will want to see profit-and-loss statements, and accounts-receivable aging. If your business is just starting, the challenge will be to demonstrate how businesses similar to yours perform in your industry. You would certainly be striving to at least meet, if not exceed, the industry norm. As a start-up, it will be very important to provide a pro forma balance sheet to demonstrate how soon you will become profitable so the bank can see how and when the loan will be repaid. This would include anticipated earnings, expenses, and your forecast for profit-and-loss performance. Provide clear explanations to support any of your assumptions, especially if they don't line up with industry trends. You may have knowledge of some new technology or change in legislation that will make your projections achievable when your industry's history might suggest otherwise.

FACT

It's not good to over borrow. In the same way banks will frown upon too much debt liability in your personal credit history, they will not like to see too much business debt. If too much of your cash flow is used to repay loans, it may not be available to accrue in a meaningful way to help you grow or improve your business operations and services.

If you have loans from any of your shareholders, and these can be put in a second position (meaning the bank would get its money first), the value of the shareholder loans could be considered as equity. This could improve the net worth of the business on paper, moving it from a negative to a positive position, and making it a more attractive risk for the lender.

CHAPTER 9

Putting a Financing Plan in Place

Once you have done a thorough financial self-examination, determined how much money you will need to borrow, and established the facts to support your creditworthiness, it is time to review what types of loans will best suit your needs. You may discover you need a combination of types and sources. Expect the approval process to take at least two to three weeks, assuming no complicating factors arise in the loan review process.

Traditional Loan Offerings

Loans can be structured in a couple of different ways. A term loan has a set period of time in which to repay the loan, and usually a fixed interest rate. The entire amount is available for you to use for the reasons you have proposed to your lender. Typically, these funds are used to cover expenses such as equipment purchases, property, furnishings, and other items that over time would be amortized. The usual repayment period for a real-estate loan is up to twenty-five years. Loans for purchasing equipment might mature in ten years.

You can also borrow by establishing a line of credit. This reserves funds for your use to cover expenses in peak times before income is generated. If your business will have seasonal fluctuations, a line of credit will help smooth out the peaks and valleys of income and expense.

ESSENTIAL

Lenders will look for collateral from your business to back loans. Facets of the company, such as your accounts receivable, contracts with customers, inventory, and equipment, may be considered of value in securing your loan. These would be converted to cash in case the loan was not repaid according to its terms.

This debt form does not require you to pay to borrow those funds until you actually use them, a big advantage. In many cases, the terms require you to repay the money quicker than with a term loan, or the credit line will be available only for a fixed period of time. You can always renegotiate the terms. As your business grows, you may need a bigger line of credit to work with; or as interest rates fluctuate you may want more favorable terms.

Special Loan Programs

If your proposal to borrow money does not fit into the standard parameters of the lending institution, you may be eligible for special loan programs, sometimes referred to as microloans. The Small Business Administration, a federal agency that backs most small business loans anyway, guarantees specialized loans. Many state and local municipalities also have programs to back bank loans. Instances where these "outside the box" loans come into play include cases where an owner cannot come up with a required down payment, or perhaps does not have enough assets to offer as collateral to back a loan. Sometimes needing a small loan, say under $25,000, actually draws a red flag and triggers an alternative program. Another reason for a special loan may be because the business is just getting off the ground and has no credit history.

Loan Sources Other Than Banks

Surprisingly, insurance companies are willing to offer debt instruments that can provide you capital. They are not set up to provide short-term revolving debt, but can write loans with a seven- to fifteen-year term. The interest charged to borrow in this manner is tied to the current treasury rate. The insurance company would add some percentage points to that rate to cover their risk and generate a return on the monies they lend.

Commercial finance companies can offer you short-term revolving debt in the form of a credit line. They use your receivables or inventory to back this type of loan. It is more expensive, with interest rates running one to four points above a bank rate. However, you have the flexibility to pay down the loan the minute you collect your receivable. In this way you are only paying on the money actually used. This is a flexible loan that can be very handy depending on your cash flow requirements.

Interest rates are an important factor in the overhead costs of your business. Some lenders will offer you a lower rate if you are willing to ride the tides with fluctuating interest rates in the market. Although it may be tempting to shave off a bit in initial interest rates, it may be more prudent to accept a slightly higher, but predictable, rate for the life of the loan.

Vendor Teammates

Obviously you will pay for everything you buy for your business, be it equipment, paper clips, or your inventory. You pay for things like postage stamps on the spot, but a great many of your other expenses can be negotiated for extended payment of thirty or more days. The time you can hold on to your cash moves you closer to generating income. Try to get the most favorable terms possible with your vendors. By extending you generous payment terms, they become quasi-lenders. Needless to say, it is imperative to honor the terms and pay when expected. Once you have a track record as a reliable payer it will be easier to approach them if you get into a crunch.

ESSENTIAL

If you start a business by "bootstrapping," you forego any outside financial assistance and restrict your needs to the most basic. A fancy office? Forget it. How does your basement sound? Maybe you don't need a sign right away. Begin with used equipment, maybe even another's cast-offs. Conserve your cash for the basics. Once the cash is flowing, maintain your conservative spending habits.

Silent Partners

Equity financing is money invested in your company by individuals or entities who are buying a piece of your business. Their reason for getting involved is different than a lending institution's. Instead of earning interest on their money, their objective is to share in profits or recoup their investment from the sale of the business. Initially your equity investors may be family members, friends, colleagues, industry friends, or even, to some degree, your employees. As you grow, you might seek equity cash from high-wealth individuals, sometimes referred to as angel investors or venture capitalists. These investors are seeking a juicy profit either through a public stock offering or by the acquisition of your entity by a corporation. Unlike a lending institution, their investment is not backed by your assets. They are not in the business of "renting" money and getting a predictable return. Rather, they are taking a bigger risk, and seeking a bigger return.

Angel investors are everywhere, but you will not find a directory listing their contact information. To find them, you need to put yourself into contact with everyone you can possibly think of who might be interested in backing your business. Then ask them to introduce you to any of their friends or colleagues who might help. In other words, get out there and network. There may even be investment networking groups in your area you can join or that can help you circulate your proposal. Angel investors are particularly attractive because they can be the source of equity funding you will need in the early days. They can generate as few as a couple of thousand dollars to amounts as high as seven figures.

Access to venture capitalists tends to be through referrals instead of a direct approach. They are deluged with plans for many multiples the number of companies in which they can invest. A referral may help your plan get a serious read. Venture capitalists typically want to be in and out of an investment within three to five years. This crowd is looking for very high returns on their investment so they are constantly combing proposals for opportunities that offer them a chance to get in on something that has an excellent chance of growing quickly. Generally speaking, they are less interested in niche companies.

Because equity investors will literally have a stake in your business, they will be scrutinizing your proposal for a number of factors. Expect to be able to answer the following:

- Are you opening a new market that has tremendous growth?
- How rapidly will your business reach market dominance, either locally or in your field?
- Where will your profits be generated?
- Can high profit margins be sustained as competition comes after you?
- Do you have a plan and a timeline to sell?
- Is your product or idea the newest "new thing"?
- Can it be protected from imitators with patents or proprietary technology?
- What obstacles do you foresee and how will you overcome them?
- What industry experience do you and your team have?

Venture capitalist investors will likely have a behind-the-scenes influence on the day-to-day management of the company, but can intensify their involvement if they sense management is making decisions that will hurt rather than improve their profit prospects. Keep in mind that they will expect to have certain milestones set forth and will want reports on your progress toward meeting them.

FACT

Know the impact of debt versus equity financing. With debt financing, you retain control of all aspects of your business. With equity financing, your investors can exert some control in your decisions, even to the point of making you sell the company. If family or friends are equity investors, it could change your personal relationships, not necessarily for the better.

In all cases, you will need to make a solid presentation that shows how the money will be used and why you and your business are good risks. Showing your passion for your undertaking will go a long way, too, in convincing any investor of your seriousness. To demonstrate the worthiness of your business as an investment, you will be asked for a pro forma plan for your endeavor. The lending institution or investors will want to know why your business can succeed, so you need to show how you will distinguish yourself. Most important, they will want to understand how you will price your products and services. The real litmus test for the viability of your idea may be how soon your profits exceed your expenses.

Even before you seek funding, you will want to rough out some scenarios in which your sales will grow from very limited to a level healthy enough to cover expenses and provide you a profit. Demonstrating the viability of your projected sales and income will be very important for convincing your lender you are a worthy credit risk.

How Soon to Profitability?

If there is one question both you and your lenders or investors have at the top of the list, it has to be: When will you turn a profit? Even in advance of writing a full-blown business plan, it is extremely useful to get a break-even analysis down on paper. Sure there will be a bit of speculating, but you must summon your best guess on a whole set of assumptions and expectations to map out the point at which you will be bringing in more than you are shelling out.

The idea behind this exercise is to determine the sales revenue you will need to cover your costs and begin making a profit. You can use the exercise to test different price points or to calculate how long you will need capital to carry the business before it generates enough cash to sustain itself. By testing out your pricing and profit margins, you might discover that you actually cannot make a profit. Not to worry. Hopefully you have discovered this before becoming overly invested in what you have proven will be a losing proposition.

To construct a break-even analysis for your business, follow these steps:

1. **Figure out the fixed costs of your enterprise.** These are expense items that do not fluctuate from month to month. They include rent, equipment leases, insurance, phone, electricity, and any other predictable obligations. For your test calculation, pad the fixed cost estimate just to be sure you have a conservative projection.
2. **Determine your cost (the variable cost) for each unit. Note that a unit can be a tangible commodity or a service.** The cost of a commodity, whether it is a salad bowl or a toilet bowl, is easy enough to determine. The direct cost of a unit of someone's time needed to provide a service is less straightforward.
3. **Determine the gross profit per unit.** The gross profit (contribution) is the difference between what the customer pays and your cost to buy or provide it. You may know what industry norms are for profit margins, or you may need to experiment to see what the market will bear.
4. **Calculate your breakeven.** To do this, divide your annual fixed cost figure by the gross profit or contribution per unit and you will see what you need in sales revenue just to cover the fixed costs and the variable costs of your product or service. That just gets you to break even. Higher sales start to generate the profits you seek.

If you are unable to reach breakeven with your expected costs and revenue, make adjustments to your plan. Delay some overhead expenses if you can. Find cheaper workspace, or hold off hiring until you have the established revenue stream to support staff. Negotiate for better rates from your suppliers. Raise your prices.

Using the following example, you can see how a break-even analysis works. The following chart shows how to plot where an imaginary chocolate shop business turns from losing money to making money. The fixed costs will include rent, insurance, cleaning crew, payroll, utilities, telecommunications, and equipment leases. Variable costs are for the purchase of chocolates wholesale, per pound. A simple breakdown of costs, pricing, and sales helps pinpoint the target sales goal to move into profitability.

Fixed cost	$800.00
Variable cost	$6.00 per pound
Selling Price	$15.00 per pound
Gross Profit	$9.00
Breakeven	$800.00/$9.00 = 90 (approximately)

The table below shows profits on sales of 0 to 225 pounds of chocolates. Sales under ninety pounds result in a net loss. After ninety pounds, profits begin to climb.

Pounds	Fixed Cost	Fixed and Variable Cost	Sales Revenue	Profit
0	$800.00	$800.00	$0.00	-$800.00
10	$800.00	$860.00	$150.00	-$710.00
20	$800.00	$920.00	$300.00	-$620.00
30	$800.00	$980.00	$450.00	-$530.00
40	$800.00	$1,040.00	$600.00	-$440.00
60	$800.00	$1,160.00	$900.00	-$260.00
80	$800.00	$1,280.00	$1,200.00	-$80.00
90	$800.00	$1,340.00	$1,350.00	$10.00
100	$800.00	$1,400.00	$1,500.00	$100.00
120	$800.00	$1,520.00	$1,800.00	$280.00
140	$800.00	$1,640.00	$2,100.00	$460.00
160	$800.00	$1,760.00	$2,400.00	$640.00
180	$800.00	$1,880.00	$2,700.00	$820.00
200	$800.00	$2,000.00	$3,000.00	$1,000.00
225	$800.00	$2,150.00	$3,375.00	$1,225.00

Balancing your pricing can be a bit tricky. There are the hard factors you have to consider, such as the cost of the goods and your overhead. Then there is the dynamic of the market. Is yours a product or service that has lots of competition that could force you to keep pricing low to attract customers? The overall economy can affect what you can charge. If the stock market is doing well, people feel a little freer with their cash, even if they are not big investors themselves. If general business reports are glum, folks tend to keep their hands in their pockets. Some businesses are more seasonal, making the products difficult to sell during the off-season. In all cases, the goal is to sell at a profit. You may need to prepare more than one model for your break-even analysis, using different pricing assumptions. In the real-life experience of the business, you will soon discover what pricing levels work.

When You Have the Money in Hand

Once you have your initial capital, whether your own or from outside sources, the race begins to the day your sales revenues generate positive cash. There is cash and there is cash flow. Cash is the greenbacks you have sitting in the bank. It is not your inventory, nor your accounts receivable, nor any other asset. It is liquid and it is available to meet your obligations immediately. Cash flow is the movement of money in and out of your business. Cash flow occurs even if you are not making a profit. During periods when you are not bringing in more revenue than you are spending, you have negative cash flow. When your cash receipts exceed your expenses, you have positive cash flow.

In the early days when the business is getting going, you may have negative cash flow as you spend some of the capital you have secured. It is an extremely good idea to include cash-flow projections with your other business plans to make sure you don't get to the end of your reserves before positive income kicks in. As a business owner, it is critical that you understand your cash needs. You will need to have ready access to additional cash if you need it, such as with an established credit line. Keep lines of communication open with all of your lenders, investors, and creditors. There is no greater feeling in the world than making deposits into your bank account knowing your creditors are not nipping at your heels.

CHAPTER 10

Regulations and Legal Matters

Once you have figured out a basic plan for your business, there will be some regulatory and legal matters to attend to. Though the processes may seem tedious, it's very important that you operate legally to protect your investment in the business. Although there are plenty of resources to access on your own, using the professional services of an attorney to guide you through this process will be money well spent.

Licensing and Regulations

Financial brokers, insurance brokers, doctors, dentists, veterinarians, attorneys, pharmacists, and certified public accountants are among the many professionals who are required to have a license. Likewise, many companies must be licensed in order to conduct their business. It's up to you to contact either the town hall, the records bureau, the secretary of state, the Department of Consumer Affairs, or other governing body to determine which licenses you need to conduct your business. The Small Business Administration (SBA) can also help. Go to *www.sba.gov/smallbusinessplanner/start/getlicensesandpermits/index.html* for basic licensing information. Many cities now provide this kind of licensing information online as well.

FACT

Trade associations and professional associations are useful resources for licensing and compliance information. They are composed of members who are all in the same business so they are used to answering typical questions from individuals starting out in that line of business. They may also provide training for compliance with various regulations.

In most cases, business licenses are not costly, but they can make the difference between staying in business or being shut down—and even a temporary shutdown can cost you a lot in revenues. It can also damage the reputation of your new business. Certain cities make it clear that you must have a business license in order to operate. For example, any business of any type in the city of Chicago will need a business license. There are nearly 200 different types of business licenses in Chicago, and your business will certainly fall under one heading if not several. So if you're starting up a business in Chicago, make a visit to city hall.

Along with having a city, state, or county license, you'll need to address other responsibilities that come with owning a business. Businesses selling or preparing food, including vendors, will need special licenses or permits or both and will have to follow the codes set forth by the health department. Outdoor cooking or selling of potentially flammable objects will be closely watched by the fire department and you will need to adhere to their local ordinances. The local sanitation bureau and various other departments may have regulations that you'll need to comply with—or risk facing fines or even being shut down. The local chamber of commerce is a good place to inquire about such local regulations.

Some businesses need to adhere to federal regulations. Radio stations, for example, must follow Federal Communications Commission (FCC) rules. Internet-based businesses have presented many gray areas in regard to application of standard regulations set forth by governing bodies such as the FCC and Food and Drug Administration (FDA). Thus far, it has been difficult to impose restrictions on the Internet because websites are based in different states and different countries and can, therefore, cross national and international boundaries. For example, you cannot open up an online casino based in most areas of the United States. However, you can start a casino outside the United States and U.S. citizens can play for real money at your website.

ALERT

Most business licenses have expiration dates. Don't forget to make note of the date your license expires and what the renewal process entails. That way you won't be scrambling around at the last minute trying to find what you need to get your license renewed.

It's in your best interests to be aware of all regulations and licenses necessary for your profession, your business, and your community. Here's a to-do list for licensing:

- Obtain any and all required federal, state, and local licensing.
- Familiarize yourself with all zoning ordinances and local regulations.
- Establish a system to periodically check the expiration dates of all licenses.
- Post all licenses that require posting, and put all others in a safe place.

Inspections

The fire department and health department are among several agencies that can inspect your business. Code violations can result in a fine the first time around, and the fine can become increasingly steep for repeat offenders. Certain businesses, particularly those involving food, plants, or chemicals, can expect more frequent inspections. This doesn't mean that other businesses can assume they are exempt from fire, health, or other similar codes, of course.

If you will be renovating space or an entire building you will need a building inspection—and in some areas, a building permit—before you can even begin work. Check with your city hall before starting any work to see what the local requirements are.

Zoning Ordinances

It's no coincidence that all the fast food chains are in one area of town and none are situated among a row of private homes on the lake. There's more to this than just preventing a lovely view from being ruined. Communities enact zoning laws to maintain the structure, property values, and way of life in neighborhoods. Zoning laws are primarily designed to separate commercial and residential areas. However, there's often much more to it than that. Zoning laws may also guard against a business opening up that is too noisy, smelly, or rowdy; uses hazardous materials; or promotes or sells materials unsuitable for minors.

Beyond the ordinances regulating which kind of business may be operated in a certain area, there may be other restrictions. For example, signage may be limited to a certain size or approval may be required for advertisements.

ESSENTIAL

Some towns can provide you with a color-coded map showing the various zoning districts. Having this visual may be helpful as you plan your location. Some towns also have mixed zoning, which may be good to know about. Contact your local city, town, or county clerk's office for maps and other information.

It's usually fairly easy to get a basic idea of the general zoning laws in a specific neighborhood by simply driving around. A fast food restaurant may not be found on the main commercial street of a residential neighborhood. A topless club will not be down the block from a school. A bar won't pop up on a quiet residential street.

Even a home-based business can be subject to zoning requirements. If you are anticipating a steady flow of clients to and from your home, or have commercial vehicles making deliveries, your neighbors may have a surprise for you in the form of a zoning restriction.

Check out all local zoning ordinances before you set up shop. Some will actually surprise you, while others are those that you would expect. The county clerk, community planning board, and city hall are places to go for more information.

Leases

Once you find a location that suits you, you'll need to have your lawyer carefully review the lease. You need to know exactly what is expected of you and what you're entitled to expect in return from your landlord. A multiyear lease can represent a significant financial commitment. Make sure it fits in with your business plans and financial resources.

Keep in mind that just because someone offers you a lease doesn't mean you can run your type of business from that location. Check the zoning restrictions before signing the lease. Conversely, just because the zoning ordinance says you can run a certain type of business in an area doesn't mean the landlord wants you running that business in her building. Landlords don't want a business that will cause their other paying tenants headaches, or will jeopardize their standing in the community or their ability to maintain a high rental price for neighboring stores or office space.

When looking at a lease, find out if you can sublease the space. This way, if business doesn't grow as quickly as you anticipate, you can fill those empty offices temporarily.

Other points to have clarified in your lease are the availability of certain amenities, and who is responsible for paying for them—you or your landlord. These include:

- Utilities—lights, heat, air conditioning
- Parking—number of spaces
- Signs in the lobby or on the building

- Snow removal
- Elevator access
- Internet connection

Make sure you cover all your bases so you aren't left with any surprise monthly charges.

Fictitious Name Forms

If you choose to run your business under any name other than your own, you will have to file a fictitious name form or doing business as (DBA) certificate in the county where the business is being conducted (usually at the city, town, or county clerk's office—it varies by state). This form indicates that your business is being run under a specific name. Prior to filing the form and paying the fee, you'll need to do a name search to make sure the name isn't already being used by another business. The wider the scope of the business, the broader the name search will have to be and the costlier it may become. A local business named Silver Star Cleaners doesn't need to worry about finding another Silver Star Cleaners three states away. But if you're doing business under that name in several states, you will want to do a name search in each of those states.

Keep in mind that just because you operate under a DBA, it does not mean you are protected from personal liability for the debts of the business. The only way to make sure your personal assets are not on the line is to form a corporation, a limited partnership, or a limited liability company.

Trademarks, Patents, and Copyrights

Incorporating in your state will protect you against another company incorporating under the same business name, but not across state lines. Also, this protection only works if you started using the name first. The law really is "first in time is first in right," so if someone was using the name first, you lose even if you register. When you register a name or phrase you will need to sign an affidavit saying that following due diligence, you believe that no one else is using this mark.

But what about your brilliant invention or original work? If it's your business, your creation, or your original idea, you'll want to protect it from being used by another business. The three most common forms of protection for entrepreneurs are trademarks, patents, and copyrights.

Trademarks

A trademark can be a name (one word or several), logo, symbol, design, slogan, series of words, or combination thereof that makes your product or service uniquely distinguishable from others. Companies use trademarks to help protect the image and brand-name presence that they are trying to establish. For example, the name "Pepsi" is a trademark name, and the phrase "You deserve a break today" is also registered. If you're looking to build a nationally known brand or company identity you should consider registering your name or slogan as a trademark.

You can apply for a trademark with the United States Patent and Trademark Office (USPTO) as long as you use the trademark for commerce regulated by the U.S. Congress, or have a bona fide intention to do so. You can obtain an application from, and file it with, the USPTO (*www.uspto.gov* or 703-308-9000). You can also perform a trademark search at the USPTO website to see if others have already registered the name or trademark you want to use. Applications need to include the name and address of the person or business filing, a clear representation of that which is to be trademarked, and a list of goods and services. There is also a filing fee.

ALERT

After holding a trademark for five years, you will be required to file an affidavit to keep the trademark active. Don't neglect this or you could lose control of the trademark. Not only will you have to go through the entire filing process again, someone else may grab the trademark before you do.

Patents

If you create or invent an original product you might want to patent it. A patent protects the invention you've created from being pirated and created or sold by someone else. Not unlike a trademark search or a title search, you'll need to conduct a patent search, which will let you know if your very own original invention has already been invented and patented elsewhere.

You can conduct a patent search at the USPTO in Washington, DC, or at one of the nation's patent and trademark depository libraries located in cities all across the country. For information on patents and the locations of these key libraries, go to the website for the USPTO at *www.uspto.gov*. It may be in your best interest to have an attorney look over your application and help you fill it out.

There are several types of patents you can apply for, including a utility, design, plant, or international patent. There is also a nonprovisional patent that is good for only one year but allows you to obtain a patent more quickly. If you think others may be developing a similar product and you want to beat them to the punch, you can get a nonprovisional patent first and then a provisional patent. You must, however, apply for the provisional patent when you apply for the nonprovisional patent. Provisional patents for new products are good for twenty years, except for design patents, which last for fourteen years.

Copyrights

While trademarks protect a name and your image, and patents protect tangible products (not ideas), you can protect creative works such as artwork, music, books, brochures, advertisements, and computer software programs with a copyright. These are handled by the U.S. Library of Congress. For a small fee you can obtain a copyright by filing the proper application. Go to *www.copyright.gov* for more information and application forms. Or write to Copyright Office, Library of Congress, Washington, DC, 20559. Copyrights are good for up to fifty years after the death of the person who has registered.

Screenwriters and even authors can also obtain protection from the Writers Guild of America, East or Writers Guild of America, West by following their submission guidelines. You do not have to be a member to register a property with the guild. Go to *www.wgaeast.org* or *www.wga.org*. The guild dates and seals a copy of the work in an envelope, which you sign for, and then locks it away in their files. You hold a claim ticket and can use it to open the file in the event of an infringement upon your work.

Even if you don't file the document you create, you may benefit from simply noting on the document your name, the word "Copyright," and the year you first published or used the document in business.

Agencies, Agreements, and Regulations

There are numerous agencies governing various aspects of business—from foreign trade to communications to child labor laws. It's to your advantage to know about such agencies so you can find answers to your questions and concerns regarding policies, laws, and regulations. The U.S. government's official website for small business, Business.gov. (*www.business.gov*), has a laws and regulations section with links to sixty different federal organizations that are designed to assist you with such business needs and concerns. Business.gov is sponsored by the SBA.

FACT

Many companies do work for or with government agencies. To work with the government you will need to register your business with the U.S. Small Business Administration. Go to *www.bpn.gov/ccr* and click on Dynamic Small Business Search or call 202-205-6460 to request a guide called "Selling to the Government."

Whether you locate the agency you need through the Business.gov website or in another manner, it's important to remember they're there to help you. They also have subdivisions and online research sections that can be of service. The agencies you may need to be involved with while running your business include:

- Environmental Protection Agency (*www.epa.gov*)
- Federal Aviation Administration (*www.faa.gov*)
- Federal Railroad Administration (*www.fra.dot.gov*)
- Federal Trade Commission (*www.ftc.gov*)
- Federal Transit Administration (*www.fta.dot.gov*)
- International Trade Administration (*www.ita.doc.gov*)
- Maritime Administration (*www.marad.dot.gov*)

- U.S. Citizenship and Immigration Services (*www.uscis.gov*) [formerly Immigration and Naturalization Service]
- U.S. Consumer Product Safety Commission (*www.cpsc.gov*)
- U.S. Customs and Border Protection (*www.customs.gov*)
- U.S. Department of Commerce (*www.commerce.gov*)
- U.S. Food and Drug Administration (*www.fda.gov*)
- U.S. Department of Labor (*www.dol.gov*)
- U.S. Patent and Trademark Office (*www.uspto.gov*)

CHAPTER 11

Locating Your Business

One of the most important decisions you will make for your business will be its physical location. The Internet certainly opens doors, but often an old-fashioned door is the one a customer wants to pass through. In today's business environment, access in both the real and virtual worlds may be the way to go. This chapter will help you figure out where and how to situate your business venture.

The Right Space

You probably have a mental picture of where you envision your business located. It might be worth consulting with a space planner or other expert to help you get a realistic idea of the most efficient way to use space. Do you really know the average square footage needed for each employee doing desk work versus doing design work? Your budget may determine how much space you can afford initially. Even though you want to be conservative, with any luck at all, your business will grow. So you may also want to consider how you'll obtain more space than you will presently require. Can you find and afford a space slightly larger than you need at present? Or can you find a space with the option for expansion later without taking on the unnecessary overhead right out of the gate? Another option is to sublet extra space to another new entrepreneur, but then you have to worry about being a landlord while you are getting your own business launched.

ALERT

When searching for a place in which to do business, you may find your options are limited and you have to make the space fit your needs. Remember, you can add paint, put in new windows, and have the wiring inspected or redone, but you cannot perform miracles. You'll have to say no to certain marginally acceptable locations, even if it means continuing your location search a little longer.

Commercial realtors, advertisements in local papers, and word of mouth are three key ways in which you can find a space for your business. However, before checking out an office or retail space, review a checklist of the needs of your business. Among the questions to ask yourself are:

- How much space does my business require?
- How much equipment will I need in my space?
- Can I start out working from home or share space somewhere?
- Do I need to be in the heart of town or can I be in a low-traffic area?
- How much of a commute am I willing to make?
- Do I need to travel by public transportation?

- Will suppliers, vendors, distributors, clients, or customers be able to reach this location easily?
- How much can I afford for renting or buying?
- How much fixing up or renovating am I willing to have done?

Storefront Businesses

A retail store has special needs, the most important of which is high visibility. The business needs to both fit in and stand out at the same time. By fitting in, you want to be similar to the other businesses of the neighborhood. An upscale store won't thrive in a poor section of town, while an auto parts store may not fit well on a quaint commercial street with boutiques and restaurants. You also want to stand out in some manner so that people passing by will stop and look.

There are a number of important factors to consider when it comes to opening a store or restaurant. Weigh the following:

- Nearby competition
- Need for your type of business
- Visibility by foot and vehicular traffic
- Street-front window size and signage
- Convenience of parking
- Office and support space
- Storage space for supplies and merchandise
- Shipping and loading areas
- Local regulations regarding garbage pickup, deliveries, snow removal, etc.
- Utilities, including power, water, heat/air, and phone
- Rental costs and lease terms

You'll need to gather up all the information available and determine whether your business will thrive in this location. The public transportation, roads, off-ramps, and accessibility will play a vital part in your decision process as well. A restaurant that can be seen from the main road but is not accessible unless you turn onto a side road may lose a significant number of customers who drive past it not realizing they had to make a turn onto the smaller road. The next restaurant on the main road is then the beneficiary of your lost business.

Sometimes retail leases differ from commercial space leases. In some cases landlords require retail tenants to install heat and air conditioning, bathrooms, and other facets of a workspace that would customarily be included in office space leases. Make sure you understand your obligations as a tenant before signing on the dotted line.

Often, a retail business will be best suited to a shopping center where you're one of several businesses and your location comes with built-in accessibility from the main road, plus plenty of parking. You can benefit from other stores and businesses, such as a movie theater that draws customers to that particular shopping mall. Another benefit of a shopping center is security. Often there are security guards for the center or a system already in place that you can utilize.

Sometimes it's difficult to get a location in a shopping center or mall, because they're booked in advance. Often the developers are looking to rent to big-name franchises or businesses with which they, and customers, are already familiar. Another drawback is the necessity of conforming to the rules of the center or mall, which may limit the size of your signs or style of your window displays. In most instances you will also have to operate on their daily or hourly schedule, which can give you staffing challenges.

Shopping malls are only one clustering of stores. You may benefit from setting up in a small town center with similar size shops. You may not get the same volume of foot traffic, but your overhead will likely be far more manageable.

If yours is a business that is more seasonal in nature, such as a gift shop in a beach resort town, you may need to consider the economics of closing down for a period of time in the off-season. Can you carry your overhead for a period without any cash flow?

The Seen and the Unseen

There are many intangibles and they are all worth checking out when it comes to a retail business or restaurant. Location is always a key factor in your potential success or failure, whether you're selling goods or offering a service, such as shoe repair or manicures. Service businesses can often do with less storage space and may have fewer concerns regarding shipping and loading docks.

You might, for example, contact the local chamber of commerce, explain that you'd like to open a business in town, and see what kind of reception you get. Some towns and communities will welcome a new business such as yours with open arms. Others are overcrowded and don't want the additional traffic problems, competition, or possibility of attracting what they perceive as "the wrong element," in their (often misguided) opinion. Get a feeling for the people who make the laws and dictate business decisions in the community. They can make your entry into the community either smooth or tortuous.

Finding Good Help

Another important aspect of opening a business is determining whether you will be able to hire a staff at affordable wages. This will depend on the skills needed to run your particular business. If you can survive with part-timers and college help and are in a town with a young population, you may be just fine. However, if you need a more highly trained level of employee, or individuals with more advanced technical skills, then you'll have to consider whether such employees can be found in the neighborhood where you're considering starting up. Research how much you'll need to pay in wages.

The Ideal Location

The best retail location is the one that people can find easily, draws walk-in customers, and is easily accessible by car or public transportation (depending on whether you're in a rural or urban area). It's a location where your business can grow thanks to a supportive business community, little direct competition, and a strong demographic base for your products. It's also an area where you feel safe and can attract a high level of experienced personnel.

Office Space

Unlike a retail business where drive-by and walk-in customers are essential, an office does not usually need to worry about high visibility. Yet many of the other concerns about finding a space for your business remain the same. You still need to consider utilities, security, rental costs, and commuting distance from your home to the office. Parking is still an issue, although not as consequential, unless you anticipate a big staff, or a large number of visitors right off the bat. And indoor appearance will generally be more important than outdoor appearance, unless you clients visit often.

Many business owners look for the right tone and atmosphere that will enhance their employees' productivity. Most want to know that restaurants are nearby. Day care facilities, health clubs, and other lifestyle-support services are growing concerns for business owners. The more a facility or area can offer to employees, the more attractive it will be to the highly skilled individuals you are looking to attract. Office parks often offer a host of facilities in a secure setting. Many are attractive because they are situated in the suburbs, or exurbia, offering easier access. Depending on the real estate climate at any given time, they may be difficult to get into, since they are custom built for such office-based businesses and highly sought out. Or, if it is a down time, you may be able to negotiate extremely favorable terms, locked in for a few years.

ESSENTIAL

If you're going to spend most of your waking hours at the office, choose a place that is functional and makes you feel good about yourself and your business. If you are squeezed into space that is laid out awkwardly, communication and efficient traffic flow may be difficult. An office should have some character and represent the image you're trying to project with your company.

For a more temporary environment in which to grow, you might lease short-term space from another company that is perhaps slightly larger than your business and has some unused room to spare. This can prove advantageous if they provide some essential services, such as security for the whole office space, a common eating area, and even some technical assistance. It may even be a complementary business to yours, where client referrals may occur easily back and forth. You may, however, be asked to chip in on repairs or maintenance expenses or other aspects of the overall space. Cover all the details when you sit down and meet with the owners of the space. Also make sure you know what it takes to get out of the sublease.

Manufacturing Space

If you need to set up a full-fledged factory, you'll need plenty of space for manufacturing and storage, as well as a location that can accommodate extensive shipping. If you build boats, you need to know that a large truck can get down the street you're located on and that a freight elevator can hold a boat. The bigger the products you make, the more size matters, and the more limited your choices will be. You also need to take into account the number of employees you will need, and have sufficient parking available.

Licenses and ordinances also play a large role in the space you select. More so than retail locations, your location will need to stringently meet the requirements of the Occupational Safety and Health Administration (OSHA), as well as of the local health and fire departments. In choosing manufacturing space, you will want to determine:

- Square footage and flexibility in the layout of the space
- Temperature fluctuations
- Whether the space can accommodate machinery/equipment
- Technology connection access
- Amount of storage space
- Availability of office and support space
- Accessibility for shipping and delivery
- Compliance with safety codes
- Security of premises

You will need to look over the area and visualize how you can set up a productive manufacturing business. It may be worthwhile to use the services of an expert to help with your layout planning. You need to create a system where you and your personnel can work with the equipment to make the product as efficiently as possible. Function is more important than appearance, since your goal is to make products and send them out rather than draw customers to you.

The actual location of the plant can range from your den where you make carved birds to a massive warehouse for manufacturing helicopters. It's to your benefit to be at a reasonable distance from your customers. If you need employees specifically trained with certain skills, it helps to locate in an area where you will be able to find such skilled individuals.

ESSENTIAL

There may be occasions when customers will visit your plant, so you should have at least a small waiting area with clean comfortable furnishings. Manufacturers such as commercial printers often have customers come to approve press proofs. An area in your factory with properly lighted tables is the kind of customer amenity that may distinguish you from your competitors.

Watch the zoning restrictions carefully. If you plan to be noisy or use hazardous materials, you will need to seek out industrial areas, since other neighborhoods will likely not want your business.

Home-Based Businesses

Many businesses start from and remain in the home. Working from home is highly desirable for many reasons. Plenty of commuters dream of trading higher salaries and perks for the privilege of rolling out of bed and into the office without so much as shaving.

The success of a home-based business centers on you and your ability to self-motivate and remain committed to your work. One person working from home can remain focused and motivate himself or herself to put in a productive forty-five-hour workweek, while another will stray over to the television set, play computer solitaire, and end up putting in twenty-five hours on the task at hand (which is the enormous task of building your business).

Setting up your home office means finding a location in the home where you feel comfortable working. Sometimes it takes a bit of trial and error to find the right spot. If you have a spare bedroom that can be converted to an office, everything can be contained behind a closed door. If you need to use a computer that is shared with other family members, you might find yourself saying, "I just need to jump on there for a minute," to your entranced teenager.

You need a place without distractions. You also need a place near electrical outlets for your computer, printer, fax machine, and any other equipment. Include filing cabinets, your phone system, and any other necessities, and lay out the space in a manner that puts everything within easy reach. Dormant files you do not need to access on a daily basis can be stored in a garage, cellar, or other out-of-sight location. Keep your work area as clean and efficient as possible. It is a good idea to position your workspace near a window for fresh air, sunlight, and an occasional glance at the world outside.

Advantages of working at home include:

- Maximum flexibility for organizing your own time
- Significant time and money saved by not commuting
- Home comforts, including your own kitchen and bathroom
- More time around the family
- Some equipment already on hand
- A low-cost starting point

Disadvantages of working at home include:

- **Losing focus.** It can be easy to get distracted by housekeeping, errands, television, or neighbors stopping by.
- **Working too much.** When you work at home, you're always at work.
- **Loneliness.** Working at home can become lonely, as you find yourself missing the companionship and camaraderie found working with others outside the home.
- **Inconvenience of meeting with clients.** When an important client is sitting in your living room and Baby Lizzie starts wailing, you'll think again about having an office away from home.
- **Limited expansion potential.** If you suddenly find that you can't handle the workload of the business yourself, you may want to bring in an assistant or hire other employees, and most often you can't do this from a home-based office.

- **Increased liability insurance.** You may need to pay higher insurance in case a client falls on your doorstep and sues you.

You can run a web business from your home or from an office. Since it's operating in cyberspace, no one will really know the difference. In fact, much of the work on websites is outsourced and involves people working from numerous locations. It's very important to consider your technical needs when determining whether you can run such a business from your home. If you decide to find an outside office, make sure the facility you choose is wired to meet your needs. This may mean checking out what services, such as which Internet providers, are available in the area.

Shared Services

An option for a home-based business is paying for an office identity. Companies that provide what is called shared services can offer you a range of support to give you a more professional appearance without assuming long leases or other expensive overhead. When you purchase an identity package, all you are paying for is a professional address and telephone service. Someone will answer the phone with your company name. Your mail can be sent to and from an address that isn't 14 Mulberry Lane.

The downside to this plan is that your caller never reaches you directly; you must always call back. For someone starting out who needs a professional appearance, this can be a short- to medium-term solution. A very limited office area can usually be rented on a month-to-month basis. It may be fairly easy to add space as you grow. Common areas, such as a professionally appointed lobby with a receptionist, add to your solid appearance. Often, conference rooms can be rented on an as-needed basis. Back room services such as photocopying, mail sorting, faxing, etc. can be purchased on a fee basis.

Shared services are certainly not the least expensive way to get yourself set up, but may fill the bill while you get going. Once you have more reliable cash flow, it may make sense to negotiate your own office space and take on equipment leases yourself.

CHAPTER 12

Furnishings and Equipment

Whether operating in the real world or in the virtual world, your business will occupy physical space somewhere. Planning a budget for your investment is the nuts and bolts of your business and sticking to it can be a make or break difference for the feasibility of your venture, especially in the early days. Once you determine the total summation of everything you will ultimately need in your physical place of business, take a hard look at what your absolute minimum needs are to get started.

Assessing Your Needs

Before you rush to your local office supply store or cruise through the many online options, take a hard look at your bare-bones start-up needs. Once you have an idea of the inventory of items necessary to get the job done, weigh the advantages of traditional and more creative resources. Anyone can buy retail. But what about tracking down someone else's cast-offs? Check local ads for gently used desks, chairs, conference tables, storage units, and the like. Depending on the nature of your undertaking, you may be able work with just about any mish-mash collection as long as it is serviceable—or you may need something better.

One of your first steps should be to decide what equipment you consider absolutely necessary. Typical major equipment includes:

- A communications system, including telephones and voice mail
- Computers
- Computer software
- External hard drives
- Printers/scanners/fax machines
- Filing cabinets
- Storage units or shelving
- Desks or workstations
- Postal meters and mailroom necessities
- Various chairs (computer chairs, conference room chairs, and so on)

Retail outlets will also need cash registers, display cases, shopping baskets or carts, and much more. Manufacturing companies will need the necessary machinery to build or assemble the products. Security systems will also be necessary for all types of businesses.

Will Clients Be Visiting Often?

The more often you plan to be meeting with clients in your location, the more important it will be to project the right image and decorate accordingly. Whether it's trendy (for a company dealing with style mavens) or more traditional (for a legal or accounting office), you'll need to look for furnishings that make the desired impression. If, however, your office is just for you and your ten employees and not the outside world, you may think of ways to create a comfortable work atmosphere while cutting some corners.

How Many People Will Be Working in the Office?

Perhaps not everyone needs a workstation with a computer. Laptops are popular, and Blackberries (and their cousins) are able to perform many of the traditional functions of a computer in a convenient, hand-held device. Whatever type of hardware your staff uses, you don't want to be short. You need to carefully review the requirements for each position that you intend to fill. If your budget can handle it, have a few extras in case you experience technical failures or your business grows and you need to take on new people. Also keep in mind that some people may work off-site and other tasks may be outsourced.

How Much Space Do You Have to Work With?

Just guessing at square footage requirements without planning for the actual usage can be a waste of time. All space is not created equal. A long skinny space may not be nearly as efficient as a square space with the same area. Remember, equipment takes up space, so when measuring for people, plan accordingly and leave some empty spaces. Pay attention to fire regulations and other such rulings when you consider cramming twenty people into a space designed for ten. Also consider access to your building before making any purchases of large items.

Comfort and Layout

Assess the space and the number of people who will be occupying the premises during the workday. People need a degree of personal space, and with that in mind, you can fit only a certain number of people into an office without overcrowding and creating an unproductive—and even unhealthy—work environment.

Cubicles, workstations, or tables with data ports have become very popular in the modern business world, eliminating the need to build walls throughout the office space. Laptops can give employees greater flexibility to carry their work with them when traveling outside the office to see clients or vendors. An open environment often creates a better team atmosphere than you might find with traditional offices with closed doors. However, the personal space and privacy issues need to be addressed. If you're going to set up cubicles, make sure they're roomy, comfortable, and allow for individuals to add their own personal touch. Employees who can personalize their work area are more likely to feel a greater sense of identity with the company.

ESSENTIAL

Keep in mind that certain tasks can be outsourced, while others can be performed by telecommuting employees. In some instances, you can have more than one person sharing a desk, if each person is only working from the office one or two days a week. Depending on your situation, you might also consider using modular furniture, which can be rearranged as your company grows.

Customized workstations help employees work more efficiently. For the sake of comfort and efficiency, you need to consider:

- **Distractions:** Think about whether there are any distractions from either outside sources or inside sources, such as office machinery and equipment, or delivery people walking in requesting signatures.
- **Acoustics:** You don't want sound from radios, computers, or even phone conversations bouncing off the walls, so consider the type of paneling or soundproofing that will create a quieter work atmosphere.
- **Lighting:** It's essential that every workstation or office has appropriate lighting.
- **Access to shared equipment:** If everyone needs to use the photocopying machines, then have them in a central location (but separate, to reduce noise).
- **Electrical wiring:** It's important that wires be carefully handled and contained for safety purposes. Since most offices require numerous cables and wires, have an electrician review your wiring needs.
- **Common space:** There should be a place where employees can take a break from their daily routine and socialize with their coworkers or just read quietly over a cup of tea for a few minutes. As an added ben-

efit, you can count on the best information exchanges taking place in these informal meetings.

- **Temperature and climate control:** You may want a policy about changing the thermostat. And remember, you don't want your high-end computer equipment next to the window that gets the most sunlight.

Telephone Systems

Along with computers, your telephone system will generally be your most important technological need. If you're working from home, you should consider a two-line phone or a separate line for business calls. When you set up an office, you'll need to consider setting up a phone system that's adaptable as your business grows. It's important to address the particular technological needs of your business and avoid simply buying the latest model with bells and whistles you won't be using. When evaluating your phone needs, consider the price, the service support, and the features of the system.

ESSENTIAL

When determining the number of phone units you will need, begin with one for every workstation or desk. Next, identify places it would be convenient to use a phone, such as your reception area, employee lounge, and work spaces like your manufacturing floor or warehouse.

Review all phone-related features closely and determine which ones you need. Call forwarding? Call waiting? Speakerphones? Speed dial? Many of these are standard features, along with caller ID and, of course, the ability to put people on hold.

You might want to explore VOIP options (voice over internet). Particularly for small businesses there may be some great cost savings opportunities. Just bear in mind that your phones will be inextricably linked to your computer. If it is down, your phones are down.

Shop Around and Compare

The entire telecommunications industry is in such a state of rapid change it is worth spending time to search for the best deals. You may find communications businesses in your area that can offer both telephone and computer services.

Select a long-distance provider that has a solid reputation, has reasonable rates for weekday usage (which is when most of your business calls will probably take place), and has quality service, including service visits when necessary. If you can't reach the service department or they don't come when you need the phones repaired, you should consider switching long-distance carriers. The competition is fierce, so you shouldn't have to stand for inadequate service. Also make sure that the bills come promptly and are understandable. Complicated phone bills can result in your paying too much. Make sure you aren't billed for features or services you don't have or want.

Cell Phones at the Office

There were over 2.6 billion cell phones in use worldwide as of the end of 2009, illustrating that they are the preferred way of communicating for nearly every man, woman, and child on the planet. You'll need to assess whether it is better to provide your employees with cell phones restricted to business use or to develop a policy to help subsidize their personal phones that are used partially to conduct your business. Limit personal cell phone use, including texting and tweeting in the office. Your employees may think they are honoring your wishes not to abuse personal calls on your system by using their cells at work. However, the more time employees spend on their cellular phones, the less time they're working. Remember to keep your own usage in check as well. Model the behavior you expect from your staff.

Fax

Some companies still use a fax machine, which will need a phone line, either dedicated or shared. Despite the advent of e-mail, there is still a need to fax invoices, take orders, and send (or receive) other important documents, especially ones that require signatures. Seek reputable vendors, compare prices, and make sure the features you're getting are the ones you need. Stock up on cartridges, because they don't last very long.

Cost-Effective Decisions

Look at how each equipment purchase serves the best interests of the business as a whole. Even a television for the lounge can be a productivity booster if people enjoy watching it on their lunch breaks and they get back to work more quickly. Or if your business needs to have updates on a 24/7 cycle, such as anyone in financial services. Keep in mind you generally don't need to buy top-of-the-line products. High-end products are necessary when you need the features (on a regular basis) or need to present a certain image to clients. In this case, however, you can fool most of the people most of the time with near-top-quality furnishings.

Green Choices May Equal Greenbacks

Many smart business owners are taking a second look at the ways they are outfitting their offices with an eye toward helping the environment and the bottom line. Certainly using second-hand furniture is a green choice. So is using a water filter instead of paying for costly water in plastic bottles. Ask employees to keep personal dishes in the office kitchen instead of supplying disposable items. If your town offers recycling be sure to provide appropriate containers for the staff to keep up this good habit.

Leasing Is Worth a Close Look

As you take a look at the cost-effectiveness of your office equipment, consider whether to buy or lease. Leasing or renting smaller items like paper shredders is not cost-effective. However, you may want to lease some of your larger equipment, including copiers, fax machines, furnishings, and computers. If you're starting out and don't want to make large purchases, or can't afford to, this may be a way for you to meet your equipment needs without a major cash layout up front. However, over the course of a one- or two-year lease, you may end up spending as much as or more than you would if you had purchased the item to begin with. For this reason, you will want to do a thorough cost-benefit analysis before deciding which route to pursue.

Here are some advantages to leasing:

- While you may be required to put down a deposit up front, your initial expenditure is not as great as it is to purchase items.
- You can get better equipment for your money.
- You aren't stuck with obsolete office equipment after a couple of years.

Here are some of the disadvantages to leasing:

- You may spend more on the item, over time, by leasing than if you purchased it.
- For items that don't depreciate greatly, such as furniture, you don't have any resale possibilities and can't claim the items as assets because you don't own them.
- Leases are very difficult to break.
- You're responsible for someone else's property, which means if you damage leased equipment, you may find yourself paying additional money.

Deciding whether to buy or lease is a matter of evaluating your start-up budget and determining what you can afford to buy and what you can't. Copiers have become multitaskers and now can be used for printing, faxing, and scanning, too. They have become sophisticated to the point of including software that can track use on behalf of a client or for a particular project. Leasing can allow you to take advantage of such updates in technology without a huge capital outlay. Computers, on the other hand, while they also become obsolete quickly, are often so integral to the company that the investment in purchasing such equipment is worthwhile from many angles, including tax purposes. Furnishings such as desks, chairs, and filing cabinets not only can be purchased from a wide range of affordable sources, but can be resold if owned, making them assets.

Cost Cutting Ideas

You have a wide range of options for furnishing and equipping your office. Besides your local Office Depot, Staples, or office furniture store, you can also check in with the folks at eBay (*www.ebay.com*).

QUESTION

Used, remodeled, refurbished, or recycled furniture, as well as used office equipment, can help you save significantly on your budget. As is always the case, you'll need to be a savvy shopper and compare costs of a new version of the same item. You will also need to evaluate the condition carefully before making a purchase. In the case of equipment, you might be able to take over the original warranty, if the item isn't too old and allows for a transfer of the warranty.

Some places to find used office furniture or equipment include:

- Auctions—both online and in the real world
- Estate sales
- Businesses that are remodeling, relocating, or going under
- Classified ads
- Craigslist

On occasion, you might find someone who has outgrown his or her home office and has some items that would help you get started, especially if you are trying to furnish your own home office. It's advantageous to look around at what you already have and make use of those items. You may have a desk lamp sitting in your closet, for instance, or at least a lamp small enough to use as a desk lamp.

Once you get the furnishings and equipment in place, you'll need to fill the drawers and stock the shelves. Stores, manufacturers, and corporate offices all need a wealth of supplies. Commonly needed supplies include paper for copiers, fax machines, and printers; legal pads; notepads; pens and markers; paperclips; postage stamps; envelopes of various sizes; file folders; staplers; scissors; calculators; calendars; printer cartridges and toner; rubber bands; various tools; and numerous preprinted forms, including invoices and/or receipts. Retailers will need credit card forms as well as boxes, bags, and packaging supplies. Manufacturers will often need a variety of specialized tools. And everyone will need a coffeepot, coffee cups, and some kitchen items.

Keep supplies well stocked and put someone in charge of them so they don't walk off in great quantities. Ask whoever is in charge to make sure to order new supplies before the old ones completely run out. But don't over-order. This is one of those "profit-leak" places you will want to watch closely.

Technology—Get Up to Speed

The two primary technological items that most businesses require are computers and telecommunications systems. Fax machines and scanners are also useful; and for retail businesses, the modern cash register and price scanner are a necessity. Projectors, presentation tools, and manufacturing technology may also come into play, depending on your business.

When it comes to technology, you need to be a good shopper. This includes comparing prices, looking for first-rate service policies and tech support, and checking to see what's covered under warranties.

Computers

Before buying a computer, it's important to assess your needs. Make an initial list of how you anticipate using your computers and how many people on staff you'll have working on them. Some of the ways you might need to use a computer include:

- Inventory control and bookkeeping
- Word processing
- Project management
- Graphic design and layout
- E-commerce
- Networking for interaction between several users
- Running advanced, highly technical programs

You'll also need to consider your office layout and space as well as the technical capacities of the facility. Does the space have T1 lines or will you need to install them? Then you'll need to assess the technical know-how of your employees, or the time needed to train them. And always filter your decisions with the price factor.

Finding the Right Computers for Your Needs

It's not hard to find computers. Every major office supply company has plenty of models, and all the popular manufacturers have websites and plenty of advertisements touting brand-new products and special deals. Of course, the newest, hottest, most hyped model isn't necessarily the one you need. Quite often, the second or third model down from a manufacturer is better for your needs. It may be easier to obtain, and you may find it at a good price, since the newest models are the high-ticket items. Don't pay for a host of computer features that you do not need. Shop for your specific needs.

Speed is a relative factor that often fools computer buyers into spending more than they need to. No matter when you buy your hardware, something will come along that's faster by the time you've got the computer set up in your office. So don't get overly concerned about comparing speed between models. The speed is important, but your Internet connection is also a major factor.

Computer System Components

For anywhere from a few hundred dollars to $10,000 you can have a desktop computer up and running in your office. Most often the price of an appropriate model should land between $1,200 and $2,000. If you're buying several computers, you can work out a bulk rate. The investment in the hardware and software do not reflect the last dollar you will spend, however, as you will need ongoing tech support and software upgrades. If you do not have a gifted technology specialist on your staff, you can find this type of support from a subcontractor. Either way, you will need to budget for this expense.

As far as features you should look for in the computer itself, key areas of concern are covered in the following sections.

Random Access Memory (RAM)

RAM is a representation of the size of the computer's ability to multitask and operate multiple programs quickly. The more RAM you have, the snappier your computer's operations will be, especially if you run memory-intensive programs or several programs simultaneously. You should look for at least 128 megabytes (MB) of installed memory, with the capacity to add more.

Processor Type

The central processing unit (CPU) is the brain of the computer. It will determine how well and how quickly the computer handles programs. While speeds range from 300 to 2,000 megahertz (MHz), some systems will work better than others at the same speed.

Drives

You need drives for inserting disks for storage or for running programs. You might seek out a recordable CD drive if you are planning to store large amounts of data or are planning to make CD presentations.

External drives, sometime referred to as thumb drives due to their very compact size, have become a very easy way to store large documents or graphics without eating up huge memory in an individual CPU.

Operating System

The operating system is the program that manages the programs; the foundation upon which all the software runs. Windows VISTA, XP, 7, and Mac OS are the most popular operating systems. Computers come with an operating system in place. If you buy a Macintosh computer, you get Mac OS, while most PCs (non-Mac computers) come with the latest version of Windows. If you want something other than Mac or Windows, you can get it—you'll just have to ask. Check out online sites for good information such as *www.compinfo-center.com.*

Hard Drive Capacity

Your hard drive determines how much data your computer can hold. You'll find hard drives with capacity from anywhere around 6 gigabytes (GB) to 80 or more. The price will rise as the size of the hard drive increases, so consider your needs for stored applications and documents. You may not need the biggest hard drive out there, so why pay for it when it may just sit empty? It is possible to add capacity as your business needs grow.

Monitor

You can do fine with a fifteen-inch monitor. But a seventeen-inch monitor is just that much better on the eyes, and not much more expensive. A decent monitor tends to be serviceable longer than other computer components.

Shopping for a Computer

Like anything else, you should compare prices and features when shopping for your computer. Whether you plan to buy in a local store or online, spend some time browsing computers in person to get a feel for the latest models. The more comfortable you are, the more likely you'll be able to do some mixing and matching and not simply buy the configuration as presented by the manufacturer.

Shopping Online

You'll probably get the best prices if you go directly to one of the manufacturers' sites, such as *www.dell.com*, *www.apple.com*, or *www.ibm.com*. You can also do well with the top computer online e-commerce sites, such as *www.buy.com*, *www.computers4sure.com*, or *www.globalsources.com*. You'll also find websites selling reconditioned or discontinued models, but always make sure you shop on reputable sites. Search carefully, take your time, and check out policies on warranties, customer service, and shipping.

Computer Stores

Often, you'll pay a little more at a computer store, but you should get better service. (The operative word is "should.") A good computer store has knowledgeable salespeople working to fit you with the best models to suit your needs in an effort to get your return business. Inquire about their repair services, and if they can offer you any extended warranties (at a price, of course). Best Buy is known for launching the cleverly named Geek

Squad, which will make onsite tech repair calls. A poorly run computer store is trying to push whatever they have in stock and provides insufficient answers to your questions. Pay attention to the kind of service you're getting, and move on if it doesn't meet your needs.

Office Supply Stores

Generally, you'll find a more limited selection at office supply stores simply because they do not specialize in computer sales. However, you may stumble upon a good deal, often on the last model, which they need to roll out since their shelf space is limited and they have newer merchandise to fit in. This, however, may limit you to buying a specific configuration.

Software Options

Once you've found the computer to meet your needs, then comes the software. You'll be able to find software for just about anything you want to do for your business, including accounting, presentations, inventory, and graphics. From simple word processing to detailed project management, numerous programs exist.

Although there are more software programs promoted for Windows users, Mac enthusiasts have been glad to see the rebounding of Apple and more Mac programs on the way. The current market has a wide range of products available. Being an astute shopper means reading up on the various offerings in each category and reviewing their features. When shopping around, compare prices, look over the system requirements, and read user reviews. Word of mouth is also an important source for computer information, because you can talk with people who are actually using the programs and see what they think.

Popular sites for software shopping include:

- *www.amazon.com*
- *www.cnet.com*
- *www.softwarebuyline.com*

Although options are continually upgraded, some of the software to look for includes the following:

- **Accounting:** QuickBooks Pro, Peachtree Complete Accounting, and MYOB Accounting Plus
- **Planning and contact management:** Day-Timer Organizer, Lotus Organizer, Franklin Planner, and Microsoft Outlook
- **Office suites:** Microsoft Office, WordPerfect Office, IBM/Lotus SmartSuite
- **Business presentations:** Microsoft PowerPoint, allCLEAR, Patton & Patton, and Corel Presentations
- **Spreadsheets:** Microsoft Excel and Lotus 1-2-3
- **Word processing:** Microsoft Word, WordPerfect, and WordPro
- **Project management:** Microsoft Project, SureTrak Project Manager, and FastTrack Schedule
- **Graphics:** Adobe Illustrator, Adobe Photoshop, Freehand, and CorelDraw

You can purchase software from many e-tailers, or you can go to the manufacturers' websites and buy directly. When shopping online, make sure you check the in-stock availability of the item, look for product features, compare prices and return policies, and take note of shipping charges. Well-known manufacturers and e-tailers have an edge in the marketplace because they provide customer service and have been proven reliable.

Computer Networks

Businesses that use multiple computers often set up a computer network. The network allows them to share and exchange information. For example, you can have common files that several people can access and work on with relative ease (although not at the same time). Networks eliminate the need to save files onto disks for someone else to use. One main schedule can be posted and everyone in the office will have access to it. Computers on a network can also share a printer and a modem for Internet access. In a business where people are frequently interacting and collaborating on a project, a network can be very valuable.

FACT

While networks can be very helpful, there are also associated problems. If the network is down, it slows everyone down, not just one person working on a file. So it's advantageous to have people do their work off-network and then transfer the files onto the network. It's also important that sensitive materials, which aren't for everyone's eyes, don't end up on the network unless proper security measures are employed.

Setting Up Your Computer System

If you're not sure how to set up your computer (whether for a network or individually), get help from someone who's well versed in the area. It's not hard to find a computer expert these days, whether it's a real consultant or someone you know who just happens to work in the field and is kind enough to help you out.

While it's tempting to put all the components together in a hurry and fire up the new computer, it is to your advantage to be meticulous and follow the directions to the letter. Set up a surge protector, have an antivirus program ready to load, and make sure you put the computer in a location that's dry and won't get too much heat.

Take your time when setting up your computer. Getting it set up correctly the first time is a tremendous time-saver. Save all documentation, installation disks, and even the box in case you need to return it.

Get Online

Whether you are a one-person operation or a company growing by leaps and bounds, you cannot avoid being online. There are numerous Internet service providers (ISPs) to choose from. Your business and how much you'll use the Internet will help you determine which method of connectivity you'll need.

Dial up is out of fashion mainly because it is frustratingly slow. If your business is in a location where this is your only option you will have to use it. Otherwise, you will definitely want to opt for a more reliable, fast link to the Internet. If your business depends heavily on the Internet, you might select a digital subscriber line (DSL). Cable modems are also a popular method of connecting. If you're already hooked up to cable for your TV, you can use this same cable for your Internet needs. Cable lines allow you to be constantly hooked up to the Internet. Like DSL, they're costlier than dial-up, but faster and more reliable. They can, however, slow down if numerous people are using the cable.

Wireless networking, known as WiFi, can give you an even faster Internet connection than DSL. One of its great appeals is that there are no wires involved, which makes networking multiple computers easier in some environments, such as a home office. An increasing number of public spaces including airports, coffee shops, and even parks now offer WiFi.

If your business is an Internet-based business or if a portion of your business is dependent on Internet sales, you should have a dedicated T1 line that is all yours and not shared with anyone. This is a dedicated connection that provides constant service. Naturally, you'll pay much more for it. However, you'll have greater bandwidth. And if your business depends on your website, you'll need it.

Computer Policies

Just as it's important to buy your hardware, install your software, and train your employees on how the system and the network operate from a technical standpoint, it's important to establish computer-related policies. Set up your guidelines from the outset. Computers in the workplace are not for solitaire, personal e-mails, or getting a jumpstart on holiday shopping. While you may want to allow your employees some freedom to check out the latest news stories, stock quotes, or sports scores, you do want to maintain a level of professionalism. Setting up policies and even blocking access to tempting online activities such as chats may be necessary.

While you don't want to become Big Brother, you also need to let it be known that you may occasionally monitor to see what sites are being visited. You should check the system and web logs periodically to see what activities are going on. This will also help you guard against hackers. Don't let unauthorized individuals have access to your server. If you encounter suspicious activity, monitor usage more closely and have employees change their passwords.

ALERT

A worldwide crisis of computer viruses has put businesses on the defensive. Many invest in software to provide "firewalls" against these menaces. Having a strict policy for your employees on the types of sites they cannot visit, and warning them never to open suspicious e-mails can help deflect some of these crippling invaders.

You also need to make it clear who the "computer person" is in your office. Every business has someone who handles the computer problems that arise and integrates any new equipment. Having one person handle the computer configurations and the network is advantageous. In some cases it is a subcontractor who gets the "help!" call.

Set up guidelines regarding what does and does not belong on the network. For several reasons, you may also want your employees to have passwords. It's very important that you establish your computer policies before you hit the power buttons.

CHAPTER 13

Getting Online

Perhaps nothing exemplifies doing business in the twenty-first century better than buying and selling online. The Internet is a fast-paced environment where developments and opportunities are constantly exploding. It is an exciting place, yet one where missteps can hurt. In this chapter, a number of key issues are spelled out. Whether you plan to use a website to supplement your business or will operate solely in the virtual world, there are a number of steps you will need to take for success.

Taking the Website Plunge

Not all websites are the same, nor are they intended to be. You may need your site for e-commerce, actually making sales online. Or you may use it as another marketing tool, such as an online brochure, to promote your business. In today's fast-paced world, keeping printed material up-to-date and in the hands of your potential customers can be slow and costly. Having a website has become mandatory for virtually all businesses. It has become the cultural norm. So, you will want to put your best foot forward with your site, making it as attractive and useful as possible.

ESSENTIAL

One of the exciting aspects of operating in the virtual world is that, by definition, everyone is "thinking outside the box." This may be a chance to broaden your services. Say you want to sell used books. You might find customers starting to ask for used DVDs or used CDs. Presto, you have new products!

Think seriously about the purpose of your site. Do you envision it as a functional place where you will actually conduct business? Will it establish you as a credible presence in your industry? Do you want your business mission to be presented here as another key marketing tool? Will the site improve customer service? Will you want to collect data from those who come to your site so you can stay in touch with them?

Next consider what your customers will expect from your site. How easy can you make it for them to find your site? Once there, you will want them to understand the objective of the site. If it is an information-only site, you won't want viewers to be frustrated trying to find a way to interact with it. At a minimum, you will want to furnish contact information for customers to reach you, either via e-mail or other conventional means.

As you get ready to create a site, do an assessment of what you already have that you can use, such as marketing brochure copy, photos, or graphics. If you have been listing your products with other larger sites, like Amazon.com, consider whether you can transfer any material easily to your own site.

When you are dreaming of what the site will be, think about how a user will move around in it. Imagine your homepage as the roadmap, then sort out each section of the site and its utility to the user. Can you, or should you, use roll-over buttons or animation to jazz it up? How about embedding short videos? Are you ready for YouTube primetime? As you develop criteria for your website, cruise the web and see what other businesses have done. You will undoubtedly find sites you like and those you don't. This knowledge will be a big help as you envision the big picture for your site, and even more so as you get into the specific design and operation details.

Building a Website

The good news is that there are a range of options when creating your website. Whatever route you take, treat the site like any other business expense. Set aside dollars to create, set up, market, and maintain it. Once you make the commitment to create a website, remember it will be as much a reflection of your business as the sign on your door, the look of your premises, the level of customer service, and of course the quality of your product or service. Be sure it shows the same degree of professionalism you bring to every other aspect of your endeavor.

FACT

For just a few dollars, you can download Color Schemer software. You can use this software to find the best colors to use in your web design. It can allow you to match colors you have in images or get creative by adding new colors into your design.

If you are really watching your dollars, you may want to take advantage of one of the do-it-yourself website-building programs, such as SiteDelux. These programs offer templates; you only need to enter your copy and add pictures, and voila, you have a website. The downside to using a template is that you are limited in your creative options, and it is possible another business's site could look startlingly similar to yours. Some web hosting companies offer templates as part of their services. You can shop and compare.

If you want to get a little more creative and come up with a truly unique site design you might try one of the "what you see is what you get" (WYSIWYG) programs such as Microsoft's FrontPage or Adobe's DreamWeaver. A little more skill is needed for these but they operate with software you may already have in your computer. If you are really ambitious you can always take a class to master hypertext mark-up language (HTML), which is the computer code that brings you what you see on your computer.

AllBusiness.com offers the following recommendations as design resources:

- Usability.gov (*www.usability.gov*): This is a website hosted by the Department of Health and Human Services. It offers help with design basics and usability statistics, and provides best-practice guidelines.
- Useit.com (*www.useit.com*): This site is run by Jakob Nielsen, a noted usability expert, who offers the ultimate in guidance on his site.
- The Web Content Accessibility Guidelines 2.0: This is a resource from the World Wide Web Consortium specifically written for tailoring website usability for people with disabilities. These standards can be used broadly to make your site useful for any visitor and thus are definitely worth following.

Hiring a Professional Web Designer

Professional web designers have the skills and the creative talent to transform your ideas into reality using the medium of the web. Their experience can save you frustration in the long run. From the very outset it will be important to have a clear understanding of what your goals are and how the designer can help you meet them. If you find a designer who already has knowledge of your industry, it may make things go smoother and faster, although not necessarily. Of course, you will have to pay for this talent and experience. And, there is the expense of maintaining your website to consider. This could become a hidden cost that eats into your profits.

You will need to consider the big issues, of course, such as driving more customers to your business, but you will also need to get down into the nitty-gritty details. If you do not have a logo, this is something your web designer can help create. If you need your designer to help with writing text, you will want to negotiate how that approval process will work. It is always a good idea to set reasonable response times for both sides so the project doesn't languish because either you or the designer is awaiting another round of drafts.

Think about what you want for an overall look. The visuals will set the tone. You may just need straightforward product visuals and shopping cart functions. Or you may need to have images conveying solid dependability if yours is a service such as a law practice. Your credibility may be enhanced by listing any licenses you hold, as well as client testimonials.

When choosing a professional web designer, find one who meshes well with your style, budget, and need for responsiveness. If you have waited to hire a web design professional until after you have designed your own site, you may be in a better position to give concrete guidance on what you need. In either instance, this is an important relationship for the success of your online operations.

Getting Referrals

Be forthright in asking to see examples of a designer's work and requesting customer referrals. Don't just ask for referrals; you need to actually take the time to call them. Of course you will want to know how the project worked out overall, but probe into some of the particulars. How much discrepancy was there between the approved bid and the final invoice, and what were the factors? Was the designer able to furnish detailed invoices? Ask how the interaction went throughout the web development process. Was the designer able to hear the client's wishes and take the web concept to another level, or did she do exactly what the client envisioned and no more? This may be the most important answer to consider, especially if a strict budget is in force. How is the site working? Has the client had many customer complaints?

One key measure is the reliability of the site. It may be the best-looking site on the planet, but if it is down or not performing the intended functions, you might as well be closed for business. Perhaps the best test of a designer, or any vendor, is how she responds when there is a problem. Seek details on how quickly and competently the designer handled problems along the way.

The boundaries of the contract are another key point. It is important to be clear how much support can be expected following the initial setup of the site. There will always be kinks to be worked out in the development stage. Ask the referral whether they plan to maintain the site themselves or continue on a contractual basis. The bottom line is that you need a web designer who has the talent, skills, and experience necessary and is someone with whom you can communicate.

ALERT

Second only to making a site user friendly is making it search-engine friendly. Incorporate key words into site content descriptions. Webmonkey (*www.webmonkey.com*) offers beginner resources. Major search engines also provide assistance in optimizing your site.

Web Designer Fees

Be sure to have the fee structure clearly negotiated before any work begins. For example, if you contract with the designer to complete the work by a specified date, and that deadline is missed, will she be able to continue to charge you her hourly rate until the work is finished? You might want to know how your project fits into the designer's schedule. Discuss ahead of time what kinds of issues could disrupt the project schedule. Will you be her major focus or will you be fighting for attention with other simultaneous projects? She should be able to give you an idea of how long your project should take, setting up reasonable expectations for both of you.

The Fine Points

In addition to getting yourself a groovy-looking website, your designer should have the goods to build one with all the appropriate technical features needed. Find out which web standards her designs will follow. Be sure to have her test your design with multiple browsers. Find out if she knows how to add back-end functions. For example, if you want to have images rotate through your home page, does the designer have the capability to get you set up with Adobe Flash or a similar multimedia platform?

Ask who will host your site, and if she gets a commission from the hosting service. You may want to update your site after it is initially designed—find out how you would do this. Be clear about who owns the rights to the copy, or to any images, video, or animation on the site. Clearly it needs to be you. Don't make any assumptions and risk a nasty surprise later.

Web Hosting

For small businesses wanting the impact of a web presence without a Fortune 500 company-level of investment, choosing a web hosting company may be the way to go. You simply hire one of these firms to provide the infrastructure and data management needed to get you on the web. There are literally thousands of web hosting companies and related services. As you consider using one, think about what features you need for your site. Two of the most popular are e-mail access for customer contact and a shopping cart for e-commerce. Some companies offer tools for site construction as well.

There are nearly 10,000 web hosting services to choose from. Larger host companies have larger servers that can manage more data, and may be more reliable. However, they may provide a lower level of service and support. Across the industry, there is a 2 percent cancellation rate. Try to get the cancellation rate for any company you may consider. It may give you an insight to customer satisfaction.

Finding a Web Host

Most web hosting companies are geared toward either small businesses, such as BizLand (*www.bizland.com*), or home crafters. Some are highly specialized, such as PureHost (*www.purehost.com*), which is targeted to small businesses owned by women. Believe it or not, 50 percent of web host customers find their site of choice through word of mouth. The rest may see ads that run in the major technology trade publications such as Wired or PC Magazine. A number of industry directories and related sites are available, including:

- *www.CNET.com*
- *www.justhost.com*
- *www.ixwebhosting.com*
- *www.inmotionhosting.com*

Subscription Choices

In most cases when you use a web hosting site you will contract for a subscription rate for a set period of time. Depending on the company, you may be able to sign on for a monthly, quarterly, semiannual, or annual rate. Costs range from a few dollars to more than $100 per month. The perception may be that if you pay more you get more, but that is not necessarily true. It is difficult to comparison shop—some say it's similar to buying a mattress. Look for and take advantage of money-back guarantees or free trial periods. If you are willing to share some web real estate, companies such as Netfirms (*www.netfirms.com*) will give you free web hosting in exchange for displaying advertisements on your site.

Domain Names

The Internet Corporation for Assigned Names and Numbers (ICANN) is a nonprofit worldwide organization whose responsibilities include tracking every domain name to be sure it is unique. It also monitors that each domain name is connected to the proper IP address. By going to their site, *www.icann.org*, you can research names. However, you may need to secure a name through a reseller who has blocked a group of names. To determine if the name is already taken, log on to Whois? (*www.whois.com*). Once you register a particular name, you will pay a nominal fee annually to secure it. Some businesses reserve a group of names that are very similar even though they intend to use only one. This can help reduce the risk of having a competitor owning a name too uncomfortably close to yours. As you contemplate a name, try to come up with one that is short, easy to remember, and somehow ties to your business. Check out what your competitors have used and see how you can differentiate yourself from them.

Finally, be mindful of how much information you furnish when you register for a domain name. This information can be easily accessed and may reveal more than you wish.

Your domain name is key to your business identity and the ease with which customers will be able to find you, therefore it's not something to take lightly. Some web hosting packages may include a free domain name for the first year. Otherwise expect to pay a nominal fee ($10 to $35) annually to protect your domain name.

Preparing to Launch Your Site

Once you have gone through the rigors of setting goals for your website, and then designing it, you will want to run through a few final steps before going live. First, review your initial goals for the site. If it was meant to be informational, have you included the information so that visitors can find it easily? If you wanted a tool to make sales, is it organized to work efficiently?

ESSENTIAL

When creating the individual pages of information for your site, brevity rules. There is nothing more aggravating than plodding through layers of a site trying to find something. Make sure you have done a good job of organizing your information in logical groupings.

Beginning with your homepage, make sure the icons are obvious and are easy to use and understand. Check to be certain you have succeeded in getting all the pertinent data presented in an attractive and easy-to-understand manner. If you have a search function for your site, make sure it works in a user-friendly way. Test to confirm whether your links make the connections intended. Make sure a visitor to your site will be able to tell which items are links and which are not.

Test how easily a user can move around on your site. Have you built in effective shortcuts to find any page? If your site is structured in an intuitive way, a search engine may not be needed in every case. The user should be able to figure out how to find the information he's seeking.

Visuals Are Key

Everything from the font size to graphics and animation should make the time someone spends on your site productive and satisfying. Make sure the visuals don't compete: the background shouldn't fight with the message, or make it difficult to read the copy. As you look over the final creation, see if you have included extraneous components that do not add to the usefulness of the site. Sometimes, too many nifty elements get thrown in during development that in the end are really unnecessary. Keep your target audience in mind. They may not want to perform too many tasks, or watch a ninety-second video, before they get to the objective of their visit to your site. Likewise, you can keep your site from getting bogged down by using small product images. No one likes waiting for a site to upload.

Navigation

Think of the construction of your website as if it were a salad. Separately, the components are a bunch of vegetables. Together they make a splendid lunch. Your navigation tools should make it as easy to find a page on your site as it is to identify the radish in the bowl. Give each main category on your site its own tab or button. Most sites run these along the left side, or across the top of the homepage. The navigation of every page should follow the same format. Consistency is king. And information should be organized from the perspective of your end users. What may seem perfectly logical to you may not speak to the goals they want to achieve at your site. Feel free to study other sites, including your competitors', and see what navigation methods can be adapted for your own.

Search Engine

The real secret to the success of your site is the element you do not see: the search engine. It cannot be overstated how important it is that search engines can actually find what users want.

One way to test how many of your site's pages are being picked up is to log on to Google and enter your site name in the search box. This should turn up any URL history of the site. If it does, one option offered is to "find web pages from the site yourdomain.com." Click on this link and make sure the number of pages the engine finds matches the number you have on your site. If the engine finds fewer than there should be, it means that the engine robots cannot find all of your pages. The robots use links as they traverse the web. You may have pages that are not linked, or some pages may be dead-ended.

The best way to ensure that you are fully linked is to make certain all of your site's pages have internal links, which link them to each other internally. External links, known as hyperlinks, connect you with other sites and will help a search engine find your site. An excellent way to help robots to find your site, as well as to help users navigate the site, is to have an up-to-date site map.

Search engines are programmed to weight the ranking of a search result based on how many times a particular site is hit. The more people go to a site, the higher it will be ranked in suggested responses to a search request. Try to get your site linked to as many natural connections in your industry as you can. In the early days, while traffic is building to your own site, get it listed in the various website directories such as Yahoo! or Open Directory Project.

ESSENTIAL

To prevent any confusion once you are live on the web, take the time to test your site on each of the major browsers. Subtle differences in their respective protocols can affect how your site appears. For more help visit AnyBrowser.com (*www.anybrowser.com*).

A subtle, but important, factor for directing traffic to your site is having the right keywords in the title or descriptive copy that points users to your site. This may take some trial and error. There are companies who, for a fee, can massage your descriptors to increase not only visitors to your site but also increase the number of visits that end in actual sales. Another way to pull in customers is by purchasing keyword ads on the major search engines. Closely allied to your keyword descriptors are the meta tags tucked into your HTML directions for web browsers. It is important that the language here uses the keywords someone would likely enter to begin a search for your site.

As the creator and owner of your website, you will want to run through all the measurement tests. However, to get a truly objective evaluation you may want to solicit real or potential customers to test it and give you feedback before you go live. Even if you pay them a nominal fee to perform this service for you, it can save you from big headaches and who knows how much money by identifying the kinks before a public blow-up can happen.

Spyware and Adware Trouble

Nothing is more discouraging when using the web than to discover that your system has been infected with an adware or spyware invasion. The first clue may be that your computer is processing at glacial speed, especially when trying to perform tasks online. Your homepage may have changed without your input. New icons may appear on your desktop. Annoying pop-up ads may be proliferating. Any or all of these may be telling you that some insidious application has latched onto your system and may be stealing data. This can be dangerous because your personal information can be captured and broadcast without your knowledge.

By using a combination of software and fastidious work habits, you can minimize invasion of these applications. First and foremost, avoid opening strange e-mail attachments. Consider running virus-filtering software on your e-mail server. Next, stay away from "free" download offers that include adware in their software. Make sure your employees, or any contractors who may have access to your computers, conform to your policies for protecting the system from these threats. It is key to have your virus protection program set to automatically update itself every day so you limit the time of exposure to this nasty stuff. Should you find you are plagued with any of these applications, run a program to purge them from your computer. You can get either Spybot Search & Destroy or Ad-Aware programs for free directly from *www.download.com*.

Wrapping It Up

In order to get your site on the Internet, you first need an Internet service provider (ISP). This is how you get access to the Internet. Next, you need a web host. As discussed earlier, your evaluation of a particular host should include the services they provide and, perhaps more importantly, the amount of server capacity they offer. Lastly you need a file transfer protocol (FTP) program, which is the software that actually places your files on the web host server. If you use any of the WYSIWYG programs, FTP access is generally included. Similarly, most web hosting companies include it in their offerings. In most cases, once you have your FTP established with the specific server information and your unique user name and password, you are good to go. After that it should be quite easy to add or change files on your server and modify your website as you wish.

CHAPTER 14

Selling Online

Once you have worked all the bugs out of your site, it is time to put out the virtual "Open for Business" sign. Stay alert to the activity on your site. The Internet has created an expectation of immediacy in communications. If your web business is a supplement to a three-dimensional business, you may find yourself pulled in different directions. Be ready to adjust. It may become necessary to add staff to respond to orders and inquiries. Your competition may force you to be creative in your promotions to retain customers. Flexibility is the name of the game.

Service Business

While the Internet has truly opened up world markets to the entire spectrum of producers, when it comes to service businesses, it is the person—not the product—that is most often being sold. Some services lend themselves just fine to the online world. Travel specialists, for example, can help a client in Boston as easily as Brisbane from a base in Boise. However, if a service business involves house calls, it is limited to time and space. For this genre of business, the bare minimum online presence should be in Internet yellow page listings. Unlike your landline, which would be listed in a big fat yellow book produced by the carrier in your area, your website could be listed on many online yellow pages sites. People seem to have their favorite online directories. Check out these:

- *www.anywho.com*
- *www.superpages.com*
- *www.switchboard.com*
- *www.yellowbook.com*
- *www.yellowpages.com*

ESSENTIAL

Providing immediate contact between a buyer and seller of very expensive items, such as real estate or high-end jewelry, is a popular trend in online selling. Some online services are offering a way to connect with a live person with the necessary expertise, not just a call center on some remote continent, to gather further information beyond what is posted on a site.

As with your telephone listing, you pay for an Internet yellow page listing. As these markets grow and converge, it is increasingly possible to make combined purchases for listings in local yellow pages and online directories. Talk to your local sales rep for details. Online marketing agencies are another source from which you can purchase placement. Try *Leads.com (www.leads.com)*, Local Leads LLC (*www.localleadsllc.com*), Elite MLM Leads (*www.elitemlm leads.com*), or InstantLocalLeads.com (*www.instantlocalleads.com*). Market research results showing that a significant portion of those who go to online yellow pages are ready to buy are the most compelling reason to get into these directories.

Subscribing to search engine marketing, such as with Google, Yahoo!, Ask.com, MSN, or AOL, won't get you the same percentage returns, but your name will be out there in a giant pool, and you can be automatically included in their "local" directories as well.

Retail Sales

Successful selling online, just as in the material world, is a combination of the three famous virtues: quality, service, and price. If you have progressed to the point of having a product to offer, you have undoubtedly gone through all the steps to assure its quality. Whether you are offering car parts or handmade quilts, to ensure customer satisfaction in this consumer-conscious society you are going to have to stand behind your product. Selling online may seem easier, but the same standards apply, and in fact it may be more challenging to deal with returns, repairs, or other quality-related complaints. Be ready for the complete flow-through—from acquiring or making your inventory, presenting goods for sale, completing the sales transaction, delivering products in good condition, and handling any service issues that may arise. As your business grows you may need a full-time staff to deal with returns and exchanges.

FACT

Business-to-business transactions also take place online. As with retailers, in some cases the online sites are a supplement to a brick-and-mortar location. Some e-entrepreneurs are using the web for industrial sales—and doing it only online.

If you find that online sales are more profitable, you may want to follow in the steps of other smart marketers and find ways to drive traffic to your site. The giant discount shoe retailer, DSW, often offers discounts and promotions that are only available online—not in their stores. You might consider having a weekly online special good for only one day. As your customers learn about it they will be looking for the deal of the week.

Keywords Bidding

Drawing the right buyers for your items is managed in the virtual world with its own set of tools. A uniquely media-specific tool is keyword advertising. You can buy keyword ads that match words your prospective buyer enters in a search engine. Say you are going to sell a gentleman's Seiko steel tank watch. You will get a far more targeted response if you buy the words "gentleman's Seiko steel tank watch" rather than just the generic "watch."

The price for keywords can be bid up depending on the demand. You submit a per-click price you are willing to pay for the word or phrase you want to use to drive traffic to your site. You also commit to a budget amount you are willing to spend in total. Using our watch example, say you bid $50 per click and set a budget amount of $5,000. If yours is the highest bid for your keywords, your ad will pop up at or near the top of the list when someone searches for those words. Your "kitty" of $5,000 will not be tapped if someone reads your ad, only when someone actually clicks on it. For $5,000 at $50 per click, one hundred shoppers could click on you in first position. If your bid was $50 but someone else bid $51 your listing would remain under the radar. More obscure words are less in demand and thus less expensive to reserve. You may have a number of different keywords reserved at any given time for whatever you are selling.

If one set of words is not effective, try to massage the copy. Try to direct those who respond to your keyword triggers to the specific page on your website that has the product being offered. Save them the step of moving from your homepage to the innards of your site and you'll not put up any barriers to their purchase. Try any of the following companies for help in making the most of your search words strategy: Facebook (*www.facebook.com*), Twitter (*www.twitter.com*), Squidoo (*www.squidoo.com*), HubPages (*www.hubpages.com*), or Yahoo Directory (*www.yahoo.com*).

Get Linked with Compatible Sites

Shoppers cruise around online with almost wild abandon. Your challenge is getting visitors with attention spans of nanoseconds to your site and keeping them there. One strategy growing in popularity is getting your business linked on compatible sites. Conversely it is in your interest to have links on your site to other appropriate sites. For example, if you are a florist, it would be great to be linked on local photographer, bakery, and function hall sites. In turn, by having links for these businesses on your site, party planners can enjoy the efficiency of "one-stop shopping." Each of you will be giving validation to the other in this reciprocal promotion.

This exchange of links doesn't need to be restricted to local businesses. If you have a particular product you are selling online, such as vintage linens, it might make sense to find similar online retailers who are selling estate flatware or antique china and have cross links.

Auction Sales

Is there a person on the planet who has not heard of eBay and dreamed of turning those Pez dispensers in shoeboxes at the back of the closet into hard cash? Online auctions have exploded far beyond a virtual marketplace for exchange of trinkets and trash. Serious business is conducted and the rules of engagement are rapidly evolving. Online auction selling can be connected to a your traditional retail business, or it may be a completely separate endeavor for you.

ESSENTIAL

There is a tremendous number of resources for advice on how to use online auction selling successfully. There are scores of books and websites, such as *www.auctionbytes.com*, devoted specifically to industry issues surrounding auction selling, particularly on eBay. You might even try training classes to sharpen your skills.

Here are some tips and truths to keep in mind as you contemplate online auction selling:

- Start small. Test the market by selling a few things before investing in a big inventory.
- As with any business endeavor, create a business plan that includes financial goals, legal structure of the company, inventory acquisition and management, and target growth.

- If it is a business, run it like a business. Keep records of all transactions, file tax returns, etc.
- Sales tax rules can be tricky for online sales. Make sure you are compliant.
- Research and take advantage of special software programs that can enhance your sales. There are tools available that can guide you in understanding timing patterns of bidding, track your auctions, and give you important data about your customers.
- Title words are the bait for your buyers. After experimenting on your own, look into services that can hone your descriptive language and drive more sales.
- Most major sites have ratings for buyers and sellers. Watch for comments about your buyers.
- It is perfectly acceptable to wait for payment to clear before shipping your goods.
- If you amass a truly large inventory, one way to keep it fresh is to operate multiple online stores. Pull items off if they are not selling and re-list them at another time.
- Stay up to date with your technology investments, both hardware and software. If you are down you are out.

As you plan or expand your business, weigh how online auction selling fits into your overall strategic plan. Initially, you may need the vast reach of these sites to get your products out there in the market. Over time, it might make sense to use the auction sites to drive buyers to your own website, where the sale of the same product will net you more income. In all likelihood you will operate with a combination of the two. Established customers can be enticed to buy directly from your site. The auction sites can continue to attract new customers. You will need to keep a balance between the expensive auction sites with their tremendous customer base, and your more narrowly focused but less expensive proprietary website.

Payment Options

If there is one dimension to your online selling that you do not want to have a problem with, it is getting paid. There are a number of payment choices that can increase the security of transactions between you as seller and your buyer. Nothing is foolproof, however, and you will need to weigh the risks and benefits for your individual business. One of the available options is to use third-party payers who can facilitate your buyers, paying you with certi-fied checks. At the other end of the continuum is the strategy of establishing merchant accounts with banks that can process credit card payments. Per-haps the best-known payment system, thanks to the phenomenon of eBay, is PayPal. Begun as an independent company, it has since been acquired by eBay and is used for buying and selling transactions on that site. Their mer-chant accounts, however, do not have to be used solely for eBay. You should also research getting a merchant account established through your bank or another commercial institution. Regardless of which payment system you select, there is a risk of not getting paid. In the normal course of processing payment transactions there can be glitches with too many or too few funds going in or out of your account, which will require follow-up to resolve.

Naturally there is some cost associated with using a third party to col-lect payment for you. These are expenses that fall to your bottom line. It is worth investigating which merchant account providers are out there and which one best matches your particular needs. See if there is any flexibility in the fees and discount rate. Feel free to ask to see a sample monthly state-ment. Find out if their services include reports such as order analysis, which can be very useful in tracking your products and the seasonality of your business. You definitely want a highly competent and respected service for this function. Even the best of the best seem to be vulnerable to hackers, however, so be sure to negotiate an agreement that protects you as much as possible in the event of fraud. It will be important to reassure visitors and prospective customers on your site that their credit card information will be protected. It may be tempting to seek details about the buyer for demo-graphic profiling, but probing too far can make folks skittish.

ALERT

Look out for red flags when trading online. A major no-no for anyone is wiring money. Never, ever, wire money anywhere. As a seller, have your payment system and your shipping linked—don't release mer-chandise until you are sure you have payment.

Taking credit cards for payment may require special hardware as well as software. Find out if there is a minimum or maximum threshold for transactions as part of your package of services. Depending on how many transactions you anticipate, it may be more advantageous to have real-time rather than batch processing. Ask about the pros and cons of each.

If you have sales going through a third party such as Amazon.com, you can expect to pay listing fees. These may be per-item fees, or if you have enough volume to warrant it, you can register as a pro merchant for a flat monthly fee. The real knife in the heart is facing a steep commission of 15 percent per sale plus a bit of the shipping charge they collect. However, when you are signed up with a seller account, the minute that sale is made, you are paid. Some sites such as Half.com (*www.half.ebay.com*), which is owned by eBay, do not charge a listing fee. In that case a fee is assessed once a sale has been made.

It may be worth comparing each company's bundle of merchant services, including dispute resolution services and transaction screening. When reviewing merchant payment systems be sure to consider other charges, such as set-up, monthly, gateway, and transaction fees. Inquire whether there are any fees associated with fraud protection. Your buyers' identities and personal information have to be secure in whichever system you select. Probe to discover how this is assured. Once you have the facts, you will certainly want to research the reputation and reliability of the company. The worst time for you to discover you cannot penetrate a phone tree to get to a real person to resolve a dispute is when you are in the middle of one.

You want to achieve all the noble goals of your business endeavor, bringing quality products and services to market. However, you will not be able to sustain it if your money-handling processes are not in order. Money is still real in the virtual world. All of the responsibilities for managing it are there with perhaps some added challenges. This is one area you absolutely have to get right in order to succeed.

Stand Out from the Crowd

Your online world needs to be tied to your real world using all the tools you can. In some cases you may want to run banner advertising on other sites to pull business to yours. Research industry-specific directories and submit your information for inclusion. Be sure to incorporate your web address on all of your traditional communications pieces, including everything from your stationery to brochures to print ads, even in the yellow pages if you are listed there. Many savvy business operators use direct mail to drive customers to their website.

There is one thing to be aware of here: The uprising against the tsunami of unwanted, and in many cases downright offensive, e-mails triggered the CAN-SPAM Act, spelling out very specific restrictions for e-mail blasts. Some of the regulations to be mindful of when using broadcast e-mails are:

- **Opt Out:** A recipient must be given the opportunity to ask to be removed from your list. You then have ten days to honor this request.
- **Play in Your Own Backyard:** The government frowns on snitching e-mail addresses from other sources or creating ad hoc lists.
- **Closed Door:** If someone opts out of your list you may not share her address with anyone else.
- **It May Be an Ad:** You have to call an e-mail an advertisement if the recipient did not ask to receive it. For those folks who have opted in to receive your e-mails you are exempted from this requirement.
- **Truthfully:** A big no-no is trying to trick the recipient. Be square with the sender info and the subject line content.
- **No P.O.:** Somewhere in the e-mail you must include your company's brick-and-mortar address. P.O. box numbers are not allowed.

There are many ways to draw customers. You can use special promotions, seasonal or introductory offers, first-time-user discounts, you name it. Entice interested parties through online ads, e-mail newsletters, anything that gets them motivated to find your site.

ESSENTIAL

You can build your customer base with a quality e-mail newsletter, which is easy to read, timely, and useful. Once recipients become accustomed to your high-quality effort, they will look forward to opening and reading it rather than clicking and dismissing it.

The measure of your success in converting visitors to consumers on your site is known as the conversion rate. Simply, it is the calculation of how many sales (or sign-ups, or whatever action you want the site visitor to take) occur in relation to the total number of visits to the site. Experience shows most people surfing the web make multiple visits to a site before committing to a purchase.

CHAPTER 15

Product and Services Management

Whether you are selling Limoges china or lion-taming equipment, you will want to find sources with the best prices and reliability. If you are making your own specialty product, you need great resources for your materials. Having enough product on hand to meet demand without having too much money tied up in inventory can be a balancing act. This chapter covers such important issues as product procurement, pricing, and brokering, as well as information about how pricing and services can draw more business.

The Importance of Inventory

If you are in the retail or the online e-commerce business, the first priority is making sure you have the quality products your customers are looking for, when they want them. Points to cover when planning your supply strategy, either for finished goods or materials you will convert into items for sale, include:

- Where to order
- How much to order
- Which goods to order and which ones to avoid
- When to reorder
- How much to have in inventory at a given time
- What to do if the merchandise you receive is unsatisfactory

How well versed you become at buying and merchandising will factor heavily into your level of retail success. Larger, more established companies will hire buyers, experienced in the area of sales, to stock the shelves and track the sale of goods. When starting a retail business this will be your job, along with anticipating upcoming trends and knowing what to buy and what to avoid.

Just in Time Inventory Management

One of the ways companies have been able to marry customer service with cash flow is by shortening the time between making a product and selling it. All of the upfront expense required to create a product usurps resources that cannot be replenished until a sale has been made and payment collected. A cabinetmaker must purchase materials: wood, paint, stains, hardware etc. It takes time to make pieces. A huge inventory sitting in a warehouse waiting for a customer means valuable cash is tied up.

A savvy business owner who can offer a catalog—printed or online—of choices in a furniture line can wait until orders come in before beginning the manufacturing process. This can be a bit of a dicey balancing act. You don't want to lose customers by forcing them to wait too long to get your product. On the other hand, by reducing as much as possible the time between investing in manufacturing and receiving an order, you will come out ahead of the game.

Product Procurement

You're opening a store, but where do you find the merchandise to sell? You have a few options. One is to attend trade shows, which are one of the most significant opportunities for retailers to meet representatives from major manufacturers, get business cards, and establish a relationship. Nearly every industry has trade shows, either regionally or even locally, if you're in a major metropolitan area. You can also contact manufacturers directly. Find out who the sales representative is for your region, or if the company sells through a distributor or a wholesaler. Research the trade magazines for your industry and read them thoroughly. You'll find listings, ads, and articles about manufacturers. Finally, there are general directories for suppliers, manufacturers, and distributors, as well as industry-specific directories. Look for them at business libraries and online.

Buying from Reps

You'll be making your purchases from either the representative working for a specific company, an independent representative handling several manufacturers, or through the manufacturers themselves. But first, become a savvy buyer. Read up on the sales trends in the industry. Learn which items are hot, and which are not. If, for example, you were opening a gift store, you'd attend gift trade shows and read up on the latest trends in trade magazines and journals. You'd scour gift store websites and browse the shelves at actual stores with an eye for what's prominently displayed and at what price. The best way to learn about your new business is to immerse yourself in it.

When you buy items wholesale you need to consider:

- What are the sales terms?
- Is there a minimum order?
- Can you return items that don't sell?
- What is the method of shipping and are there additional charges?

- How long must you wait to receive the items?
- How quickly can you restock?
- What do you do if the items show up damaged?
- What happens if the shipment never arrives at all?
- Can you buy on credit, and if so, what are the terms?

Your relationship with sales representatives and vendors is very important. If you establish a good working relationship, you can then trust each other and work together for many years. The bottom line is, you need each other. Vendors make money if you continue to buy from them and you make money if their products sell to your customers.

ALERT

Be wary of distributors who are too aggressive in trying to sell you a line of products not familiar to you. Know the brand and the products before buying—do your homework. And if you take item X, don't get suckered into taking items Y and Z, too. Pawning off poor merchandise with the good merchandise is an old trick.

After you become established as a retailer, you'll find that reps contact you. Be selective in what you order, since, after all, you only have so much shelf space. If you overstock, you're prepared should an item be in heavy demand. On the other hand—and this is more often the case—you're stuck with an item that isn't moving as fast as you would have hoped, or has gone out of style.

Keeping the Inventory Fresh

You will generally need to turn your stock over a few times a year. Besides how well an item is selling, you'll need to consider how often new models or styles come out and how much you want on hand at any given time. Naturally, if you're dealing with perishables, your turnover will be daily or every few days.

From web pages to catalog layout to the design and layout of your store, how well you present the goods you're selling will impact heavily on their sales. One school of thought will suggest that bestselling items be up front so people will be drawn into the store to buy them. Another theory is to have hot-selling items farther back in the store so that people will have to pass your other stock and possibly buy other items. You can put one or two samples or demo items in the window to draw customers in. However, if a customer sees the one in the window and then doesn't bother to look around, you can lose the sale and your trick will backfire. Study the layout of other stores to get an idea of how you want yours to be set up. Then work hard on a logical traffic flow that will create an easy-to-navigate store and allow customers to see the merchandise.

ESSENTIAL

In department stores, you usually have to wander through the maze of fragrance counters to find the basics department. This is no accident. The more tempting (and highly profitable) products such as fragrances and cosmetics seduce the shopper on the way to the necessary purchases. Experiment with directing traffic to your high-profit items.

Buying

When you start out, you won't be making many deals. You'll be writing checks and buying merchandise C.O.D. As you build your retail business and establish relationships with vendors and sales reps, you will have greater negotiating power. You'll discuss the terms of the deal, such as a discount for a cash purchase, specific details of delivery, and possibly additional merchandise. In some cases, vendors will even split the cost of advertising with you on one of their products in a cooperative advertising arrangement. Rarely do deals include returns to the manufacturer of unsold merchandise, except in the book industry and a few others.

Of course, you'll need to prove yourself a good retailer and build your reputation to forge relationships with vendors, sales reps, distributors, and manufacturers. Over time, you'll go from looking for goods to stock to turning products away. Practically everyone who publishes a book, creates a software program, or develops a toy or game contacts an e-tailer like Amazon.com. Amazon.com can accommodate many of them because they don't need to stock the shelves. They can order just a few copies of a book and wait to see how it sells before ordering more. Their reputation helps them maintain ongoing relationships with an enormous number of publishers and manufacturers. New businesses should start small and increase their orders as sales increase. However, if you need to stock shelves, you'll become more and more discerning as numerous salespeople try to sell you their latest products.

When deciding which items to buy, consider the cost per item and determine the markup. (Is it worth your while to buy the item? Can you make enough money on it to warrant putting it in your store?) Read up on the latest trends and newest products in your industry, and stay ahead of, or at least keep pace with, your competitors. Every time your competitor has a new product available and you don't, you're losing a sale and signaling to customers that you aren't as up-to-the-minute as you should be. Consider the seasons and place orders in advance, making sure you buy far enough in advance to have items on hand for peak sales seasons, such as the end-of-year holidays.

You will make decisions on style and image. You will want to create a certain image for your store and order items that fit that image. You should look for unique items that other stores may not carry even if you only carry a few and cannot mark them up as much as you would like; these may draw customers or grab their attention once they're in the store.

You need to have a good eye for quality merchandise. This means knowing your industry and knowing the difference between the real thing and knock-offs. You need to know the types of products that your customers will buy. Study the demographics of your industry, your location, and your store or website. Know which products can be sold with accessories or other related items to get the most from a customer's buying decision. A model train set, for example, comes with numerous pieces that are sold separately.

Soak Up Information Everywhere You Can

You can learn a lot from others who have run retail businesses for many years. Successful retailers love to talk about how they built up their empires, and as a future empire builder, you need to soak up as much of that collective wisdom as possible. Join associations or the local chamber of commerce. Look at trade journals and gather as much information about retailing as you can. STORES magazine, at *www.stores.org*, has a wealth of retail information plus an industry buying guide that will help you put your store together, from the sign in front to the bags customers carry out when they leave. You'll also find links to numerous retail-based sites at *www .retailindustry.about.com*.

Pricing Your Goods and Services

How much you charge for goods or services is crucial to your success as a businessperson. Your pricing decisions will affect your sales volume, profits, image, inventory, ordering decisions, and more. Prices that are too high can alienate customers, while prices that are too low can hurt your profits and ultimately your cash flow.

Keep good records of the cost for each product so that you know your bottom-line amount in case you need to clear out an item at the lowest price without taking a loss. This means that if you order from different distributors, you should know the various costs and can come up with a cost average. For example, if you purchased a brand of dog food for your pet shop for $0.69 per can from one distributor, $0.67 from another, and then found someone else selling it at $0.65 per can, and each time you bought 100 cans, your total expenditure for 300 cans is $201. Therefore, if you had to reduce your selling price to $0.67 per can to be competitive, and if you sold them all, you'd break even (less any delivery cost).

Product Pricing

In a retail business, you're concerned with the cost of the merchandise and the retail price at which you can sell the product. The difference between these two amounts is your markup. Therefore, if you're buying screwdrivers at a cost of $2 per item, and selling them for $6 each, your markup is $4 per screwdriver.

There are numerous factors that come into play when you're pricing goods and services. However, the strongest driving factors are:

- Suggested retail price by the manufacturer
- Competitive prices on this product as found in other stores

Consider the costs of running your business. You need to pay your employees, your rent, and other bills. If your expenses add up to $10,000 per month, and you expect to sell 5,000 units a month, then you need an average markup of $2 each on whatever it is you sell to cover these fixed costs.

Consider the popularity of the item. Is this a hot-selling item that will move off the shelves just as quickly at $20 as it would at $17?

Consider your customer base. Do your customers look for high quality? Are they shopping at your store for convenience and personalized attention? If so, they won't mind spending more. If, however, they are looking for bargains and are very price-conscious when they come to your store, then you need to provide them with prices that match or beat the competition.

Pricing to Draw More Business

Think about drawing additional customers to your store. If a lower price will draw more customers and increase overall traffic in the store, then you might price an item at close to cost, which will result in less profit per item but more overall sales plus more store traffic.

Think accessories. Hobby items are perfect examples of products that can lead to plenty of potential sales on accessories. If you have any type of item that offers numerous accessories, you can take a lower markup on the main item. A dollhouse itself can sell at close to cost. Then you can get a higher markup on the furniture and other accessories needed. You can also work a deal that if a customer buys item A, they get a percentage off on items B, C, and D if they buy the entire set.

Think about seasonal and holiday shopping. The price for a dozen roses around Valentine's Day shoots through the roof. Also, as different seasons approach, you will see more demand for certain items. Likewise, as the season passes and you're left with items on the shelves, you'll need to mark them down to clear them out.

Know your neighborhood. If you're in an elite part of town, you'll be perceived as a high-end store, so price accordingly.

Consider who sets the prices. If you own a franchise, you may not have the final say in determining prices. Manufacturers often suggest retail prices, but generally they can't hold you to them. However, they also don't have to continue to sell to your store.

Think volume. Consider whether the item is one that you expect to sell in large quantities, producing a good overall return, or if it's a rare item that will only sell a few units, meaning you'll have to turn a profit on each one to make it worth your while.

Be mindful of trends. If you're dealing with clothing or other items that will change in style within a few months, then be ready to mark down the item so that you'll be able to move it out as the trend fades.

Determine what added benefits you can offer. If you charge more but throw in gift-wrapping or other services, you may attract customers for the added perks. While you're spending money on wrapping paper, you're also building an image and satisfied customer base with each purchase made. Build customer loyalty with "frequent buyer" incentives, for example, "Buy ten loaves of bread and the eleventh one is free." Another great asset with frequent buyer incentives is the ability to collect contact information such as e-mail addresses and get a direct pipeline to your regular customers.

There are numerous methods and theories regarding retail pricing. Keep in mind that it's an ever-evolving process, one that will change with new products, higher costs, more or less competition, and the economic picture. Don't stick to one hard-and-fast rule for pricing. Unless you're a very specialized retailer, you probably will have a range of markups for various products. This is quite common in what has become a greatly diversified marketplace.

Services

People in the service industry are always weighing the question of what to charge. Rates vary based on numerous factors. One of the biggest pitfalls for selling services is setting prices too low by not factoring in all of the costs of running the business, even if it is a business of one. First, service providers must consider their overhead costs, including rent, legal fees, accounting, bookkeeping, and so on, plus the materials needed to do the job, if applicable. Then the specific service must be competitively priced. This can be tricky because service providers offer different specialties. The reputation and background of service providers also needs to be considered. An established financial planning company can charge more because they have forty years of experience and people are willing to pay more for that expertise.

When determining how much you will charge for services, consider the range of competitive prices in your industry. Know how much your operating expenses are, including overhead costs, material costs, and marketing costs. Consider your profit goals. How much are you trying to make and how much do you need to charge to get there? Set realistic goals based on national figures for your industry. Weigh these with your own level of experience, specific expertise (including degrees or certificates), and your region or area. A New York City-based service provider, for instance, might charge 25 percent more than the same type of business based in Richmond, Indiana.

Create an hourly rate. Even if you quote a flat fee, determine it by how many hours the job will take and how much you can bill per hour, factoring in all of the other variables. Always estimate that a job will take 20 to 25 percent longer than your initial calculation.

Make sure you will be reimbursed for out-of-pocket expenses. If you need to make an out-of-town trip on behalf of your client, be clear about who is responsible for associated expenses.

ESSENTIAL

Consider selling accessories. If you own a nail salon, you may set a price for manicures and pedicures, but you also may make extra money by doing a little retailing of polish and related items. Many service-based businesses today are making extra money from such peripherals.

Whether you're running a house cleaning service, fitness center, financial planning service, or dog walking service, you need to evaluate what the market will pay. The key for you to understand is how much profit you're making above and beyond your expenses.

In all aspects of pricing, for any kind of business, make sure you think out a strategy for your prices very carefully. Do your break-even analysis and be ready to change your prices when necessary.

CHAPTER 16

Marketing Your Way to Success

The most brilliant business idea in the world, with all the necessary funding, equipment, and employees, will go nowhere without a solid marketing plan. Before you go to market you need to know the market. To muscle into the market you should be able to show a good reason to draw customers away from competitors. This chapter will get you started with market research, help you identify your target market, and give you publicity and advertising pointers.

Start with Market Research

If you plan to sell to a particular market, it's important to know all about that market. Research means finding out what customers want, don't want, and why. Surveys, questionnaires, and focus groups are a few ways to find out the needs and desires of your potential customers. You may also be able to tell a lot about your customers by observing them and taking note of who they are and what they're interested in when they're in your store. Get some basic information when they call for your services or browse your website. When customers make a purchase or any kind of inquiry, you can ask them where they heard about your business. Have you ever been asked for your zip code when you are checking out at a chain store? They capture this information to learn where their customers are coming from to shop in that store.

There are many factors that will impact on your marketing plan, including the following:

- Your budget
- The type of products or services you're offering
- Your scope (are you selling locally or going on the web to handle worldwide sales?)
- The amount of volume you can handle
- Your methods of distribution
- The amount of personal service you are able to provide
- How quickly you expect your business to grow

Consider the unique attributes of your business while designing questionnaires, surveys, or any other type of research-gathering materials. For example, if you're planning to do business worldwide, be prepared to conduct surveys in other languages and be aware of cultural nuances that may affect how your product is perceived.

Market research can tell you many things. You can learn about the pricing, trends, and competition in your industry. You can gain a greater understanding of the actual value of what you're selling in the market, meaning what people are willing to pay. You may also uncover trends in the marketplace that can be advantageous. For example, if surveys indicate that healthy foods are the hottest items on the menus for the lunch crowd at competing restaurants, then perhaps you can have a special fixed-price health lunch, and even offer calorie or carb counters and other health-related information at your dining establishment.

QUESTION

What is the difference between primary and secondary research?
In primary research, you gather information from surveys, question-naires, tests, focus groups, and other direct means. Secondary re-search draws on other sources, such as data services, the census, books, magazines, or websites. Primary research is more precise be-cause it is tailored to the exact questions you want answered. Second-ary research is faster and cheaper. Ideally, you will use both.

Look at trade magazines and reports from organizations and groups in your field to get the latest industry news. Visit websites and subscribe to such industry publications. If your business is local, you need to know the sales trends in your community. Libraries, websites, company reports (annual or quarterly reports from public companies), and the local chamber of commerce are just a few places to look for local business information. Manufacturers will want a broader picture, depending on how large they anticipate their customer base will be.

Surveys

Keep surveys short (ten to twelve questions maximum), whether they're given online, in-person, or by telephone. Phrase questions in a straightforward (nonjudgmental) manner, with neutral language, and keep questions one sentence long. Keep it relatively simple and even entertaining if possible, so respondents will want to continue. Get the age, sex, and approximate income level (provide ranges to select from) of participants. People are more likely to fill out a written survey or answer questions in person because they consider telephone calls annoying. Internet surveys are considered particularly valid for a backward reason. According to Larry Zussman, director of One-to-One Marketing for Xerox, people responding to them tend not to lie or give what they consider the "right answer" because they perceive the responses do not matter.

Focus Groups

Focus groups are wonderful ways to get insightful answers to questions and opinions about your product. You will want to have a neutral group in a neutral location with a neutral host and provide a pleasant atmosphere—sometimes including snack foods. Often focus groups are watched through a one-way window or mirror or taped for future evaluation. Keep the session to an hour and a half or two hours at the most.

During the time of the session you want to get the most meaningful feedback possible. The facilitator conducting the focus group should press the participants to give specific feedback. For example, if you have an independent financial planning service you have to charge fees. The folks in the focus group might not like the idea of paying a fee, but when pressed, may acknowledge some fee has to be charged. The focus group goal might be to establish the threshold of tolerance for your fees.

ESSENTIAL

It's vital that your market research studies provide a close representation of your target audience. In fact, by your third focus group or series of surveys you may be intentionally including 90 percent men or 90 percent women because that percentage most accurately profiles the population buying your product or using your service.

Know your product, know (or learn) your market group, and then test the product on the right group. For example, if you're testing your new wedding planning website, test it in front of engaged couples or engaged women, but not in front of a room with 50 percent divorced men who have no interest at present in getting remarried.

Tracking

Keeping close tabs on who buys what product or service is a way of gathering information. Are all your credit card receipts from the same zip code? Do customers always seem to visit the same pages on your website? Simple statistical information can be gathered by tracking your business transactions. This can provide market research information and help you define your target audience. You might simply notice on your store video camera that the last sixty-one customers who bought items were males in their early to mid-twenties. Pay attention and you can gather inexpensive marketing data.

Identifying Your Target Market

Just as children's games say clearly on the box what ages the game is geared toward, nearly every product or service has some demographic group that will be most interested in spending money to own it, use it, or rent it. The number of businesses that have failed because the owners haven't taken the time to determine their target audience is staggering. Know your target market, and remember it doesn't have to be twenty-year-olds. In fact, the group with the biggest buying power in this country is over forty, not sixteen to twenty-three. A growing market is the over-sixty-five demographic, particularly women. There are almost 40 million people in the United States over the age of sixty-five, and more than 55 percent of them are women.

Yes, a store selling air would have everyone as a target market since we all need air, but our interests, likes, dislikes, tastes, and needs are different based on many factors, including age, location, income level, ethnic culture, marital status, and so much more. There are many reasons why the one-size-fits-all approach usually doesn't work when marketing a product or service.

Some questions to ask yourself when outlining your target market or demographic group include:

- What is the age range of the customers who want my product or service?
- What is their income level?
- What level of education do they have?
- What is their marital or family status?
- Is this a product or service they need, or a luxury item?
- How will they use this product or service?
- What will draw them to my product or service?
- Which gender will be buying my product or service more often?
- What special features or attention are they looking for?

- What do they like or dislike about the product or service in general?
- Is this an impulse buy or something they are saving up for?
- Where do they gather their decision-making information?
- Is this something that will be come a repeat purchase?

These are just a few of numerous categories into which you can break down your target market. You don't want to make a marketing plan that is ultimately so narrow that it limits your sales to a few perfect customers. On the other hand, if you think your product or service is perfect for "everybody," you have not defined what makes it special, and for whom.

Reaching Your Market

Let's say you've established that your ideal customer is a single woman between the ages of twenty-five and forty-two, with an income in the $35,000 to $55,000 range, who resides in the suburbs of a large city, drinks diet soda, watches soap operas on television, speaks to her mom twice a week, dates men three to five years older than herself, and has a cat. Well, perhaps you didn't get that specific (you generally don't need to), but the point is, once you've established who your audience is, you need to know how to reach them.

Pricing

Before venturing into the methods of getting your name out there, it's important that you consider your pricing strategies. In a new business, you may need to establish your reputation and brand name with potential customers by keeping your product or services below average market prices. Otherwise, you'll need to provide special services or incentives that your competition cannot provide. If a new product and an established brand-name product are priced the same, the established brand will most often be the winner.

You might also use time-factored pricing as a promotion point. For example, you can promote a lower price if customers buy before a particular date. Be careful not to lower your prices below cost or make prices so low that customers don't return when you're selling at your regular prices.

ALERT

Note that just as you are watching your competitors' pricing, they are watching yours. Be prepared to trigger a response matching a competitor's pricing offer. During the holidays e-tailers may use free shipping as a lure to get customers to make purchases on their sites. Once a few of the big guys try it, soon everyone needs to offer it to remain competitive.

Pricing is also linked to perceived value. If someone is expecting to pay a certain amount for a product or service, he won't question that amount. If you're able to cut costs, you can lower the price. However, it is not necessary. For example, if you're selling soda at $1 per bottle and buying bottles in mass quantity at $0.59 each, you're making $0.41 per bottle sold. If everyone is used to paying $1 for a soda in your area, then no one will think about the price. If, however, you can suddenly get bottles of soda at $0.49 each from a different distributor, it doesn't mean you have to lower your price to $0.90. If you stay at $1 per bottle you're staying at the market price, which means more profits for you. If, however, you want more volume because there aren't enough people coming into your sandwich shop, you might lower your price—and promote the new price through fliers, signage, and advertising. Keep in mind, though, that people can become spoiled by lower prices.

Promotion and Advertising

If you have a product or service and you want to make money from it, you'll need to promote it. Promotion includes selling, sales promotion, and advertising. Selling can include talking with customers and making sales calls. Sales promotion can include anything from how you arrange the sales items on a selling floor or set up the homepage on your website to attending trade shows.

There are numerous ways to get your name out there, and once you've done your market research and established who your target audience is, you'll need to put together your promotional budget.

Promotions can be seasonal, such as offering a free Christmas ornament to customers who spend over $50 in your boutique during November.

Promotions can be tied to events, such as when you become a sponsor of a road race to support a local charity, or underwrite one of the area Little League baseball teams. Promotions can be tie-ins with other events. Think of all the children's meals at fast food chains themed to the newest movie release.

Direct Mail

Often referred to as "junk mail" by its recipients, direct mail can yield a greater response if you target the consumer for your product or service correctly. Magazines seeking subscribers have long relied primarily on direct mail, and today numerous products and services also seek significant returns from direct-mail marketing. Direct mail differs from a mail campaign to your regular customers because it involves buying or compiling a specific list that best suits your target market or demographic needs. Certainly, many people will toss what you send into the garbage. However, if you send out 100 direct-mail pieces at a cost of $100, and make three sales of $60 each, you're making $80. You've also put your name in front of the other ninety-seven people, four or five of whom may remember you at a later date or have a friend who needs whatever it is that you're selling.

ESSENTIAL

An offer should be included in every direct marketing piece. The offer can vary depending on the importance of the target recipient. With direct mail, your goal is to make at least enough profit to cover the cost of the mailing, including printing, postage, the price of the list, and so on. Study other direct-mail pieces and create a professional-looking direct-mail piece—one that appears personal and presents the benefits of what you're offering.

Timing is everything when it comes to direct mail. Plan your mailing for opportune times. For example, you won't want your direct-mailing piece to get caught up in the holiday postal overload. Make your piece stand out. Use color, a photo, or a clever quote. Postcards can be effective direct-mail pieces. They're cheaper than letters and grab attention immediately.

Avoid mixed or confusing messages. Use a tone that reflects the demographics of your readers. If your piece has too much to read, people will toss it. Don't insult or put down your audience. Don't tell them why what they're doing is wrong or stupid and why you have all the answers. Rather, tell them you can improve upon their way of doing things.

FACT

Direct mail should grab the attention of the recipient and prompt him to take action. With digital printing technology it is possible to customize a message for your targeted recipient. Creative (or some would say deceptive) packaging, such as a mailing piece that looks like a check is enclosed, will improve the odds of your piece getting opened.

E-Mail Marketing

E-mail marketing is a very effective way of reaching a worldwide audience. Internet users hate spam, or the electronic version of junk mail that comes when companies buy lists of unwilling participants. Most savvy folks have spam filter software on their computers to rebuff the avalanche of unwanted messages bombarding them daily. The same people might not mind junk mail in their mailbox—in fact, they're used to it—but e-mail is considered more intrusive. Even if your message does get through, the delete button is easy to hit before it is ever looked at.

To make the most of e-mail communications, you need to have good lists of existing or prospective customers who will accept your solicitations. It's to your advantage to market yourself clearly on your website or even on another website of a similar nature. You want people to sign up for e-mails from you, or agree to receive them. Blind e-mails from massive lists generally annoy people, and don't work if they are blocked.

If you do plan to use e-mail, keep the message concise and make sure people can get off the list if they want to. The website *www.constantcontact .com* is designed to help small businesses set up effective e-mail marketing programs. It can help with developing a monthly newsletter to send to your list, and offers other services, including one to help you track responses.

Signage

Signs draw people into an establishment and keep the company name highly visible to new and old customers alike. The lettering, the colors, a logo, and anything else that makes your sign stand out are significant. Passersby are only glancing at your sign as they drive or walk past. A simple three- or four-word sign is easier to comprehend than one containing two sentences.

Along with your actual signs, you can take advantage of inexpensive but effective advertising with posters and fliers. In major cities, there are numerous construction sites and other such areas that have advertisements posted all over them. As long as the posting of bills is allowed, this is an inexpensive way to be seen by numerous people. The traffic that passes by in a major city is tremendous. College campuses are also great places to post fliers.

Handouts can also be an effective way of letting people know about your hottest products or specialized services. Instruct those handing out such materials to be courteous and to avoid sticking them in people's faces.

Be clever. Anywhere you think people who are prospective customers might see your company name is where you want to have it placed. Just abide by laws, rules, and regulations—or you could be fined.

Advertising

Posting bills and fliers is advertising, so is direct mail, but these are less expensive methods than major newspaper or magazine ads. And they pale in comparison to the cost of a TV advertising campaign. Depending on the nature of your business, you'll need to evaluate the types of media available. If you're planning and promoting an annual one-month festival to be held every October, then you'll use your ad money to advertise in a big way in August and September. However, if you're selling products or services year-round, you'll want the budget to last for twelve months.

Newspapers

Newspapers provide a means for reaching a particular region (or the nation, if it's a paper with a wide circulation, such as *USA Today* or the *New*

York Times). You can time your ads to run when you choose, and reach a large audience. Keep the ads simple and make sure they provide a means by which customers can reach you—phone number, e-mail address, and so on. Remember to place your ad in the section best suited for your product or service, such as Sports or Lifestyle. You can also include incentives like coupons. Be forewarned, however, that photos and artwork don't always look good in newspapers.

Look at the ad rates carefully and measure the size of ads that you might want to buy (ads are sold by column inch). Generally you will need to run your advertisement several times so people become familiar with your ad. Sunday papers can be good because people save them. PennySaver and similar publications aren't newspapers but they can be good for small inexpensive ads, depending on your product.

Magazines

Magazines allow you to reach a more targeted audience. Also, your ad will have a longer shelf life than it will in a daily paper, which gets tossed or put in the birdcage. Trade magazines can be beneficial for business-to-business sales or industry recognition. Select magazines that are best suited for your product or services, and remember that they usually have a long lead-time. Get a calendar showing when ads are needed at the magazine. Magazines allow for marvelous artwork, so you can be colorful and creative. Provide art electronically to conform to today's production norms. Make sure the copy suits the magazine and its readership.

Radio

Radio is an excellent way to reach a targeted market, since different demographic groups listen to different stations. Radio allows you to be creative with sound effects and you will spend a lot less money than you would by advertising on television. Be concise and conversational in your tone, get to the point quickly, don't be obnoxious, and try to be entertaining and snappy—whether the copy is produced or is read by on-air talent. Make sure the location of your store or website is clearly stated and the phone number is repeated twice if you're a one-location business. Look for high-traffic times like morning or evening drive times.

ESSENTIAL

When looking into radio advertising, consider easy listening stations or light music stations, which are played in establishments like restaurants or even over telephone lines when people are put on hold. The listening audience for such stations is often larger than the ratings reveal because of all these secondary listeners.

Television

Be creative when it comes to television. For example, if a local talk show needs a hotel for their guests to stay at, you might provide rooms free of charge in exchange for a promotional announcement. If you run a limousine service, provide free transportation for all guests in exchange for a daily mention of your company on their show. Such deals are worked out all the time. And then there are infomercials. They're expensive, but they can be very effective for certain products.

Outdoor Advertising

Billboards are a great way to put your brand name in front of the public. Be imaginative and keep it simple. Remember, people are driving by and have no time to read five lines of copy at sixty miles per hour. A new curious place for advertising is a small sign attached to the gasoline pumping hose. Vehicles roam cities acting as street-level billboards. Taxis can have roof signs. Public transportation such as buses and subway cars offer opportunities to grab the attention of commuters with displays inside and out.

ALERT

Get recommendations before signing up with an ad agency or consultant. Also, make sure to monitor your ads to be certain that they run when they're supposed to and look—or sound—as you wish. If the ad didn't run properly, or at all, you must make sure the media source knows it.

Trade Shows

Trade shows are another great way to be seen. Design a booth that grabs people's attention and displays your products or services. Have plenty of literature and friendly, knowledgeable personnel on hand. Nothing beats that face-to-face contact, even if it is a brief encounter in a hectic trade show environment. A more in-depth conversation can be had afterwards. Conventioneers attending trade shows expect to leave loaded down with all kinds of giveaways as well as literature or CDs from the exhibiting companies and organizations. There is a wide price range for the seemingly infinite choices of clever giveaways to remind the attendees of your business or service. If you can't afford to be part of a trade show, at least attend and make sure you put your business card in the hand of everyone you meet.

Other Creative Options

Other forms of advertising are all around you. You can promote yourself with T-shirts, sweatshirts, pens, notepads, or baseball caps. Newsletters (online or offline) can also spread the word about what you're up to and what you offer potential customers. Put your name on a takeout menu, or sponsor a local event. Putting your name before the public—preferably your target market—is your goal. Advertising can be one method of doing so, but there are other means of getting publicity. Keep in mind that repeat advertising is more effective than one-time advertising, so budget accordingly.

If you're operating an online business, you may benefit from online means of exposure, which include:

- Linking with other sites
- Registering with several top search engines
- Using specific keywords to increase the likelihood of your company name coming up during a search
- Swapping ads with other sites
- Joining Internet organizations and being written up in newsletters and on other sites
- Mentioning your company name on newsgroups, in chat rooms, or in forums
- Marketing and promoting your company offline

Social Networking

Social networking sites like Facebook, Twitter, and YouTube are no longer the sole reserve of high schoolers. Increasingly businesses are setting up Facebook pages as another way to stay in touch with clients By setting up a specific Facebook business page you'll be more accessible to tech savvy customers who check in on Facebook regularly to see what is new in their world. You want to become part of their regular search as a favorite vendor or source for what is happening right now Updating a Facebook page regularly ensures that your company name will be visible to your target audience every day—and it's free!

As traditional media such as print advertising contracts, social media is gaining in impact in the business world. Some are using Twitter to stimulate customer loyalty by promising information that will be found exclusively through this media. MiniLuxe Nail Salons and Boutiques in greater Boston promote "Twitter Thursdays" when they offer special discounts on products or services available only to clients who follow them on Twitter.

You should assess who you are trying to reach for customers. If your target audience is using social media, you don't want to overlook these important tools. Build your fan/follower list by linking your Facebook and Twitter pages to your website and e-mail signature. If you have an e-mail list, send out a message announcing your social media presence and invite customers to follow you. You can send updates to customers about new products, special sales, and other events. Post photos or videos that will interest your customer base. Invite fans and followers to a private sale or an anniversary celebration. Hold contests and invite feedback. The possibilities are endless!

Publicity

You need not always go out and spend top dollar on advertising and promotional ideas to get your name before the public. Stories about your business in newspapers, magazines, on the Internet, or as part of radio or television newscasts can be remarkably successful ways of increasing business. Unlike advertising, you don't pay for these directly, but you may pay for a publicist or public relations agency to help put you in the limelight, or at least in a few key stories.

When you're starting out, you can do some of this work yourself through writing and sending (or e-mailing) press releases to anyone and everyone who you think might be interested in a story about what your business is doing. Send information about new products, upcoming events, new technology or inventions, interesting news, mergers, or anything else that could potentially become a story. Look for a clever attention-grabbing hook. Think up an eye-catching title and include the who, what, where, when, and why of the proposed story. Double-space your press release, keep it to one page (two maximum), and make sure you include specific contact information.

ALERT

One of the biggest reasons for the downfall of several major web-based businesses was the overextension of their advertising beyond the value or profitability of their product. This can be the downfall of any business. If you're spending an average of $10 to promote a $7 item, you're in trouble.

Press kits are important and should include a collection of recent press releases, clips from stories that were written about you or your company, and an overview of what the company is all about, plus bios of the key players. If you have them, include papers or speeches you have authored. A professional-looking press kit is a very important business tool. You can start by having a few kits printed to serve your immediate needs, but as your company grows you will want to look at places like *www.presskits .com* for a selection of professional personalized kits. Your kit should reflect the image of your business.

ESSENTIAL

You can position yourself for good media coverage in stories related to your industry by establishing yourself as a recognized authority in your field. Getting yourself published in trade publications makes you an expert when general media is doing a piece related to your industry. Always make yourself available for background information even if you are not going to be quoted.

Public Relations

Public relations involves more than trying to place your name in front of the media. A good public relations firm can help you maintain a positive image on those occasions when things go wrong. This includes cleaning up negative publicity that may result from incidents, activities, or accidents involving your business. If one of your products was recalled, you'll need to spend time working with your PR department to reassure the public that your company has addressed and dealt with the problem. Your reputation and how it plays in the media is very important. If you're a media darling, you can thrive. If David Letterman and Jay Leno make jokes about your company, you might still thrive. However, if your company has a seriously bad reputation or is part of a negative news story, this could cause you to lose significant business.

Another great way to promote yourself is by sponsoring local activities or events. From a local track meet to a major golf tournament, sponsorship can be a marvelous way to put your name before the public in a positive manner. You can also host seminars, classes, or other such events. Joining trade associations, attending conferences and seminars (press kits in hand), and putting yourself and your company name in front of groups of people who are in your industry or are interested in what you do can help you spread the word.

Word of mouth is another way of gaining free publicity, one that you can get started by getting people to talk about your product or service at any place from cocktail parties to Boy Scout hiking trips. Tell your friends and family to talk you up! Remember charitable work can't hurt either.

CHAPTER 17

Networking

There is no point in having a business and not letting the world know about it. Besides the usual promotions, ads, signs, direct mail, and online newsletters, you have a very important secret weapon to ensure your success—you! Make the effort to participate in as many industry and business organizations as time permits and you will unlock the door to learning more in your field and drawing more customers to your business.

Join Your Tribe

Maybe you have a knack for coordinating paint colors and fabrics. Friends have admired your clever touch and have sought your advice for years. Friendly inquiries begin to evolve into referrals to people you don't even know. Now you are on the brink of becoming a professional interior designer. Your talent is certain. You have ferreted out great resources for fabric and trim, but you could use some advice on finding the best workrooms to produce your designs.

You won't get that question answered in the yellow pages. But if you look into the relevant national professional group, in this case the American Society of Interior Designers (ASID), you will garner all kinds of helpful information about the industry you are entering. All fields have these vertical groups. Many have requirements for membership that you may need time and experience to gain. Even if you are ineligible to join right off the bat, their membership counselors can guide you to other industry places where you can seek help.

ESSENTIAL

If you can't find a local membership group in your field, start one! There may be a national organization already in place and you could be the initiator to launch a local chapter. The national group can provide guidance for standards to be met for membership, how to establish bylaws, and other helpful information to make a go of it.

Also remember that there's no limit to the number of professional organizations or societies you can join. As long as you can handle any membership dues and time commitments, join away! Having your name appear in more places can only help you get exposure for your business. Try to attend meetings, conferences, and other gatherings of organization members as often as possible. This will help people match your face to your name.

Civic Organizations

If your business is serving your local community, whether it is a pizza shop, a dry cleaning business, or a silk flower emporium, you need to be known.

Besides listing your number in the yellow pages and running ads with the local newspaper and radio or television stations, you need to be personally visible beyond the doors of your establishment. A great way to accomplish this is by joining a local civic organization such as Rotary, Lions, or the chamber of commerce. Coming to know your fellow business owners will provide a type of camaraderie not available to you with your employees. You can share ideas about business operations or local market conditions. This is a place where you could get wind of some zoning changes bubbling up at town hall.

FACT

The biggest advantage to belonging to a local civic organization may be the chance to collaborate with others in promoting your businesses. Maybe you can have the local tax preparer offer their clients coupons for a free cup of coffee when they buy a meal at your restaurant during the month of April. Perhaps a group of retailers will jointly sponsor a sidewalk sale during slower times of the year.

Typically these groups meet monthly, and have a program speaker on a topic of general interest to the group. They also usually raise money to support local charities or sports teams, or to provide scholarships to worthy graduating high-school students. It is a great resource for professional help such as local legal counsel or accounting services, as well as qualified tradespeople like plumbers or electricians.

These meetings may also give you the inside track on what is happening with your competitors. Another gift shop owner may be getting ready to sell and would give you right of first refusal; or a big box store may be looking to come to your area, posing a pricing challenge to your hardware store. Knowledge is power, and sometimes the local grapevine is the quickest way to get the information you need.

Associations and Organizations

Whether you are a lawyer, plumber, interior designer, or computer service geek, you are not alone. Many before you have walked the path you are walking and have the battle scars to prove it. You don't have to go it alone professionally, trying to figure out what works and where the pitfalls are in your particular field. Tradespeople have clustered in unions, which help protect wages but also provide a standard of competence for their members. Would you rather have your brother-in-law rewire your family room for all your high-tech toys, or a certified electrician who won't burn the house down in the process?

So, too, for virtually any profession or interest group you will find a society or association whose goal is to support its members with some or all of the following:

- Industry updates
- Continuing education
- Certification programs
- Government relations—or lobbying—on your industry's behalf
- Group purchasing discounts
- Customer leads
- Marketing support
- Leadership programs

There is even an association of associations, called the American Society of Association Executives, which can provide you with information on local and national associations for your field. Visit their website at *www.asaenet.org*.

Industry Awards

One way to stand out from the crowd in your field is to be designated a star by winning an industry award. The Academy of Motion Picture Arts and Sciences has the Oscar. Broadway has the Tony. Your field surely has a means to recognize excellence. Often, these awards are established by the professional association or society for a particular industry. Categories such as best practices, marketing, advertising, and more are established, criteria are set, and deadlines imposed for submission. Judging is done by a group of experts in the field. In some cases awards are earned after meeting certain criteria and there is no competition per se.

Think of the AAA diamond awards for hotels and resorts. Each diamond is given only when particular standards are met. Some are as finite as whether the bathrooms are painted or papered. Yet there is nothing to say two four-star resorts couldn't be right next to each other and continue to earn the same rating year after year.

Just starting out in a new business, you may not be able to go for an industry award right away. Yet, you may be able to bring past glories along with you. If you earned "mechanic of the year" for three straight years while working at a local auto repair shop, and now you are branching out on your own, there is no reason you cannot toot your own horn and feature these awards in your ads and promotions. Who wouldn't want an award-winning mechanic working on his transmission instead of a run-of-the-mill worker?

It will take some research to learn how awards are given in your field and by whom. Once you know the categories, guidelines, and submission requirements, don't hesitate to get your business compliant and ready to apply. If you need to be nominated, find out how to go about it. There is no reason to be shy about letting the world know you have been recognized as the top dog groomer, best hair-coloring salon, or source for the city's best chocolate turtles.

Everyone loves a winner, and many local newspapers and magazines run readers' choice contests in just about every category of business imaginable. These truly are popularity contests and are not based on any industry standards. Often several levels of awards are issued—gold, silver, bronze, honorable mention, etc.—thus many businesses wind up with bragging rights. Really aggressive businesses will ask their patrons to vote for them rather than sit back and hope they make it on their great products and services alone. There is nothing wrong with asking for votes, as long as you don't try to "buy" them.

Professional Networking Groups

Civic organizations are generally open to any established business in the community. A professional networking group has a slightly different twist. Some groups are structured with the intent of generating leads for their members. Often these leads are presented at breakfast meetings. To make it worthwhile to join they may restrict membership to only one person per field. If you own a printing company you would be happy to meet with owners of many other businesses, from caterers to sales trainers, because they are all going to need printed materials: menus, manuals, or, at a minimum, business cards. You wouldn't like it if your networking group included other printers who would be going after the same business.

The good news is there is no limit to networking groups. Should one be closed to your particular niche, another can certainly be found. You might even seek one in a locale you are contemplating expanding into as a way of making some entrees. And just as with local chapters of national professional organizations and societies, if you can't find one in your area, start it up!

Volunteering as a Strategy to Meet New Customers

When you join a professional society, a civic organization, or a professional networking group, you are looking to gain knowledge or new business in your field. If you become active in one of these organizations you may join one or more committees and offer your services as a volunteer for the advancement of the group. There are plenty of other volunteer opportunities that may draw customers to your business as a result of your visibility in these nonprofessional groups. Among the many places that are always interested in volunteer support are:

- Hospitals
- Youth groups
- Disease/health charities such as the American Cancer Society
- Disaster/relief groups such as the American Red Cross
- Houses of worship
- Cultural institutions
- Schools
- Alumni organizations
- Public affairs groups, such as the League of Women Voters or the Democratic or Republican Party
- Amateur sporting events

Some groups require membership to participate in their volunteer opportunities, such as the Appalachian Mountain Club or the Junior League. However, most are just happy to have willing people help out. In either case you may be able to help the organization by contributing "in kind," meaning goods or services from your business instead of money. Whatever method you choose, volunteering will serve to expand your knowledge and experience, as well as get your name on the map.

Social Networking Sites

Facebook may have been spawned on a college campus but it is a serious engine for connecting people, and increasingly, businesses. Keep your eyes open and you'll notice more and more companies have a line in their ads or on their websites saying, "Find us on Facebook." A word of caution about Facebook, however. You will want to maintain a line between your personal page and your business page. Some folks continue to say or disclose things about themselves to the great worldwide web that they would never do in polite company. Keep in mind your professional reputation can be dashed by some silly impulsive disclosure on the personal pages.

LinkedIn is another popular site, more oriented to business, for making connections and reaching out to prospects. You may not get direct new business from sites like Facebook or LinkedIn, but you certainly don't want to miss the promotional opportunity they present.

CHAPTER 18

Employees: Choose Well, Manage Well

As soon as you reach the stage where you literally cannot do it all, it is time to bring in the troops. Hiring employees, even if some are unpaid, brings your business to a new level of complexity. There are creative or traditional ways to bring in people to get the job done. Being clear about the task at hand and the level of skill needed will help tremendously in deciding how to meet your growing staffing needs.

Prepping Before Hiring

Prior to hiring anyone, you need to prepare, and preparation means focusing on a number of details. If you're going to hire someone, you'll need to be ready to do the following:

- Get a federal ID number as an employer
- Recruit qualified individuals, review their skills, and contact their references
- Train and supervise others
- Adjust to various personalities
- Delegate responsibilities
- Recognize that some things may be done successfully in a manner different from yours
- Make sure you're a good communicator and listener
- Know the going rate for wages and how much you can afford to pay
- Pay employees on a regular basis no matter how business is going
- Establish rules and guidelines so that your employees know your expectations and don't take advantage of you
- Pay unemployment taxes, Social Security, and Medicare when due
- Have desks, phones, computer terminals, and other supplies ready
- Know how to lay people off or fire them

Are you prepared to do all of this? Can you handle conflict between employees? Can you motivate employees to work at peak levels? As an employer, you'll have to set the tone and lead by example. You'll need to determine your own style and be consistent and fair to all employees. Hone your leadership skills in advance. Learning as you go can result in poor business practices and even lawsuits. You want to project an image of professionalism.

Crafting a Job Posting

A job posting will help you hire a person for a specific job. It also serves as a blueprint for the tasks associated with that job. You should include accurate, thorough information in a posting, without overwhelming potential applicants with too many details. Here are the key elements of a job posting:

- Date of posting
- Name of company
- Brief description of company
- Job summary, with the primary functions described
- Compensation
- Necessary background and skills for doing the job
- Benefits
- Contact information

In order to get applicants who closely resemble your ideal candidate, you must offer specific, clear information about the job. If your posting is vague or misleading, you may end up with a bunch of applicants who are completely unqualified for the job. If this happens, it will be your fault—not theirs.

Finding the Best Match for Your Needs

They say good help is hard to find, but it's not impossible. It's all a matter of clearly defining what your needs are and screening the applicants accordingly. The better you know what you're looking for, the more likely you'll be able to find someone with those skills. Take your time and assess potential employees very carefully. The human element of your company is more significant than the brand of computer you're using.

Classified Ads

If you're hiring locally, place ads in local papers. Also consider classified ads in trade publications. Keep the ad brief and make the job description (and list of requirements) clear. Explain the basic skills you require and the experience you prefer. Don't ask for unreasonable amounts of experience, like ten years in the Internet field if you don't truly need that level of expertise. Include any technical know-how that a person should have and exactly what you want to see (for example, a resume, work samples, and cover letter). Also include how applicants should get their information to you (e-mail, fax, or mail). Give a few options—not everyone has e-mail.

Some metropolitan area newspapers feature greatly expanded job-listing sections once or twice a year. If the timing works out, this is a great time to include your listing because the paper aggressively markets the section, drawing the attention of a large pool of job seekers.

Web Postings

You can post a job opportunity on your own website or on any of the many employment websites. Monster (*www.monster.com*), Yahoo! HotJobs (*www.hotjobs.yahoo.com*), and Craigslist (*www.craigslist.org*) are among the many places where individuals look for work—which makes them excellent places to post. Keep in mind, however, that the web is worldwide, so put your location up top in the ad. You don't want people from Panama City overlooking the fact that you're located in Peoria.

Employment Agencies and Headhunters

Employment agencies generally sign up far more applicants than they can find jobs for, so they may have someone to place in your business. Few agencies are very creative, so you'll need to be extremely clear about your needs. If the job isn't easily defined, you may run into trouble. Headhunters, however, take a more professional approach and deal with higher-level executives whom they are trying to place accordingly. They can sometimes be helpful if you're looking for top-level talent.

Make sure your job-posting requirements are commensurate with the salary or wages you are offering. If your budget doesn't match your grand wish list for credentials, education, and experience, you will be frustrated when you only hear from candidates who expect to earn more than you do.

Friends and Family

The business world is largely run based on the "who you know" principle, especially in certain fields, such as the entertainment industry. Consider those people you know and trust—but remember, when friends work for friends, trouble can ensue. Establish a business relationship in the office that is separate from your personal relationship.

Staff Alternatives: Contractors, Freelancers, and Interns

There are many online listings where you can post positions for freelancers or contractors. There are an equal number of freelancers and contractors who have posted their qualifications on the Internet. You can also find qualified contractors and freelancers through word of mouth. It's important to get good references and check the work and background of such independent workers, since you don't have a personnel office in their last company to turn to for information.

Here are some things you need to know about each freelancer or independent contractor you consider:

- How soon can this person commit to the project?
- Can she meet your deadline?
- What are her hourly rates?
- How many hours does she anticipate the job taking?
- Does she work on-site or off-site?
- How does this person expect to be paid?
- Does she mind signing a confidentiality agreement?

Research rates for the same job to make sure their rates are in line with what you can expect to be paying. Writing, graphic arts, and most other professions in which people often do freelance work have associations, unions, or websites where you can find compensation information.

Once you've established the boundaries and guidelines for the job and how your company works, write up a basic contract agreement. Don't get too elaborate with your contract or you may box yourself into a corner.

Include outs for both parties. From the contractor or freelancer, you want sufficient notice if he can't finish the project, and make sure it's clear that he will only be paid for the work he's done. If, however, you need to end the project at a certain time or cancel, you should also give notice and pay the person for the work they've done to that point.

ESSENTIAL

While contractors and freelancers are not employees and do not get the benefits of staff, you should still treat them in a proper, professional manner. Contractors and others who are self-employed do a lot of networking, and inappropriate practices can give you a bad reputation, which will make it harder to find good people.

Internship programs through local high schools or colleges are great places to find energetic young talent willing to learn in exchange for course credits. They can often be your future full-time employees in training. It is a great way to try out a young person who may be a rising star in a few years.

Interviewing Candidates

After you decide on your methods of searching, you'll have to go through the task of evaluating resumes and determining which individuals you want to call in for interviews. If you are flooded with resumes, it might be worth your money to hire someone to read through them and narrow down the field to the best candidates.

Weigh the benefits of education, knowledge, and experience in the field against basic work experience and an often-overlooked strong work ethic. In short, you may be best off hiring a mix of people fresh out of school and people who've been in the workforce for a while. They can balance your company and benefit from one another.

Many people think that it's easier to be the interviewer than the interviewee. However, because you're the one representing your business, there is a lot of pressure on you to act in a professional manner and in a way that adheres to proper protocol. In other words, there are questions you can ask prospective employees, and questions you cannot ask them.

ESSENTIAL

If you get a crush of responses to your job posting it might be worthwhile to do the first round of screening interviews by phone. From this group you can winnow down those who came across with enough knowledge and polish to warrant a face-to-face interview.

For example, you can ask all about past jobs, past responsibilities, favorite tasks or work-related activities, and why they've left their last job. You cannot ask if they're married, have kids, or about their sexual orientation. You can ask about goals, dreams, special skills, strengths and weaknesses, long-term plans, and preferred work style (team, individual, and so on). You can't ask about a person's religious beliefs, age, political affiliations, or disabilities. In short, personal questions are out and work-related questions are fine.

ESSENTIAL

Reread the candidate's resume just before you start the interview so you can focus on her qualifications. The resume may trigger an interesting talking point revealing how she would fit into your organization. The candidate will relax a bit knowing you took the time to at least read the resume, a small courtesy to her and requisite preparation for you.

When interviewing, stick to the subject (the job), explain the company, make no judgments, and use common courtesy. You should be able to evaluate and determine whether you want to hire someone based on two interviews and a check of his references. Sometimes, individuals are also asked for samples of their work, such as a portfolio in advertising.

It's often advantageous to ask someone how he would handle a certain responsibility or how he would act in a specific situation. The answers to questions like these may prove more valuable than the standard "Where do you see yourself in five years?" Get an idea of how an individual solves problems. You can, and should, request references, and have the person's resume in front of you as a guide during the interview. Take good notes when interviewing someone so that you can go back and compare candidates later.

Once you do decide to hire someone, establish a start date. (Usually a new employee will start in a week or two.) Provide each employee with the W-4 form for the IRS, any benefits information, the I-9 form from the USCIS (formerly the INS), and an employee handbook if you have one.

Running Background Checks

You don't have to check up on everything, but a little research can't hurt. People sometimes make gross exaggerations, and it could prevent you from hiring the wrong person.

Get the applicant's permission to call previous employers. Then check on the previous jobs, dates, salaries, and skills. Depending on the requirements of the position you are filling it may be a good idea to verify any degrees or licenses the candidate has included in her resume. Specific references given to you by the candidate are also fine to call, but they're obviously always people who will say good things about the person. These types of references should therefore be taken with a grain of salt—call one and that will usually provide you with all the praise you need for this person.

ALERT

Depending on the particular position for which you are hiring, you may also want to run a criminal background check. Day-care providers need to be sure anyone they're considering does not have a record of sexual assault. You certainly do not want to learn the bookkeeper you are about to hire has a felony record for embezzlement.

If the factual information the applicant provides is incorrect, be suspicious. Make sure, however, that if you call a company to ask about someone who worked there seven years ago, that you're talking to an individual who can look back in the files (assuming the company keeps files that far back). Just because someone working there at that moment never heard of the person, that doesn't mean she didn't work there in the past.

Be consistent and check up on all potential employees in the same manner. This way no one can accuse you of discriminatory practices.

Do You Want Love, Respect, or Both?

Significant turnover in a business can slow down productivity, curb your profits, and squelch morale. The more time spent on training new people, the less productive work is getting done. Therefore, you want to make an effort to keep your employees happy. Besides additional compensation (which isn't always possible) there are other ways to attract and hang on to talented people; you could:

- Allow for flexible working hours
- Allow for some telecommuting
- Encourage employee suggestions and feedback—and pay attention to it
- Help with child care
- Encourage and set up social outings
- Offer fitness activities, such as a lunch-hour yoga class or a fitness room
- Be understanding in the case of emergencies and extenuating circumstances, and allow for a limited paid leave in certain situations
- Set up an ergonomic office or business
- Consider job-sharing situations, where two people do one job by dividing up the tasks and splitting the schedule
- Pay for professional development seminars or courses

There are many things you can do to make your business the kind of place that attracts and keeps talented employees—and many of these perks won't cost you very much, if anything at all. It shows that you respect your people and want them to stay with your company for a long time. Planning company outings, hosting social gatherings, and buying lunch on occasion are all effective ways to build your business's family atmosphere.

While you can attempt to create an environment that will both attract and retain good workers, you can't be a social welfare provider. You deserve and should expect top performance from your employees. You are treating them as responsible adults and enabling them to make choices about their work habits. No matter how generous you are they owe you the highest level of productivity in supplying top-quality products or services to your customers. If the customers aren't satisfied, you will not have a company or employees to appreciate.

Establishing Rules and Policies

Whether your business has an official handbook outlining the rules and procedures of the company or simply a list of policies, it's important that you establish basic rules and guidelines that people are expected to follow. Put rules and regulations in writing in case someone ever questions company policies.

More and more employees are jumping at the chance to sue their former employer. Don't make it easier for them to do so. Spell everything out. Such policies should include information on:

- Vacations
- Pensions and retirement benefits
- Holiday pay
- Safety regulations (including those imposed by outside agencies)
- Sick leave and disability
- Reviews and raises
- Specific grounds for termination
- Incentives and bonuses (if you offer any)
- Sexual harassment
- Drug use, drug testing, and smoking
- Hours and work schedule
- Theft or misuse of company property, equipment, or funds
- Defined work status (full-time, part-time)
- Inappropriate use of the computer and/or Internet (or other technological equipment)
- Discounts on merchandise or services

If you have more than twenty people working for your business, you should consider putting all this information into a booklet or handbook to distribute when an individual is hired. Having such a book (or at least having the rules and policies in writing) can help you if you're ever sued.

Show Them the Money—and Benefits

You'll have to do some research to find out what the average salary is in your geographic region for the type of job you're offering. Pay rates vary in different parts of the country. Know the going pay rates before you interview, and be sure to pay people based on their expertise, abilities, and level of experience. Many jobs are based on hourly rates. Know these rates as well. Make competitive offers but give yourself some leeway to negotiate.

If you can't match the going pay rates, make up for it in other ways, such as telecommuting possibilities, additional vacation time, and so on. Someone making $50,000 with three weeks of vacation and two days a week of working from home may be happier than someone else making $60,000 with two weeks of vacation and a five-day-a-week commute to and from the office.

You should also set up some system of raises or additional incentives. Be consistent, though. Employees often find out what other employees are offered and are resentful if they haven't been offered similar perks. Be very clear with all offers that you make. Put compensation, entitled vacation, reviews and evaluations, and other such incentives in writing. And above all, don't offer what you can't provide.

In addition to salary, employees today want benefits—and can you blame them? The two primary benefits employees seek are health insurance and retirement programs. The cost of medical insurance on an individual basis can be staggering. You're not required to provide medical insurance (although there are regulations if you do offer it), but if you're a growing company looking to attract quality personnel, you'll want to be competitive. And that will mean offering health benefits.

The rules for offering health insurance are in flux, so you will need to stay on top of developments in this field. It is worth researching insurance products on the market. You may be able to get better group rates through a small business organization or an industry association. However you source health insurance you will want to review it every year. As premiums continue to skyrocket you may need to change how much you can afford to offer your employees.

Savings and retirement plans are also popular, particularly 401(k) plans. An investment vehicle, the 401(k) is set up by an employer to allow employees to put away money, tax deferred, toward their retirement. The money is invested in any of various investment vehicles, including stocks, and most commonly, mutual funds. Plans generally give the employees a selection of five or more choices of investments. You should encourage employees to take their time and decide what the best options are for their unique situations, based on the current market and the economy.

ESSENTIAL

Working with a professional employee organization (PEO) gives you the opportunity to share the human resources responsibilities with a third-party company. Your employees are leased to the PEO, which provides a range of services, including payroll management, better pricing on group health insurance, and advice on how to handle employee issues such as terminations. A PEO can also provide background checks for new hires and offer legal advice related to human resource issues.

The 401(k) plan transfers money into investment vehicles directly from the regular weekly or biweekly paychecks of the employees, who can elect to contribute up to a certain percentage of their salaries, with a cap. The amounts change annually with inflation. The employer can then match a percentage of the money invested by the employee. Fund matching may not be possible for a growing young company. However, it is very attractive to potential employees if the company is contributing 3 or 4 percent.

FACT

Benefits that might attract top talent include tuition payments for job-related education, a relocation package, additional health benefits such as prenatal care or CPR training, adoption assistance, child care, and benefit plans that cover life partners who are not married.

As an employer, you must allow employees to roll over their 401(k) plans when they leave the company. For all the details on 401(k) plans go to *www.401k.com*.

Letting People Go—Know the Law

It's not easy to let people go, especially if it's not a result of their actions but simply a matter of funding (or lack thereof). Nonetheless, you must handle the situation professionally.

There are a number of reasons for letting someone go. If you're firing someone because of his actions, you must let him know the grounds on which you're dismissing him. Your reasoning should be supported by company policy (which should be in writing), if not local or federal law. If, however, the person is simply not working up to the capacity that you had hoped for, you may need to give the individual notice in writing so he has a chance to correct problems. It is no longer acceptable to simply let him know that the situation is not working out. If after two rounds of notification the employee still is not measuring up, and you can prove it, termination should not be a surprise.

People react to being fired in many ways. While you cannot know for sure how a person will act, you want to take some precautions. Have someone else alerted to what's going on so that the individual's access to the computer and or company files can be shut down when necessary. Have a witness to the severance conversation to avoid "he said/she said" later on. Let the person respond, which may include venting his wrath. Let him talk, and be positive and understanding. Answer his questions to the best of your abilities. Arguing will get you nowhere.

In most situations, the employee will want to know what he's getting to cushion the blow. Almost every company provides its employees with some type of severance pay. This can be higher or lower depending on the specifics of the termination agreement, but they should get something unless they've broken company policies and/or the law.

There's another reason you must be careful when terminating someone. Today, the moment someone is told that he's being let go, the thing that enters his mind is not "severance package" but "lawsuit." Minorities, women, individuals over forty, people of particular religious affiliations, and just about everyone else can come up with a reason why you wrongfully discriminated and let them go. This may mean you need to review your own termination practices over months or even years. If the last ten people you let go were all over forty, the forty-two-year-old woman sitting in front of you may have a pretty good case against you.

ESSENTIAL

As with all business procedures, you need to prepare in advance for a termination, which may mean brushing up on company policies and procedures regarding severance pay, vacation days owed, and so on. Read up on the Worker Adjustment and Retraining Notification Act. Under this act you may be required to provide sixty days' advance notice.

Try to fire or terminate everyone in the same manner. If you act in one way with one employee and in another manner with another employee, it can come back to haunt you. Work out your termination plan of action in advance. If you have proof that the person has violated company policy, broken the law, committed fraud, or acted in a violent manner, then you have just and legal cause in your favor. Don't go by hearsay in any of these situations, and make sure you're correct with your information. If you fire someone for stealing and it turns out that the items were lost in the storeroom, you may be headed for court.

Do your best to make a difficult time easier for employees. This may mean writing reference letters, providing job placement opportunities, and even offering counseling. Be helpful in supplying information employees will need when filing to collect unemployment insurance. If your employees are part of a union, make sure you comply with policies outlined in any agreement made with the union.

It's important that you handle the situation of laying off employees as professionally as possible. You want to protect yourself and your company but also let others know that you're human and have a heart. Don't forget that those employees who aren't being laid off will be watching your every move. You'll need to boost their morale or they're likely to update their resumes out of fear that they'll be the next ones to go. Explain the situation to all employees and let them know that you hope business turns around. Be honest and be supportive.

CHAPTER 19

Consulting

There is nothing more personal that you can bring to market than yourself. Whether you find yourself in transition between jobs or you realize that your true calling is helping clients with an outsider's viewpoint, your time as a consultant can be extremely rewarding. To make the most of this professional status, you will need to get certain ducks in a row. This chapter covers the basics of consulting, from setting fees to structuring your business.

Why Be a Consultant?

Only you can decide whether it makes sense for you to be a consultant. Most people are attracted by the notion that it will give them a more flexible lifestyle. While that is true, because only you are the boss of you, it does not necessarily mean you will work any less. The big difference will be, when you want to take a long weekend after burning the midnight oil for seven consecutive days to meet a client deadline, you only need to look in the mirror to say, "I'll be back on Tuesday."

Some questions to ask yourself when mulling over a decision whether to take the leap to consulting are:

- Can you get yourself motivated to seek work?
- Do you like working independently?
- Are you comfortable with peaks and valleys of income and assignments?
- Do you have contacts that will lead to assignments?
- Can you present yourself in a confident manner?
- Can you look someone in the eye and ask for the money you are worth to do the job?
- How much are you willing to travel if needed?
- How will your choice affect your family?
- Do you think you want to do this long term?
- Is this just a way to bridge to the next job?

As a consultant, you are hired to help in a certain area. You come in, work your magic, and are immune to any petty office politics. If you are very clever, you will gain the confidence of the client and will be asked back to help with further enhancements of their operation. Actors get applause, and consultants get contracts that validate their talent and expertise. Your ego should be pumped up a notch or two when an organization hires you to take them to another level that they do not believe they could reach without you.

Finding Opportunity Between Jobs

Many white-collar jobs that require an education or training in a particular field are populated with committed professionals who build their expertise while they are working for an organization. Perhaps you have held one or more of these positions and now find there is no future with your employer. The reason doesn't matter; there may have been a corporate downsizing, your company may have been acquired by another and your position has become redundant, or you yourself have decided it is time to move on. If you are in that netherworld of leaving one place without being entirely certain what you want to do next, you may be considering becoming a consultant. Who knows—you may actually like it and decide to redirect your career.

Not knowing what is coming may be scary, but it is also empowering to take the reins of your life in a new way. The key is not to second-guess the reasons you are between jobs, but to embrace the opportunity this status presents.

FACT

Alan Weiss, author of Million Dollar Consulting, defines a consultant as "someone who provides value through specialized expertise, content, behavior, skill, or other resources to assist a client in improving the status quo in return for mutually agreed upon compensation."

You may have been so busy building your career that you don't realize how much valuable knowledge you have gained by your experience. If you have ever had a friend or colleague ask you to lunch just so she could pick your brain on a problem she was wrestling with, you have offered yourself as a consultant. Perhaps you did such a good job that she called you back and asked if you wouldn't mind talking to some of her other colleagues.

Perhaps you have a particular skill, such as interior design or working with dyslexic children. You may have expertise that crosses over many industries, such as how to conduct surveys for market research or how to conduct leadership training. You may surprise yourself when you take the time to self-assess the talents and experience that you can bring to the marketplace.

Making the Leap

Many people stumble into consulting. Whether they suddenly find themselves unemployed—or about to be—or realize they have a skill, talent, or expertise that can be leveraged, they make a conscious choice at some point. Entering into a new business, "You, LLC," needs to be done with all the seriousness and preparation you would expect when starting any other kind of business, be it e-commerce or manufacturing. You might find yourself hitting the ground running with an assignment before you have had a moment to make a plan. But plan you must.

ESSENTIAL

Making your monthly bill payments cannot be the first priority when going after consulting assignments. Before you start out, try to have enough cash set aside to cover your expenses for anywhere from six to twelve months. If earning money rapidly becomes the driving force, you will be distracted from serving the customer well and are more likely to fail.

There is no commonly recognized degree that a consultant can earn as there is for a doctor or a lawyer. A small percentage of high-achieving, newly minted MBA graduates will wind up working for large consulting firms. However, the vast majority of people who call themselves consultants have arrived at this status through the back door of other work experience. Whether you decide to hang out a shingle for the long haul, or choose to provide assistance to companies in your field for an interim period, you have the ability to define your terms.

Setting Fees

When it comes to the perks of being a consultant, tied for first place with the lifestyle has to be the chance to make a lot of money. How exactly to price your services is a matter of some debate. Basically, there are three approaches, any of which needs to cover your overhead, but not necessarily out-of-pocket expenses. As you weigh the best approach for you, be sure to include all expenses associated with being a "gun for hire." When you work for someone else, space and equipment are provided. So are paid holidays, vacations, and perhaps a good portion of your health insurance premium and more. When calculating your fees, you must consider your needs beyond what you had perhaps seen in a paycheck. Here are the three typical ways a consultant gets paid:

- Hourly rate
- Day rate, also known as per diem
- Value-based fee

Hourly Rate

The least attractive compensation plan, from the client's perspective, is being charged an hourly rate. It terrifies them to think that if they have a question the meter will start running. It forces them to pre-qualify the level of urgency to speak with you. They may say to themselves, "Is this really a $250 question, which could turn into a $750 answer?"

ALERT

The most common financial stumbling block for consultants is underbidding a job. Nobody wins when you work twice the amount of time as what you have contracted for. Your pay gets cut in half, and the client does not have a true appreciation of what it takes to meet their objective. You can never get back the hours you have expended.

It is also the most confining way for you. No matter what your hourly rate may be, your ultimate income is limited by the number of hours in the day and week. It would be highly unlikely that you could get away with charging for 100 hours of work in any given week—even if you actually put the time in! A client would certainly raise an eyebrow at such an invoice, perhaps wondering about your ethics and whether you might be padding the bill.

Per Diem

First cousin to the hourly rate is a per diem rate, a flat rate per day. Although you are calculating a bigger chunk of time for a higher rate, you are still limited to time and space. A savvy customer knows the going rates and you will be confined to market norms, particularly for services where a number of competitors might be considered. If you choose this method for pricing, you will need to make philosophical choices about where you want to fall within the ranges the market will bear. For example, if there is an expectation a company will pay $2,000 to $5,000 for an off-site management retreat you will need to decide if you are the "deal" at the low end of the range, or if you believe your track record warrants asking for the higher end.

Author Alan Weiss suggests a twist on the per diem pricing concept. Rather than establishing a day rate he recommends making the most of working off a flat fee price list by breaking down individual activities you will be providing and pricing them separately. This will give your client a better understanding of exactly what they are buying, and will protect you from undercharging.

Value-Based Fee Pricing

As a consultant, your overarching goal will be to build a long-term relationship with a client, based on trust. The client needs to believe in their very core that you have their best interests at heart. The "value" part of the relationship comes from the client believing that you bring something extra to the table. By working with you the client is acknowledging their in-house staff cannot perform the role or achieve the results you can on their behalf.

FACT

Using value-based pricing with a comprehensive fee means you can freely extend access to yourself by any participant in the corporation. Your client won't need to worry about extra charges if the senior vice president of sales wants to double-check on the progress of a series of trainings. The more people who know how valuable you are, the more entrenched you become in the client's organization.

If your personal goal is to achieve wealth as a consultant, Mr. Weiss offers two core pieces of advice. First, base your fees not on measurable quantifiers such as time or projects, but rather on the "client's perceived value of your assistance." Second, and this may be more difficult: "Ask for them." Practice saying your fees out loud, so you can do it with a straight face when the time comes. Really! To be successful with this approach you will need to be firm in your belief that you are doing the right thing by putting a high monetary value on your work. As you gain experience and confidence, your client will see how your work saves them money, brings order to a chaotic environment, or raises competencies of employees.

Since you are not chained to a time-based formula you will have to suffer the frustrations of ambiguity in pricing. Could you charge $20,000 or $30,000 above your bid? Who knows? Over time you will want your clients to understand your value so they remain comfortable as you charge correspondingly higher fees. You might work with them initially at a special level of pricing, and as they come to know and trust you they will be open to increasing your compensation. But only if you ask. And you should ask on an annual basis. If you have ongoing projects or new proposals, you might not see the new fee level for another year or more anyway.

Getting Started

The early days of your consulting business may be topsy-turvy. It is likely your transition into consulting comes with either doing some project work on the side while still employed, or leaving a job and having a customer follow you to continue services for them on a contractual basis. Initially the cash flow may be dicey and you might find it daunting to take care of the myriad details of getting established. If you are working from home you may want to add a dedicated phone line for the business, which all family members are strictly forbidden to answer. You may be running around getting business cards ordered, setting up a website, filing as a sole proprietor, or talking with an attorney about forming an LLC or similar structure.

ALERT

Know your own risk tolerance. One of the biggest obstacles to success for budding consultants is giving up too soon. Sure, the path of least resistance may be to take a job. But the upside to sticking with the consulting business will be manifold in terms of professional validation, income, variety of assignments, and the thrill of building something fantastic from nothing.

Take the time to investigate any doubts you may have. Once you have put them under the microscope and decided you can deal with them, put them out of your mind. Try to keep a positive attitude, which you need to convey to your prospective clients at all times, and ultimately you will be successful. Accept that there will be challenges. You will constantly be engaged in problem solving, for your own business as well as for your clients. If you want to be safe—and perhaps bored—go work for someone else.

Finding Clients Who Are a Good Fit for You

Most likely you will begin in the field in which you have already worked, but that is not necessarily where you will remain. If you have been doing sales training in the financial services industry, those skills will be equally applicable for high-tech, publishing, or manufacturing businesses. You are limited to the twenty-four-hour day, however, so be picky about which assignments you go after. If you are in Southern California and get a special thrill from the entertainment industry, make every effort to get entrée there and leave the aerospace industry to someone else.

Be honest about the type of work you prefer. If you want short workshop engagements where you are in and out, actively pursue this work. If you need the stimulation of longer, more complex projects that may require subcontracting, take your business development efforts in that direction. The joy of having a consulting business is that you can construct the model that best suits you.

You may start out with a contract that falls in your lap. To be successful, you will need to be more purposeful in going after future gigs. The single most reliable way to get more work is to do a good job with a current client and get additional contracts with them. The time you spend preparing proposals, meeting with prospects, and trying to win a competition is time for which you are not being compensated. Ideally 80 percent of your business will be with repeat customers.

Word of mouth is your best endorsement for future business. Ask your clients to refer you to their colleagues. Social, professional, and industry networking are all necessary to keep the pipeline primed.

Your words are very helpful in raising your profile, too. Write journal articles, be a speaker at civic organizations, present papers at conferences, and lead workshops. The more places people encounter your name the more confident they will be in your ability to deliver the services they need and you want to provide.

Structuring the Business

Consulting as an industry is more fluid than most. You may find yourself moving back and forth between different roles—operating as a sole proprietor, as a subcontractor for other consultants, as a manager of your own firm—or aligning in more or less formal ways with other established consultants on a project-by-project basis. In the early days when you may not be drowning in business, it may make sense to offer your services as a subcontractor to others who have more work than they can handle.

ESSENTIAL

If you seek the camaraderie of other professionals and someone to share the valleys as well as the peaks with, you may be better suited to having a business partner. If you both happen to have different but complementary skills, the relationship provides a more interesting package of capabilities to offer your clients and prospects.

One very important professional decision you will make, and perhaps remake, is whether you want to grow your business by adding other consultants as employees. Evolving from a one-person, home-based operation to an office with the commensurate overhead and potential support personnel, will definitely change the dynamic of your professional life. When you have to begin thinking about making payroll taxes, paying utilities, and generating enough business to support all of it, you are in a different mode entirely.

Small firms or individuals affiliating to share work is a model commonly seen in the consulting field. This may occur when one has an overload and does not want to turn a client away. It sometimes happens that the needs for a particular project are complex and time intensive enough to warrant the resources of multiple consulting entities. The nice thing about this arrangement is that work relationships ebb and flow depending on the market demands.

CHAPTER 20

Your Tax Obligations

No matter how you are structured and how much (or little) you generate in sales or net profits, you will need to prepare and file taxes. Knowing what you are required to file will guide you in keeping the appropriate information organized and accessible. This is one area of running your business in which you cannot be casual or you will have major headaches later. In this chapter you will find a broad overview of what you need to do to stay on top of these obligations.

Good Records Prevent Headaches Later

One of the most basic principles of paying taxes is sound preparation, which entails good record keeping. Studies show that more people run into problems with their tax returns as a result of their record-keeping system than for any other reason.

Your record-keeping system should provide a clear picture of all income and expenses. Keep information on all sales transactions, cancelled checks for all purchases made for the business, and receipts. Make sure all filed paperwork is dated and filed into categories such as rent, utilities, automobile expenses, advertising, and so on. Your system should be easy to follow and easy to update. It should also provide you with a simple way of locating necessary information by date, subject, or client.

What You Need to Pay and When

You will be obligated to pay federal and state income tax based on what you earn during the year, minus expenses and deductions. As opposed to individual personal tax returns, which are due every year by April 15, you will be required to pay quarterly estimated taxes. Quarterly taxes are due on April 15, June 15, September 15, and January 15. (These dates will be different if your business is operating on a different fiscal year.) Be sure to check with your accountant to find out exactly when your estimated taxes are due, and mark the dates on your calendar.

Your estimated tax payments should be one-quarter of your estimated total annual payment. You can use last year's numbers if you anticipate the number for the current year will be similar or lower. However, you must prepay at least 90 percent of your total annual tax liability or you can be hit with penalties. If you have any questions about estimated taxes, check out the IRS website at *www.irs.gov* or talk with an accountant.

The structure of the business will determine which return you file. If you're a sole proprietor, you file your income tax and deductions on a Schedule C form attached to your 1040 individual tax return. Your tax payments are included as part of your personal income tax return. Likewise, partners are taxed individually on their share of the partnership. Each partner includes his or her income and deductions on a Form 1065, and this is reported on Schedule E of your individual 1040 tax return. There is no separate partnership tax.

Corporations are required to pay estimated taxes. S corporations are handled in the same manner as a partnership. C corporations, however, are entities unto themselves and taxed as such. A C corporation may have a different fiscal year. In fact, a business with peak seasons may specifically set up a fiscal year that is advantageous to the seasonal business.

ESSENTIAL

If your company depends on retail sales that are heaviest during the end of the calendar year and into the beginning of the new year with merchandise returns, it might be prudent to set up your fiscal year to begin and end in your lighter season, perhaps May through April. This will take pressure off during the tax preparation season.

Corporate tax rates are different than those imposed on personal income taxes. It's a good idea to look at the comparative rates when deciding whether to incorporate. For a smaller business in the $50,000 to $75,000 range, the tax rates for incorporating may also look slightly more favorable (25 percent as opposed to 28 percent). However, you'll be paying fees to incorporate, as well as legal fees, so you may not be benefiting after all—especially when you take into consideration the additional paperwork. In addition, C corporations also lead to double taxation, in which the corporation pays taxes and the dividends are then passed on to the shareholders and taxed. Since you're the majority shareholder, you will pay personal income taxes on the dividends you earn. Talk with your accountant about ways of avoiding such double taxation.

Self-employment tax is, as the name would imply, for people who are self-employed. When you work for someone else, your employer is responsible for paying half of the combined Social Security and Medicare payments for you as an employee (7.62 percent of your salary). The other half is withheld from your earnings. In this case, however, since you are both employer and employee, you pay both halves of the 7.62 percent for Social Security and for Medicare, or a total of 15.24 percent of your salary and wages. This is in addition to your income tax payments.

Proper Deductions Help Profits

The IRS uses the words "ordinary," "necessary," and "reasonable" to determine which expenses they consider to be helping you to earn income from your business. The concern is not how much a particular piece of equipment helps you earn, but that the purpose, or reason for buying the item, is business related. Typical business expenses include:

- Rent
- Salaries
- Employee benefits
- Utilities
- Insurance
- Office and/or business supplies
- Computer equipment and supplies
- Travel for business
- Advertising and publicity
- Costs related to an automobile, van, or truck used for business purposes
- Entertainment of clients
- Legal and professional fees
- Dues and subscriptions
- Postage
- Telephone (including Internet)
- Professional licenses

If it relates to your business, it's deductible. If it's for personal use, it isn't. If it's for both, such as a car, then you'll have to determine the amount of mileage for personal use and the amount of mileage for business use. For business purposes, you can deduct 58.5 cents for each business mile as of 2008. Keep tallies of how much you use your car or any item for business, and how much it's used for personal needs.

The bottom line is justification. If you put something down as a business expense, be able to justify it with backup paperwork indicating the need to use the item for business purposes. Include the date, the name of the person or business that received the payment, the total amount, and the category of business expense into which you have listed this deduction.

Home offices have increased steadily over the past decade. More and more individuals are working some of the time, or all of the time, in the privacy of their own home. Telecommunications and the ease of overnight shipping have made this far easier to do in a manner that is comfortable for entrepreneurs and their clients or customers. If you operate your business from your home, and you conduct the administrative or management activities of the business there, you can claim a deduction for the portion of the home used for business. Accordingly, you can also claim a percentage of your utilities and insurance costs.

ALERT

> When you prepare your tax form you will notice a place where you are asked to insert a six-digit code to classify your business. If you are unsure of how to classify yours, you can use the generic code 999999. Be cautioned, however, as using this code will draw attention and your return may receive closer scrutiny.

If you're seeking to deduct business expenses, you need to be engaged in what the IRS considers a trade or business, which is an activity carried out with a profit motive—even if you haven't made a profit in the past year. Generally, the IRS looks to see if a business has made a profit in three consecutive years out of five, meaning you can show losses in those always-difficult first two years. The IRS may also use their nine-step profit motive test to determine whether or not your business is a business and not a hobby. The nine factors include:

- The manner in which the business is run
- Your expertise
- Time and effort involved in running the business
- Appreciation
- Success with previous businesses
- History of income or loss
- Amounts of occasional profit
- Financial status of owner, other than this business

- Whether the activity is usually considered for personal pleasure or recreation

When listing your deductions, always refer to the IRS guidelines, since not all expenses are equally deductible.

Employment Taxes

Unless you are a sole proprietor, you will need to hire employees. This means that you'll be required to have an employer identification number (EIN). All businesses that employ other people must have an individual EIN. So if you are a partner in more than one company or you purchase a new business in addition to your own business, you'll need a separate EIN for each business entity or company. You can obtain an EIN by filing an SS-4, Application for Employer Identification Number, online at the IRS website.

Your principle concerns when paying employees are the following:

- Withholding taxes
- Social Security and Medicare (FICA)
- Unemployment taxes
- Disability taxes

Withholding taxes are calculated depending on the filing status of the individual and are withheld from each person's salary. You will determine both federal and state income tax payments.

Social Security and Medicare (known as FICA) require you to pay 15.3 percent (12.4 percent for Social Security plus 2.45 percent for Medicare). You withhold half of these amounts from the employees' pay (6.2 percent plus 1.45 percent), and then you're required to match this amount. You pay the full amount of unemployment taxes. The rate is 6.2 percent for federal unemployment. State unemployment rates vary (check with your state). Disability taxes are determined by each state.

Paying these taxes can get a little tricky. For example, Social Security is only paid on the first $106,800 of income for 2010. Unemployment tax is paid to the state and to the federal government. However, if you pay the full amount to the state, the federal unemployment tax is only 0.8 percent up to $7,000 in income, for each employee, which is a minimal amount ($56). You'll also find that people working for you change their marital or dependent status. In addition, individuals are putting money away in tax-free retirement plans and you need to calculate the taxes after this money is invested into their individual plans. Is it any wonder why you need to hire a good accountant?

ESSENTIAL

All full- and part-time employees should be paid on the books. An IRS audit could prove costly if it is determined that you are paying people and not recording it, reporting it, and paying their withholding taxes. Likewise, if you are avoiding paying sales tax amounts you can be hit with heavy fines.

When you hire an employee, you will ask that person to fill out a W-4 form. The employee will include her income tax filing status, which you will use to calculate the amount of income taxes.

You're also responsible for having employees fill out I-9 forms from the U.S. Citizenship and Immigration Services (formerly the INS), proving that the employee is eligible to work in the United States. Non-citizens must have work visas. For more information about these forms, contact the USCIS at 800-375-5283.

Keep in mind that you need to define which individuals are considered your employees and which are considered independent contractors. In general, an individual is considered your employee if:

- He receives his primary income by working for you
- He receives direction from you on a regular basis
- He has his pay rate controlled by your decisions

Also, if you've specifically trained the person to perform a task or job, including procedures and methods by which the work is to be done, this generally indicates an employee.

An independent contractor is hired by you to do a specific job, or several jobs, but has his own established business and pay rate and also works elsewhere to make his income. In short, an independent contractor isn't under your control as an employee. If you pay an independent contractor over $600 in a given year, you're required to send him a 1099 form. There are no withholdings that you're required to pay, and the contractor is, therefore, responsible for including the income in his own personal income taxes.

QUESTION

What is the common-law test for determining the status of an employee?
According to the IRS, you can determine if a person is an employee or an independent contractor based on behavioral control, financial control, and your relationship with the individual. Check with the IRS for more details.

Payroll taxes are due either semiweekly or monthly, depending on the size of your payroll, not on when you issue checks. The IRS will dictate the schedule—you can't make the choice. If your total payroll is less than $2,500 for the quarter, you can file quarterly. You may consider using a payroll software program. Or, if your company and the number of your employees is growing, you might opt for an outside payroll service. The largest service, Automatic Data Processing (ADP), is one among numerous services that specialize in understanding and handling your payroll needs and headaches. ADP provides paychecks to over 30 million workers. You can contact them at *www.adp.com* or 800-225-5237.

If you do not pay your payroll taxes on time, you can be hit with fines and penalties. The IRS takes this very seriously! Today with online banking there is no excuse for being late with your payments.

Tax Planning with a Pro

You can't avoid paying taxes, but you can strategically plan to structure and conduct your business in such a manner that it reduces how much you have to pay. While you don't want to focus so much attention on minimizing your tax bite that you neglect other aspects of your business, you can work with a tax professional to choose the best options for your individual situation.

The government requires you to pay taxes, but you have numerous options in how you structure your business. Whatever you do, do it legally. Fraud will result in serious consequences.

ESSENTIAL

As an employer, you must annually report wages, tips, and all other compensation paid to an employee on a W-2 form. Also, report the employee's income tax and Social Security taxes withheld. You provide copies of the W-2 to your employees and to the Social Security Administration.

A good tax plan evaluates your current situation and looks forward over the next several years to determine what your anticipated earnings will look like. The better you estimate your sales revenue, income, and cash flow over the coming years, the better you'll be able to plan accordingly. Choices of claiming deductions, hiring employees, selecting a business structure, and setting up your fiscal calendar year are all aspects of your business that you can plan, in part, around tax payments.

To handle all your taxation requirements successfully, you should work with a qualified tax professional. You can look in the yellow pages, or you can ask for recommendations from others in business. You want someone who:

- Can be trusted implicitly
- Has enough time to review your situation and provide you with advice and guidance on an ongoing basis
- Has all the necessary credentials in the field
- Is familiar with your type of business on a broad level
- Knows the state and local regulations as well as the federal regulations and requirements

A good tax professional can mean the difference between success and failure in business. So take your time and choose someone you believe can help you make the right tax decisions and the best tax plan for your business.

CHAPTER 21

Bookkeeping, Record Keeping, and Administrative Tasks

While your great idea gets the juices going and creates the energy to bring you success, nothing will undermine all your initiatives quicker than sloppy or nonexistent books and business records. You need well-kept records for tax obligations and to show how the business is doing and help plan for its growth. This chapter offers information about what to keep track of, as well as tips on administrative duties and outsourcing.

Good Records Keep Things Going Smoothly

Good bookkeeping and record keeping are essential to operating a successful business. When you start your own business, you need to know why these daily chores are important, so you'll be motivated to keep up with them. (And if you're like most people, you'll need all the motivation you can get.)

To Monitor or Track the Performance of Your Business

Monitoring will tell you whether you're making money. It will allow you to gauge which items or services are selling and which ones aren't. You'll also get a firm understanding of which expenses are necessary and which ones may be higher than you'd like them to be.

Sound business decisions should be based on where you stand financially. Before you take on new employees, buy more inventory, move to a larger office, or do anything that requires a solid business decision, you'll need to know how it will impact your business financially. Good bookkeeping and record keeping will provide you with such information when you need it most.

To Pay Your Taxes

It's much easier to calculate tax return figures and pay taxes when you're working from a set of accurate financial records. Besides paying quarterly taxes, you'll be filing tax returns or other returns if you've incorporated. In addition, the many rules and regulations governing sales taxes and payroll taxes will be much easier to comply with if you know where to look for the correct numbers.

To Pay Yourself and Others

Salaries are an important consideration. Many say you should pay yourself first. But how much? You can't pay yourself or distribute profits to other partners or investors if you don't know what those profits are.

ESSENTIAL

If you're looking for a second, third, or fourth round of investors, or you want to secure a loan from the bank, you'll need to show accurate financial statements. Besides the bank and investors, the IRS and other regulatory agencies will need financial statements from you, too. You can only furnish accurate statements with reliable bookkeeping.

To Sell the Business

If you want to sell your business someday, the buyer will want to know how the business has been doing while you were in charge. The best way for them to measure its success is by reviewing the financial statements. The same holds true for merging with another business, when you will need accurate financial statements.

Establishing Bookkeeping Procedures

If you're a sole proprietor, you'll need to take a crash course in bookkeeping basics to gain an overview of these procedures. If you're running a small business with partners and/or investors, you may want to hire a bookkeeper to handle your books. The size and volume of the operation will determine whether you want to have someone on staff or someone coming in periodically to prepare final statements.

Basic bookkeeping starts on a day-by-day, sale-by-sale level. Software packages make much of this work quite simple. Whether you're using a software program or doing the bookkeeping manually, you'll need to keep a journal of sales and cash receipts. This will allow you to see your sales totals, know what items were sold on credit, and keep track of when you received payment for each item. In a retail store, modern cash registers will keep a running total of sales and distinguish between cash and credit card sales. At the end of each day, you'll enter your daily sales total into your sales journal. If you're using sales invoices, you can keep accounts for each customer updated by posting entries to the accounts receivable ledger. File all customer invoices by number and provide one (with that invoice number included) to your customer, so that either of you can refer to the invoice when necessary.

Your cash disbursements journal, or expense journal, will provide you with information on how much you're spending by cash or by check and to whom you're paying the money. You'll also keep a general journal for listing unusual entries or those made annually.

ALERT

It's absolutely critical that you save supporting documents to back up your journal entries. You will need all bank deposit slips, credit card slips, cash register tapes and receipts, invoices, credit card receipts, cancelled checks, bank statements, and petty cash vouchers.

Whether you're actually handling the bookkeeping chores yourself or hiring someone to do it for you (often, you'll want to call someone in who specializes in doing this), you should have a grasp of what's going on financially in your business. The attitude that "We'll let the gang in accounting handle it" or "You'll have to ask my bookkeeper" can lead you into trouble. Bookkeepers are hired to provide you with accurate books, and accountants will help you prepare financial statements and make recommendations. But it's up to you to make the final informed decisions. Therefore, it's important that you meet with your accountant and/or bookkeeper regularly to review the books. In the case of uncommon situations, such as buying a new building, a merger, or even an audit, you need to spend more time in these meetings and have a firm grasp of the financial picture of your company.

Cash or Accrual—Which Accounting System Is for You?

There are two basic accounting methods: the cash method and the accrual method. In the cash method, you record income only when you receive it from your customers or clients. Likewise, when you write a check or pay cash, you record that as well. This system is very simple, since you're only keeping track of cash in or out of hand. However, the problem is that most businesses are not cash-only businesses. It's very common today to extend credit to customers and to buy on credit. These types of transactions aren't accounted for in a cash accounting system. Therefore, you don't have the whole picture of what you've actually earned or spent. It's not unlike those outstanding checks that haven't yet cleared when you balance your own checkbook.

ALERT

> Be wary of any online offers or come-ons from professionals that offer dramatic shortcuts to handling the tasks of record keeping. While technology can speed up your accounting methods, anything that appears to be too fast or taking too many shortcuts is probably missing some vital steps that will come back to haunt you later.

Today, the accrual method is much more commonly used. In this method each transaction is recorded when it occurs, regardless of whether you've received or spent the cash at that moment. This will generally provide you with a more accurate picture of your profits and losses, especially in an age when invoices are paid thirty, sixty, and ninety days later, and credit is extended to customers in a variety of situations. The accrual method will give you the best picture of where you stand. If you have an inventory, you may not have a choice: The IRS says you must use the accrual system.

Another choice you may have is whether to use a single-entry or double-entry accounting system. Most software programs will come with the double-entry system. On these programs, you make one entry and the program makes the other. In the double-entry system, both a debit and credit entry are made for each transaction.

With single-entry accounting, you just record one side of the transaction in your sales journal and a separate entry in your accounts receivable ledger. Double-entry is the most common accounting system because it provides you with a system of checks and balances (after all, credits equal debits) and allows you to find errors more easily.

Keeping Track of Your Business

Choosing an accounting system is one thing. But after you've made that decision, you need to know what to keep tabs on—otherwise, your accounting system won't do you any good.

Accounts Receivable

You'll need to keep track of all accounts receivable, which is the money owed to you by customers. For each customer, you'll keep an individual list of accounts receivable. This will allow you to know how much you're owed in total and how much each customer owes you.

Accounts Payable

The money that you need to pay (your bills) is your accounts payable. You may owe money to suppliers and vendors or others from whom you've purchased merchandise, equipment, or services. If you keep a separate ledger account for each supplier or vendor, you'll be able to see exactly who is owed money and how much you owe at any given time. This will be especially valuable when you receive bills and second invoices, and you can look back and see if you've already made a payment.

ESSENTIAL

Besides finding a competent and trustworthy bookkeeper and accountant, you will very likely need to have administrative assistance in your office. It's very important that you find someone whom you can trust with confidential information, including personal data on employees and client contact information.

General Ledger

The general ledger is the place to start organizing your financial statements. It summarizes data from other journals, including cash disbursements (your expense journal) and your sales and cash receipts journal. Here you'll find the balance between debits and credits when you finish posting your entries.

Balance Sheet

One of your key financial statements is the balance sheet. This will provide you with a snapshot overview of your business at any moment in time. Included on a balance sheet are all your assets and liabilities. The balance sheet will result after postings to the general ledger. Once adjusting entries have been made, the trial balance is ready for review by your accountant.

As the name would imply, the balance sheet will need to balance, meaning your assets will equal your liabilities plus your capital. If the totals don't balance, you'll have to look for a discrepancy or error.

Asset accounts on the balance sheet include current assets, which means anything that can be turned into cash easily. The balance sheet usually reflects your system of listing categories, starting with assets that have the most liquidity, such as cash and petty cash, and extending to the fixed assets, which include equipment, vehicles, furnishings, and so forth. Also included, although not on the following list, will be intangible assets, such as patents or trademarks. The balance sheet will likely include the following assets:

- Cash and petty cash
- Prepaid rent
- Cash in the bank
- Office supplies
- Investments (short-term and long-term)
- Vehicles
- Accounts receivable
- Land
- Reserve for bad debts
- Buildings
- Merchandise or inventory
- Equipment
- Prepaid expenses
- Furniture and fixtures
- Prepaid insurance

Also include categories for the depreciation of buildings, vehicles, and equipment. Among the liabilities you will include are the following:

- Accounts payable
- Interest payable
- Salaries payable

- Dividends payable
- Sales taxes payable
- Federal withholding taxes payable
- Mortgage payments payable
- FICA taxes payable
- Self-employment taxes payable
- Property taxes payable
- Unemployment taxes payable
- Short-term loans or notes payable

Essentially, this list will comprise all that you're obligated to pay, but haven't yet paid.

Profit-and-Loss Statement

This is the statement that will generate the most attention from prospective investors. It's also the one that you're most eager to read, simply because it shows your net income or loss and gives you an overall perspective on where the business stands in terms of making money and reaching your goals.

Also known as an income statement, this is very simply a final, rounded-off (not down to the penny) summation of what you've spent in each of several areas and what you've earned. Generally you will list the following:

- Sales
- Cost of goods sold (This will include the cost to buy the goods you sold during the period for which you're preparing the statement, less any discounts offered by vendors for businesses with an inventory; start with your beginning inventory and add the sales purchases, then subtract your ending inventory.)
- Gross profits (This is the difference between the net sales and the cost of goods sold.)
- Expenses (This includes salaries to your employees, advertising, rent, payroll taxes, insurance, depreciation, repairs, office supplies, and all other expenses.)
- Net income (This is your gross profit less your expenses.)

If nothing else, profit-and-loss statements will show you how quickly expenses can cut into your profits.

Choosing Accounting Software

Modern technology is helpful, but it requires the right software for the right task, whether it's for project management, inventory, graphics, or communications. An accounting software package should be easy to learn and include features pertinent to your particular business. You should also discuss your choice of software with your accountant to make sure you're using the same program, or at least one that's compatible with both your computers.

There are numerous programs and online services available, ranging from ones under $20 to high-end programs costing several thousand dollars. In the following sections, you'll find some of the more popular programs that should cover most of your small-business accounting needs without costing you a fortune.

QuickBooks Pro

One of the most popular accounting software programs on the market, QuickBooks includes many key accounting features. You can navigate between reports and documents easily, e-mail and fax invoices, enjoy online banking privileges, manage files, modify reports, and handle almost all of your bookkeeping needs with one program. The website, at *www .quickbooks.intuit.com*, lets you view each feature and obtain support and service help. To order QuickBooks supplies, call 800-548-0289.

Peachtree First Accounting

From the general ledger to your accounts payables and receivables right through to advanced accounting features, this program should meet all your needs. The popular Peachtree accounting programs have been among the top-selling products in a competitive software field. Peachtree First Accounting includes more than fifty predefined reports and statements designed to provide you with a comprehensive look at the financial picture of your business. Support and services are also offered. To order, visit *www .peachtree.com* or call 877-495-9904.

ALERT

In your eagerness to get your bookkeeping onto your computer don't forget to review carefully the system's requirements for any software package you purchase. Do the same for upgrades. The last thing you need is to invest a lot of money in software that your computer is too outdated to run.

Netsuite Business Suite Accounting

An online accounting system, Oracle offers a fourteen-day free trial of this comprehensive service. All the necessary components of the accounting process are featured, including the general ledger, budgeting, bank reconciliation, expense reports, purchase requests, accounts receivable ledger, and more. You can customize the suite to fit your needs as you prepare your financial statements. The online accounting system allows you to easily transfer data from Peachtree or QuickBooks. After the fourteen-day free trial is over you're billed monthly ($99 per month at the time of this printing), and you don't have to worry about downloading or upgrading software. Visit *www.netsuite.com* or call 877–NETSUITE.

Sage Accpac

This program is designed to be simple to use and powerful. Offering capabilities for up to six users, Sage Accpac allows the flexibility of customizable forms and reports. The program also features online banking and electronic payment capabilities. Visit *www.sageaccpac.com* or call 800-945-8007

Record Keeping and Administrative Needs

Besides all the financial records of profits, losses, and expenditures, you'll need to maintain other records, including the names and addresses of your suppliers, accurate client records, and up-to-date employee data. It's important that all your files be accurate and updated on a regular basis. If you're keeping inventory and other such records on your computer, it's in your best interest to also keep hard copies of key information as a backup.

Your personnel files should include:

- All necessary tax information for each employee, including Social Security number
- Personal contact information, including emergency numbers in case of illness
- Employment history (resume, initial job application, and so on)
- Employment record with your company, including pay rate and vacation days accrued

For clients and customers, you will also need to maintain files, including:

- All up-to-date contact information
- Correspondence
- Record of transactions

Other files that should be on hand include:

- Permits, licenses, and registrations
- Equipment leasing contracts or receipts for purchases
- Correspondence with landlords, regulatory agencies such as the FCC, and any government officials
- Contact listings for all local and industry governing bodies, including the local chamber of commerce, zoning committee, and so on
- Legal papers including claims you've made and claims made against your company

One of the biggest, yet least discussed, causes of business failure is poor record keeping. This doesn't refer strictly to financial records. Businesses have been shut down because they let licenses and registrations lapse, and companies have found themselves in financial trouble because they neglected legal matters. It's vital to have a solid record-keeping and filing system.

ESSENTIAL

Even though a lot of business is transacted through e-mail, it's very important to take the time to print hard copies of all key documents and store them safely in your files. Businesses that rely solely on their computers are taking enormous risks. Have backup data available at all times!

Who Should Do the Administrative Duties?

If you begin as a sole proprietor, you will be "chief cook and bottle washer," meaning you will have to perform all of the record keeping and administrative tasks as well as provide your service or product. As you grow and add enough people to form departments, specified employees will help you in tracking sales, expenses, and activity reports. You will certainly want folks with accounting skills performing accounting tasks. Employees whom you can rely upon to pay attention to details and to operate in a discreet and organized fashion can handle other administrative duties. At the end of the day, you as the business owner, or you and your partners, are ultimately responsible for the accuracy, completeness, and timeliness of your records. No matter who keeps these records, they need to be readily accessible to you, but perhaps not so available to eyes not meant to see them.

That said, for some duties, outsourcing may be an option. Some of your business administration needs, such as bookkeeping or payroll, can be subcontracted either through companies or individuals who specialize in these areas. Internal reports such as daily or weekly sales or inventory management probably need to be handled by in-house employees. Only you can make the decision if it is more cost-effective to buy services outside as opposed to carrying a heavier payroll and benefits, or whether you need to have quick access to records and need your own people handling this information.

CHAPTER 22

Insurance

Insurance is a facet of your business that cannot be overlooked. In this chapter you will learn about the importance of risk management planning for your business. You will need information on protecting your investment, complying with regulations, and assuring a smooth transition in the event of an unanticipated tragedy or business interruption. You do not have to figure this out by yourself. There are plenty of resources. The key thing is not to ignore your responsibilities in this area.

Risk Management

Of all the hats you wear when starting up a business, being a risk manager may not be at the top of your list. Yet you are. Risk management is broader than just insurance. It requires you to look carefully at all of the possible exposures in your business and then figure out the best way to handle them. Insuring yourself and your business is certainly an obvious way to manage risk, but there are also steps you can take that are more efficient and economical.

Covering Assets and Earning Power

When planning for loss, many folks think of protecting their assets. And indeed this needs to be done. Yet, there are a great number of intangibles that contribute to the success of your business that cannot be overlooked. There are seven broad areas of exposure most risk management professionals would advise you to evaluate:

- **Real and Personal Property:** Be sure to have documents that can substantiate a complete list of all of your physical facilities and equipment, regardless of whether they are owned, rented, or used.
- **Processing Data:** This would include which operations are performed, any raw materials used, the nature of your machinery and equipment, source of your supplies and quality controls in place, etc.
- **Product Information:** The term idiot-proof should apply to any information you provide about the nature and appropriate uses of your product.
- **Advertising:** The exposure here is reflected in claims made for your product; not only what is said, but by whom, the chance of over-promising, even invasion of privacy concerns, etc.
- **Liability Exposures:** Depending on the nature of your business you may be subject to lawsuits if someone is hurt as a result of negligence. Doctors, for example, carry malpractice insurance. You need to protect you and your business from claims related to any injury sustained on your premises or from using a product you manufacture.
- **Loss of Key People:** The risk here includes salary obligations over a period of absence due to disability, "key man" loss, sudden loss of group of employees traveling together, or loss of particular talents or unique abilities.

- **Indirect Loss:** This refers to serious disruption or loss of key customers, supplies, a physical locale, raw materials, etc. Risk Control

Once you have a handle on the specific risks for your particular business, you can set about finding ways to handle them. Some can be eliminated. For example, you may want to make payments by check rather than cash to provide proof. Similarly, if you have a cash business, don't let the money accumulate. Get it deposited quickly. In some cases you can shift responsibility for some functions by subcontracting them. Clearly, any time you can completely eliminate a risk, that is the path to follow. In some cases you might not be able to completely eliminate a risk, but you can take steps to reduce it. Installing protections such as safety equipment or sprinkler systems are key in a brick-and-mortar operation.

Retaining or Transferring Risk

As strange as it may seem, there may be instances when you choose to assume a particular risk in whole or in part. If there are certain losses that are predictable for your type of business, and they can be planned for, you may want to establish a "set aside fund" to cover these probable losses. Retaining the risk may make sense when the predictable loss fits one of the following criteria:

- Is small enough to be covered comfortably from current profits
- Can be contained within a predetermined, high deductible while the rest of the loss is covered by an insurance policy
- Would not be a huge hit when exposure is spread over a large number of units, and a loss in only one unit would not surpass the premium needed to cover all units
- Can be amortized over a reasonable number of years, making the risk low in comparison to buying insurance to cover it

If you cannot reduce or eliminate risk in your business, or if you are unwilling to simply ignore it, your third option is to transfer the risk to an insurance company. The key instances in which you should opt to buy insurance are:

- If your loss could not be paid from current earnings due to its catastrophic dimensions or if the loss would have a terrible impact on your assets or net income
- If the money you would save by not paying regular premiums to purchase insurance could not cover a maximum loss
- If an insurance company becomes the more efficient and economical vehicle to deliver safety planning and claims servicing

The two-part golden rule for deciding whether to insure or not is this: Do not risk more than you can afford to lose regardless of the odds, and do not risk a lot to save a little.

Evaluating Your Insurance Needs

Now that you have an idea of where and when to assume risk, let's take a look at the various facets within your business where insurance may be appropriate. There are three broad areas, each with its own distinctive characteristics. Some of these may be optional, and some may be required (such as workers' compensation insurance, which is legislated in every state for all of your employees, including you!). The following checklists will give you a jumping-off point for things to consider insuring. Your particular business may have others.

PROPERTY

- Real Property
- Broad Form
- Business Interruption
- Inland Marine
- Crime
- Contents/Inventory
- Boiler/Machinery
- Data Processing
- Bonds
- Fidelity

LIABILITY TO OTHERS

- General Liability
- Fire Legal Liability
- Professional Liability
- Fiduciary Employee Benefits Liability
- Environmental Impairment Liability
- Umbrella/Catastrophe
- Workers' Compensation
- Products/Completed Operations
- Directors and Officers
- Garage Liability
- Employment Practices Liability
- Product Recall
- Intellectual Property
- Business Auto (hired/nonowned)

PEOPLE COVERAGE

- Group Health/HMO
- Individual Disability
- Pension/Profit Sharing
- 401(k)
- Group Life
- Buy Sell/Stock Business Continuation
- Key Man
- Overhead Expense

General Coverage Considerations

The first consideration for how much insurance to buy is a determination of the value of what you need to protect. Will your insurance coverage replace what you have? You will want to select "replacement" valuation in your coverage. A common choice policy owners make to save on premiums overlooks this very important standard. You want whatever repairs or replacements of damaged items are necessary to restore your operations to the same quality you had before your loss. Watch out for "depreciation" clauses that will save on premiums but leave you short-changed when trying to replace things based on yesterday's value in today's dollars.

ALERT

Don't dismiss third-party liability coverage as extraneous just because you are a small business. If someone has a grievance against your business they may come after you with the same expectation for retribution as if you were a giant corporation. A judge and possibly a jury will rule on these claims in court. They tend to be tougher on businesses than individuals.

Deductibles are the first dollars paid when a loss is incurred. Once the deductible is paid, the balance of the responsibility for the loss is transferred to the insurance company. The rate of your premiums is in direct proportion to how big a deductible you are willing to shoulder. The higher the deductible, the lower the premium. Just be sure you don't choose a deductible so high you couldn't absorb it in the normal course of business operations. As the buyer of an insurance policy you drive the choice of deductible levels. The company will work with you, giving you ultimate control of this expense item.

Buying Insurance

With such a wide array of business needs to protect, you may be feeling a bit overwhelmed about how to address all of them. When buying a business owners policy (BOP), you'll need to conduct research to find the best fit for each area of insurance need. The Internet can offer vast resources in your search for the best coverage options for you.

You may also want to use the services of an independent insurance agency that has established relationships with a variety of insurance companies and can go to bat for you at the time of a loss. They are compensated on a commission basis so it should not cost you more to deal with a reputable one. Whether you opt to use an independent insurance agency or find coverage for yourself, you will want to identify insurance companies that know and favor your industry.

As a general rule, if a business has $5 million or less in revenue it makes sense to purchase a package of policies to address the broad spectrum of coverage needed. Once a business exceeds that $5 million mark, it becomes necessary to buy tailored coverage. Most insurance companies want a three-year financial track record before they will be willing to offer BOP coverage. In some instances you can make a case based on your past experience in your industry. For instance, if you have been a restaurant manager for ten years and now you are opening your first restaurant, it is not a big stretch to say you have an established track record in your industry. If you are starting cold in a business, it is possible to get insurance coverage but you will be placed in what is called a specialty market. Unfortunately, you will pay 30 to 40 percent above market rate in the early years to get the coverage you need.

Real Property

Real property is the nuts and bolts, brick and mortar, the tangible stuff of your business. You may think its loss or damage would be the most obvious, but there are some areas that are not. These areas of coverage need to be either purchased separately or called out specifically in your package. Here are a few to consider:

- **Building ordinance coverage:** This will protect you if building or zoning laws force you to rebuild or demolish. It can be purchased for damaged or undamaged buildings and could really take the sting out of this particular bit of bad news.
- **Flood insurance:** This insurance protects you from water damage resulting from the overflow of any body of water, flooding, tides, tidal waves, or surface water.
- **Earthquake coverage:** This covers damage from earth movement, due to either volcanic eruption or earthquake shocks.
- **Rental reimbursement:** This could be extraordinarily helpful if it becomes impossible to collect rent due to an insured loss; this coverage will replace that income.

- **Signs:** Generally signs will not be included in your business package. It is possible to cover them but usually you need a separate sign endorsement added to your policy.
- **Comprehensive glass coverage:** If your business has plate glass windows or interior structural glass it can be covered against breakage, including vandalism; however, specifics such as frames, bars, and letters on the glass need to be specified in the policy.
- **Leasehold improvements and betterments:** When listed specifically, any alterations or additions you make to your leased space can be added to your property policy. This coverage is extremely important.

Contents Inventory Coverage

As with real property, contents inventory can have enhanced coverage with specialized insurance. Besides the additional coverage options mentioned in the real property section, some other areas of specialized protection to seriously consider are:

- **Loss of income**—business interruption: How long could you stay in business if you experience the perfect storm of income loss and devastatingly expensive repairs following a fire or some other calamity? Even if your property coverage takes care of the big items, the loss of income can drive you into some serious debt pretty quickly.
- **Transit:** Did you realize you are responsible for goods owned by your business while they are away from the premises? This particular coverage is applicable to both finished goods and materials coming and going under the bill of lading.
- **Valuable papers**—accounts receivable: Imagine a client who, realizing your records have been destroyed in a fire, develops amnesia about a payable she has with you. This coverage can help keep you whole after you have proven that your efforts to collect have been thwarted as a result of the loss. Similarly, should you need to finance a loan to offset collections, this insurance may reimburse you the interest charges for same. Basically, if your collection efforts escalate in excess of normal procedures you can be entitled to relief with this insurance.

- **Debris removal:** Your property coverage partially covers this part of the cleanup. If that percentage is exceeded, as with a total loss, extended coverage can add another $10,000.
- **Peak season protection:** This is something to research if yours is a seasonal business.
- **Selling price coverage:** Similar to replacement value on real property, this coverage protects not only the cost of your goods but also your profit margin. This is purchased as an extension of your property policy. Without it you would forfeit your normal profit because you would only be reimbursed for the costs incurred to purchase or produce your lost product.

Workers' Compensation

Workers' compensation insurance coverage is required of employers in all fifty states. Rates may vary and may be updated periodically. If yours is a very small, perhaps a one-person sole-proprietor operation, it is possible to ask for a waiver from this requirement. To do so will entail signing releases, but it may be worth researching.

This coverage must be provided to all employees. If you use subcontractors, one simplistic test to determine if they could be viewed as employees is this: Do you exercise control over their work? If the answer is yes, they could be considered an employee. An extension of this logic carries over to your vendors. In every case you should firmly establish that your vendors carry workers' compensation insurance or you may one day be supporting a claim of one of their employees.

Employee Versus Independent Contractor

A labor attorney can determine whether someone is technically an employee or a subcontractor in your particular situation. Answering the following questions also should help clarify things:

- What degree of supervision or control do you have over the manner in which work is performed?
- How is the person paid (hourly/per diem/retainer/lump sum)?

- Who, if anyone, withholds Social Security and other taxes?
- Does the worker carry personal workman's compensation or liability insurance, and can he provide certificates of insurance?
- Does the worker work for more than one firm? Advertise his services?
- Is there a contract in force?

Broad Form All-states Coverage

This blanket policy protects you under the laws of a state not listed in your policy. Fines are not covered. The following states cannot be included in a broad form endorsement: Nevada, Washington, North Dakota, West Virginia, Wyoming, and Ohio.

Your employee who is traveling and gets injured in another state may make a claim in that state. However, most policies revert to the state where the claimant is domiciled for settlement.

Retention Plan

Using a mathematical formula, your policy carrier may pay you a dividend based on your loss. After factoring operating expenses as a percentage of your paid premium, if your loss claims fall below the net you will receive a dividend refund. If your losses exceed the net there is no dividend but you will also not be charged any additional premiums.

Sliding Scale Dividend Plan

Similar to the retention plan, the sliding scale dividend plan pays you a dividend on a loss-sensitive basis. Any net dividend you receive will depend on how large your premium payment is, and how low your loss claim.

Safety Discount Plan

This plan offers an incentive in the form of a discount if you have your employees undergo a training program on running a safe company.

Liability

Liability exposure is an area of "open exposure" where the boundaries of a claim may not be known. A definite swing in the perception of consumer protection has been taking place in recent decades. Not so long ago the premise was "Buyer Beware." Insurance product liability policies were written to provide reasonable coverage for use by a responsible person. Now the expectation is that a product can be made safe for all circumstances, even when people do foolish things like drink boiling coffee. The reasonable person standard has disappeared. As long as the emphasis is on protecting the consumer, the courts will continue to define liability. A judge can determine if your business is liable and the amount of that liability.

Catastrophe Umbrella

This is the biggie. Because of the uncertainty of liability exposure you will want to carry the largest policy you can reasonably afford with the largest deductible you can absorb in the event of an award against your business. The limit of the protection should be enough to cover the assets of the business. This coverage is specifically needed to protect the business from large judgments as well as more typical claims.

The importance of umbrella liability has grown rapidly. It is very important that your underlying insurance dovetails with your umbrella policy so there are no gaps in coverage, particularly if a large judgment is made against your business. If your underlying coverage excludes product liability then your umbrella policy should provide coverage. Be very attentive to how these interact to meet your goal of seamless protection.

General Liability Add-ons

Here are three options that may be worth considering for your business:

- **Fire legal damage coverage:** As horrible as suffering a fire loss is, you may find yourself in the position of being sued by your landlord, or the owner of building space you have temporarily occupied.
- **Personal injury liability coverage:** This sounds like protection for physical injury but it is actually coverage to protect you for such claims as

false arrest, wrongful entry or eviction, malicious prosecution, libel, or slander.

- **Fiduciary employee benefits errors and omissions:** If your company is big enough to have an employee benefits plan, this coverage can protect you from negligent acts, errors, or omissions by either you or anyone who manages your plan for whom you are responsible.

Auto Liability

Considering all the circumstances in which you or an employee can suffer a loss involving an automobile you may want to select coverage for any or all of the following:

- **Nonowned automobile coverage:** As the name suggests, this would cover cases such as when an employee or subcontractor uses their own car while working on behalf of your business.
- **Hired automobile coverage:** This covers vehicles leased, hired, rented, or borrowed for work purposes.
- **Drive-other-car coverage:** This coverage kicks in when your employee borrows or rents cars and does not have his own personal auto policy.
- **Uninsured/underinsured motorist:** This takes care of personal injury expenses for you and your passengers if another driver who hits you does not carry car liability insurance; or if that driver's insurance coverage does not meet the minimum standard for the state.

Other Coverage Considerations

The whole topic of insurance can be tedious when all you really want to do is get on with your business. Perhaps not every topic discussed so far will apply to your business, but there are a few more areas for reflection as you map out your own risk management strategy.

Boilers, Pressure Vessels, and Air Conditioning

In your basic policy, steam boilers, pipes, and the like would not be covered in most cases. An incredible amount of damage can be caused by a ruptured system, perhaps even causing bodily injury and loss of income if your business cannot operate for a period of time. This extra coverage could be critical if you face this type of unfortunate event.

Employment Practices Liability Coverage

An area of increasingly heightened sensitivity for employers in recent years centers on how employees believe they are being treated in the workplace. This coverage can help if you find yourself in the unpleasant situation of being on the wrong end of a harassment, discrimination, or wrongful discharge claim.

Crime

Do not be lulled into thinking only shopkeepers or owners of other cash businesses are vulnerable to loss by crime. White-collar crime averages $120,000 per occurrence. And who do you think is committing the white-collar crime? Sadly, it may be people who work closely with you, perhaps even family members or dear friends. Certainly, setting up systems and procedures that can short-circuit crime benefits everyone. If you transfer this risk in the form of buying an insurance policy you accomplish two things. First, you will have the financial loss restored immediately. And second, the process of getting to the bottom of how the loss occurred gets delegated to a dispassionate third party in the person of an outside claims adjuster.

ALERT

One out of every three business failures is caused by employee theft. To protect yourself, do four main things: (1) Install security cameras, especially in a retail store. (2) Keep an inventory list of all key items. (3) Perform background checks when hiring employees. (4) Keep up-to-date records and a watchful eye on bookkeeping.

Directors and Officers Liability

This type of policy offers protection for the decisions made at the highest executive and board level. This would include allegations and claims from stock or shareholders or employees and third-party class action suits.

If you serve on any boards, for charity or otherwise, and they do not provide directors and liability protection, you might want to seriously reconsider your involvement. Holding a board position means you share in the legal responsibility for the direction and decisions of that organization.

CHAPTER 23

A Winner's Checklist

Once you are up and running, your identity established, your legal status in place, inventory and service issues humming, happy clients wanting more of your time, you cannot just sit back and coast. Every day continues to be a challenge—both exciting and nerve-racking. Both the highs and the lows can give you stomach flips. To stay on top of your game you will need to stay sharp and keep looking for ways to improve all parts of your operation.

Customer Service

Customer service is not just responding to complaints. It is, as the term implies, providing a service. It is a way to show your customers or clients that they're very important to you. Customer service can help enhance your reputation in a way that far exceeds hiring even the best public relations firm. For every customer who tells his friend how well he was treated by your company, you'll be gaining free advertising and PR. Retaining customers is just as important as attracting new ones. Too many businesses take their regular customers for granted and only realize their value when the competition lures them away. Companies of all sizes need to maintain their steady core of customers.

Part of your product-pricing policy includes the service you will offer. People will readily pay more to eat in a nicer restaurant, because the food is of higher quality and the service is better. A quality product coupled with arrogant service won't work in the restaurant business—or anywhere else. Unless you're the only store in town selling greeting cards, another card store will gobble up your customers if you don't provide good service.

For a long time, a shoe store in uptown New York City was a favorite place for buying children's shoes. The sales help were given a bonus for selling a certain number of shoes and were hired on the basis of being able to work well with kids. It wasn't that the city didn't have plenty of other locations to buy shoes for kids, but this store provided excellent service and activities for children while they waited. The prices were not the lowest in town, but people shopped there regularly. The storeowner also decided to benefit returning customers. Knowing that children's feet grow steadily and they frequently need new shoes, the owner started a policy that the eleventh pair of shoes purchased would be 50 percent off.

To establish a successful business you need to know not only what products your customers want, but also how they expect to be treated. Your customers expect:

- **Consistency:** If you're known for doing something in a certain manner, you need to keep doing it.
- **Fairness:** If you treat certain customers differently, you can put yourself in deep trouble.

- **Assistance:** You know more about your products and services than the customers do, so you need to provide assistance.
- **Responsiveness:** Customers expect prompt service—don't keep people waiting for great lengths of time and expect them to return to do business with you again.
- **Competence:** If you continue to make mistakes with their order, they won't be back.
- **Fair policies:** If something needs to be returned, let them return or exchange it.

Customers also want that little something extra. From gift-wrapping to e-mails of new products when they come into stock, you can provide the little things that make your business stand out.

Customer service isn't relegated only to retail and e-commerce businesses. Client relations are tantamount to success in corporate America as well. Note the number of company box seats at the ballpark. While you don't want to spend excessively to indulge your clients, you do want to keep them smiling. This often means doing the little things—from remembering birthdays, to sending thank-you notes, to avoiding nickel-and-diming them on their invoices.

ESSENTIAL

Many small retailers try to protect themselves with a "merchandise credit only" policy for returns. American consumers have become so accustomed to liberal return policies that it can be jarring to bring back a pair of trousers that do not fit only to walk out with a credit slip instead of cash back. Why not offer cash back for returns in seven days and merchandise credit up to thirty days?

Also keep in mind that prompt correspondence and replies to letters and e-mails from customers or clients is very important. If it takes you a week to return an e-mail or you send them a perfunctory form letter or e-mail, you can be sure they'll notice your lack of attention and will in turn lose interest in your company.

Stay Loose and Available

Managing a business also means maintaining a schedule that's flexible yet includes time for all key tasks. If you can delegate a task or a project to someone you trust, then do so. If it's something you must be involved in or you want to handle yourself, make sure you schedule the proper amount of time and allow for preparation.

ESSENTIAL

Manage your own schedule to allow yourself as much time as possible to manage the goings-on within the business. Maximizing your time also means including the little details. Sometimes attending a birthday party for a key staff member is just as important as any meeting you'll have in the course of the day.

A good business manager can manage her own time well and prioritize all areas of the business, including customer and employee needs. Conversely, a poor manager puts sales above the staff and above customer relations and looks only at the immediate profit regardless of the long-term ramifications. If you work to make a sale at the cost of a really satisfied customer or at the expense of a staff member, you may very likely lose out in the end. Likewise, if you don't take time to establish relationships with vendors or wholesalers, you may lose them and your competition will benefit. Your schedule needs to be flexible so that you can make adjustments. Business continues to grow and change, and so must you.

Employee Development

It's unfortunate to lose business because your employees simply don't know how to do their jobs. This is ultimately a reflection on you and your leadership. Remember, when your customers are interacting with your company every encounter reflects you and your goals. Your employees act as an extension of you and your values, so be sure to have the right people in the right positions. Training entails:

- Properly assessing each person's skill level when you hire them
- Clearly explaining what is expected of them in their positions
- Offering an open line of communication and encouraging trainees to ask questions
- Clearly explaining policies, including situations when a policy might not fit
- Retraining when advanced technology or new products or services are introduced

Before you can train people, you need to hire the right person for the right job. If you have a small business and are relying on your family for help, this includes politely placing (or not placing) family members in specific roles. Don't be conned into letting your niece handle your books if she has no bookkeeping background whatsoever.

At the two ends of the spectrum you can:

- Hire people who have years of expertise in an area—but who will cost you more and may not last, as they will want to move up.
- Hire people and train them in an area—they'll cost you less initially, but they may end up costing you more depending on how long it takes to train them.

Therefore, you need to assess a person's general skill level and see how close he is to meeting your needs. Too often employers are seeking the ideal candidate with many years of experience and all the skills imaginable. This prolongs the hiring process and costs more money in advertising and recruiting. Unless you're in the business of rocket science, training individuals in most industries is not rocket science.

Remember, having workers with skills alone, such as computer skills, is not as important as having well-trained individuals who know how to act and interact with others and deal with a variety of circumstances. You should seek out individuals who:

- Offer new ideas
- Take initiative
- Reflect the image you want in the marketplace

- Are willing to go the extra mile to get the job done right
- Have problem-solving skills
- Meet deadlines
- Arrive for work punctually, ready to start work
- Extend courtesy to coworkers, vendors, and customers
- Understand the need for professionalism in the workplace
- Can make a commitment to the company and their assigned role

Well-rounded employees are more valuable than those who just have specific skill sets. Particularly in a small business, both you and your employees will undoubtedly be wearing multiple hats.

Managing successfully means being flexible and listening to the needs of your customers and to the suggestions of your employees. Flexibility means adapting to change, taking in what you hear, and using it constructively. Listen objectively: Don't make assumptions about the meaning behind the message or the reason for someone's statement. Just because a customer or employee has a suggestion to improve upon something doesn't mean your method is incorrect. It simply means there is another viewpoint, for better or for worse. If you keep your eyes and ears open, you'll also plug in to the changing trends within your industry and the business community.

How you communicate with your personnel, customers, investors, vendors, suppliers, the media, and the community at large is vital to your business success. If you can communicate in a clear, respectful manner and establish strong relationships with everyone involved in the operations of your business, you'll be in an advantageous position.

Go Team!

Managing a business, unless you're on your own, means developing and maintaining a team of competent employees who will work together for the good of the business. This need to:

- Be accessible
- Foster team spirit
- Reward good work
- Have occasional brainstorming meetings
- Constructively criticize ideas, but don't criticize people

- Listen to suggestions
- Mediate and resolve conflicts
- Encourage everyone to feel involved in the company
- Be responsible for the actions of your team, and don't blame people

If you can maintain a team of individuals who are encouraged and excited about working for your company, you'll have a winning team and a far better opportunity to run a successful business.

Delivering Your Messages Appropriately

Communication also includes timing. You need to know when to communicate your message and in what medium. A combination of e-mail, telephone calls, snail mail, and personal visits will all come into play when making your communications decisions. The mode of communication will depend on the nature of the message and the intended recipient. For example, you don't send an e-mail telling someone he's been let go. Conversely, you need not travel for hours to give someone a simple message. While managing your business, you need to monitor and constantly review your listening and communications skills. Many business owners get lazy and don't pay attention to their manner of communicating.

Staying Abreast of Industry Changes

Do ongoing research on your demographic base, changes in your industry, and changes in the market. Keep track of government policies and regulations, local business news, and environmental concerns that could affect your business. It's vital that you know your consumers. If their needs are changing, you have to be aware of those changes. There is no substitute for knowledge. You'll also need to be knowledgeable about your competition. Short of sending in a spy (and it's often done), you can gather as much data as possible on what your leading competitors are up to now and in the near future. Continue to do your homework. Stay active in your industry and your community networks. Analyze the data you've gathered to determine how it impacts your business.

Information gathering includes ongoing market research. It's important to focus in on any potential new consumer group or niche that may be ripe for your products or services. And always keep your antennae up for ways to bring new, related products or services to your existing business. If you are a day-care provider, for example, you might offer a service to supply diapers, formula, or other basics at your site so parents don't have to lug them to you.

Ongoing research also includes retesting and even repackaging "tried and true" products and services. Just because something has been successful for twenty years doesn't mean it can't be changed if the public no longer embraces the idea. On the other hand, as evidenced when Coca-Cola changed its formula, sometimes tried and true continues to be what people want.

To maintain your market position and improve upon it, you must not only keep tabs on your direct competition, but evaluate where you stand. Compare the data you gather on your competitors with your own company facts and figures. At what price are they selling goods and services? Are you able to match their prices, beat them, or provide something that justifies your price being higher?

FACT

It's imperative that you uncover and evaluate any new means of communicating with your target market. Some businesses identified and utilized the Internet effectively in its breakthrough years. Others sat on the fence and only utilized the Internet after the initial excitement had lessened. The messages of the latter group were not as well received.

Staying competitive doesn't mean you have to do battle. Price wars can run you into financial trouble by propelling you into a situation whereby you're giving products or services away. Find creative ways to attract customers, establish a relationship, and hold on to steady customers. If necessary, find a niche.

Keeping Your Presence Known

Whether you operate a local or national business, you will be a part of some community at large. Your business will be based somewhere and you will be responsible for following local ordinances, paying local taxes if necessary, and so on. But there is more to it than just setting up shop, creating a website, or opening an office. It's advantageous to your company to seek out help from local business organizations and to network with members of such groups. The local chamber of commerce and other such groups can provide leads for your business and help you extend your name throughout the community.

Community involvement is also a way of helping you to build strong relationships. Local, and even national programs may ask businesses for support. Supporting the right leaders in the community can help your business draw attention, as can donating to local charities or sponsoring a local event.

The media can also help or hurt a business, particularly an ongoing business, depending on the stories they broadcast or articles they write. A positive relationship with local media is helpful when it comes to potentially controversial stories that involve your business. The media can paint a picture of you that is positive, negative, or neutral. Some ways to establish yourself with the media include:

- Sending press releases and information about your involvement in community activities
- Offering input as a business owner when business-related issues arise (just try to speak as an expert rather than taking a side)
- Providing interesting story angles and suggestions to local reporters and journalists
- Being available for interviews or offering your shop as a location should the media need to conduct interviews

Monitoring Cash Flow and Productivity

Monitoring cash flow is a major area of concern for growing (and ongoing) businesses. You need cash on hand to operate, but you don't always have it. For that reason, you need to monitor your cash flow very carefully. If employees aren't getting paid, they're no longer enthusiastic, hard-working employees. Not being able to pay your vendors won't endear you to them either. Extending lines of credit can be a way of building relationships, but don't let such relationships abuse your trust. You need to maintain available cash at all times.

How can you do that? Try to turn all sales into cash as quickly as possible. Offer incentives for cash payments or for paying off a line of credit quickly. You can also make some of your own purchases of equipment or goods on credit. If you combine the two ideas by offering a discount if a customer pays in thirty days and then buying on credit that is due in forty-five days, you give yourself a two-week gap to collect and then make payments.

Just as it's important to monitor cash flow, periodically you also need to measure productivity. If you have a system in place for this, you can identify problem areas and make appropriate changes to improve your productivity. It's important that you measure all the tangible elements that go into your business, including manpower, resources, equipment used, and anything else expended to create, develop, or provide what you're selling, making, or marketing. Measuring productivity starts with keeping track of whatever it takes to do business—from hours spent by your workers to gas expended by your trucks. You then look at the end results of time and money it takes to create, buy, or produce your product or service and compare it to your profitability.

Some products can be streamlined and manufactured on an assembly line, while others are handcrafted. Remember, not all productivity can be streamlined. Faster doesn't mean better when you're talking about a handcrafted item.

Sometimes productivity is a matter of technology. For example, look at how many businesses have improved their checkout services through price scanners and smart cash registers. The new check-out stations speed up customer activity while drastically cutting down on errors.

ESSENTIAL

If you're in good shape financially, it's recommended that you take out bank loans and pay them back quickly, thus establishing an excellent credit rating. This will help you for those times when you need a loan to get out of a cash-flow crunch. You'll be more likely to get the loan quickly and without difficulty.

In a service business, productivity is measured by the fee-for-service schedule you have established. Those fees need to cover your entire overhead. Market forces may keep a cap on the upper limits of what you can charge. Sometimes customers feel they are getting more if they pay more. You can experiment with pricing levels.

Planned Expansion

Expansion can be a great thing. However, it also means more space to manage, more bills to pay, more employees to hire, and numerous other expenditures. For this reason, expansion takes careful planning. It requires that you balance the equation every step of the way. For every dollar of projected income, you'll have some amount of forthcoming expenditures and you'll need to be confident that the scale tips in your favor. Therefore, you need to start slowly. Before adding a new sales team, add a salesperson or two. Before launching your second website, add product offerings to your first site. It's important not to commit great amounts of money and resources to expansion until you've tested the waters. Survey new territories and explore potential new markets. The bottom line is that you want to be able to manage and control your expansion. Many businesses have tried to expand too fast, taking a successful small business and growing it into an unsuccessful larger business. A breakfast shop in a suburban locale that closes in the early afternoon may not transplant to a college community that is barely getting going at that time of day.

ALERT

Planning your company's growth or expansion means utilizing new ideas, and such ideas won't come out of thin air. As you start your business, you need to make a list of ideas—ideas that may require more resources, manpower, or customers than you currently have for their execution. Furthermore, you need to collect and consider the suggestions of employees and customers. From these ideas and your initial business plan, you can build an expansion plan.

Not unlike starting a business, expanding your business requires financing. However, if you're in a position to expand, it's likely that you're successful. If you've proven your worth, you should have established a solid line of credit, making loans easier to get. Your financial plan should be attractive to potential investors. Even if your business isn't landing you write-ups in Inc. magazine, you can show that you're maintaining a positive cash flow, have a strong customer base, and have a solid marketing campaign in place.

No One Knows Your Business Better Than You

When you start out, you're owner, manager, salesperson, technology manager, advertising director, office manager, marketing manager, bookkeeper, and janitor. It's you, you, and you doing it all. As the company grows, you delegate more and more responsibility to your employees. Over time, technology has changed and new methods have come along, including advanced technology, cutting-edge advertising methods, online bookkeeping, and unionized janitors. In short, the business changes as it grows. Could you still sit down and do any or all of these jobs? Can you wear many hats in your own business, or are you, the owner, becoming obsolete? No matter how big your business, you should have a firm understanding of the job being done. No, you don't need to be an expert in all areas, but when it comes to your own business, you should be able to step in and handle any role if necessary.

You make sound decisions based on your knowledge of all aspects of your business. You'll also gain respect from your employees if you can discuss their tasks and work in an intelligent manner.

Hold On to Your Sanity

So, you treat your employees well, and you try to create a positive attitude around the office, the store, the factory, or wherever your business resides. You lead with both a gentle touch and a forceful hand. You try to maintain a steady base of customers while constantly seeking to expand upon that base. The business is growing, but with Herculean effort. You put in 40, 50, 60, 70, or even 170 hours a week (okay, there aren't 170 hours in a week, but you're working so much it feels like there are). Are you overworked? Yes. Underpaid? Yes. Underappreciated? Yes. It goes with the territory.

Whether you walk away to the golf course for a few hours, spend a day at the beach, or take a weekend away, you need to periodically shut off the cell phone and clear your head. Some even advocate working fewer hours or days a week to allow more time for rejuvenation, making the working hours more productive. If necessary, make detailed lists before you go, just to get the workload out of your mind and onto a piece of paper or into your PDA. Put someone else in charge and instruct her to reach you only in an emergency, like flood, fire, or major computer virus. Time spent away is time to refuel your body and your mind. Don't think about the office. Read a good book—and not one about business.

Only a person who is driven can start a business and see it to success. It can take three to five years for the average business to turn a profit. It's during those years that you're getting no write-ups in business journals or awards for local entrepreneur of the year. All you're doing is working to keep the business going and, hopefully, growing. You need to set realistic goals and try to meet them. You also need to appreciate the baby steps you take as your business grows. If you train yourself not to think of profits as the only measure of success, then you're making your life easier. A businessperson needs to stay in present time but keep thinking toward the future. That's not always easy when customers aren't calling, showing up, or contacting you through your website. If you can accept the fact that you'll be living off of your savings, loans, or your partner's income until the business is off the ground, you'll be in a better position to handle those lean years.

Know When to Hold, Know When to Fold

The one thought most starry-eyed entrepreneurs suppress is the possibility of the failure of their dream, either in not getting it off the ground, or never reaching its full potential. Sometimes all of the hard work, planning, gathering of resources, and bringing the product or service to market falls short of actualization. It may be an idea ahead of its time, a shortage of capital to make the entity viable, or any of a host of other issues. A sensible person will accept the reality of disappointment before too much financial damage scorches all available resources.

FACT

Did you know it is possible to have a buy-sell agreement established with a competitor or other party even when you have no intention of selling? It is a great idea to have this in place to protect family members in the event something happens to you and you can no longer run the business. It gives your designee right of first refusal, keeping the value of the business sensible, neither "fire sale" nor inflated.

No entrepreneurial venture is risk-free. Taking that leap of faith is part of the thrill of starting something new. Without a sense of adventure America would not be dotted with the tallest buildings in the world, would not be home to everything from baseball to Bourbon Street, and financial markets to farm markets that reach around the world. Businesses that make it over the long haul go through cycles of renewal, expansion, and all the attendant issues associated with starting something new. One thing that is guaranteed is that no business can simply stand still. It is grow or go. If you have the stomach for operating with a fair degree of uncertainty, and the willingness to learn what you don't know and make the most of the knowledge and resources you already have, then go for it.

APPENDIX A

Sample Business Plan

The following pages present a broad outline of a business plan for a fictional company. (Any similarity to an existing business is coincidental.) It is organized as any plan would be, to show you the areas you need to cover. It does not include financials, which you would need to provide in some detail to support your case for potential investors.

The Frugal Fashionista

"Flaunt it - Don't Own it"

Business Plan

The Frugal Fashionista
New York, New York
Phone: 999-893-1234
E-mail: *frugalfashionista@bizland.com*
Web: *www.frugalfashionista.com*

Table of Contents

Executive Summary
Industry Analysis
Business Overview
Products and Services
Marketing Plan
Competitive Analysis
Operations Plan
Management Team

Executive Summary

The Frugal Fashionista will offer fashion-forward accessories on a rental basis. Customers will be able to use high-end fashion accessories such as designer handbags, jewelry, shoes, sunglasses and scarves on a short-term basis for a fee. The appeal is twofold: On a limited budget a style-conscious individual can present herself adorned with accessories appreciated by a discerning eye while "going green." Using valuable accessories only when needed and allowing them to remain in circulation helps preserve world resources. Saving money by renting accessories enables customers to greatly expand their wardrobe particularly for those women who strive for "no repeats."

The business will operate online. Customers will establish an account by paying a membership fee. The fees will be scaled with increasingly valuable goods made available at higher levels of membership. Membership privileges include access to a rotating inventory of designer goods for rent. Rentals will be time limited with additional charges for not returning items by date of agreement.

Goods will be encoded with embedded security devices to assure an item rented is the same one returned. Inventory will continually be refreshed with new acquisitions.

By operating as an online business the market is open to potential customers worldwide. Goods are shipped with prepaid packaging for return, making the exchange as easy as possible for clients.

Industry Analysis

A few similar businesses exist online, most notably Avelle, formerly known as Bag, Borrow or Steal. Other competitive outlets are thrift stores, estate sales, or eBay. In these instances there is only a chance of finding the item desired. Plus a purchase is required leaving the client with responsibility of reselling the item, keeping it indefinitely or, worse, discarding it. In the Frugal Fashionista model, goods remain in circulation, which enhances their "green side" and helps customers stretch their fashion dollars.

A distinguishing feature of Frugal Fashionista is the easy return method, with prepaid packaging provided. Convenience is one of the hallmarks of renting, so any steps to make the experience as seamless and easy as possible will be a key differentiator in the marketplace.

Frugal Fashionista will offer 100% satisfaction guarantee to its customers that the goods are authentic, and in "as new" condition.

NOTE: This is where you would include relevant statistics that would support the likelihood of success of your venture, such as demographic growth of online purchases, trends in society or the growth of demand for your product or service idea.

Business Overview

Frugal Fashionista will be based in metropolitan New York. It will be housed in economical warehouse space with climate control storage facilities. Administrative offices will also be located in this space enabling company management to be in close touch with the day-to-day flow of orders, goods going out and being returned.

It is expected that marketing and web development will be outsourced. Additionally, the business will need the services of legal and accounting professionals.

Start up costs include purchasing an initial inventory of highly sought-after accessories that will establish the caliber of product being offered. Office/warehouse space needs to be secured along with equipment to run an online business, shipping supplies, office equipment, communications including creating a graphic identity, an interactive website, and voice communications. Staffing will include business co-owners and two full-time personnel, and four part-time customer service representatives. One full-time person will be needed to restore and refresh inventory items, and another to manage shipping and intake. General administration and tweeting will be provided by Frugal Fashionista co-owners.

Marketing will primarily occur online with ads on sites such as DailyCandy, establishing a Facebook Page (for business), Twitter, and other social media. In certain key markets print advertising may be helpful. Target clients are women ages 18-55 living or working in high net-worth zip codes internationally.

Products and Services

Frugal Fashionista's success will be built on its ability to offer "hot" fashion accessories. It will be necessary to have a wide range, but not multiples of items. Scarcity will add to the appeal of the product line.

Designer handbags, high-end costume jewelry, hair pieces, scarves, sun glasses and shoes will be offered. Products will be categorized by use such as wedding, special event, vacation, meet-the-in-laws, or job interview.
Products will be acquired by eBay purchases, Craigslist searches, and offers to buy such as discreet behind the scenes offerings of purchasing services through high-end boutiques, to name a few strategies. All items will be certified as authentic prior to being included in Frugal Fashionista inventory.
Goods will be cycled and can be put on reserve for upcoming dates, e.g., a wedding or major charity event.

Marketing Plan

Frugal Fashionista will target fashion-forward women ages 18–55. It will use traditional media such as print advertising and direct mail along with social media to reach its target audience. Since it will be an online business, special effort will be made to raise its visibility in that medium. Key words will be purchased to push up its Google placement. Ads on sites such as DailyCandy, Style.com or the Daily Beast will tease prospective customers about the benefits.

Social media will be used liberally. A Twitter account will be established which should be very appealing to those who want to know the latest up to the minute product arrivals. A Facebook page (for business) will be created. Incentives for new customers will be offered, such as a one-time discount for a charter membership. Incentives will also be offered for existing customers who refer new customers.

A virtual fashion show featuring some of the more exciting product offerings will be created for YouTube distribution. Something outrageous will be included to amp up the chances of viral explosion of the mini video.
A public relations plan will be designed for a big splash launching the business. High profile endorsements will be secured.

Competitive Analysis

This is not a brand new idea. A limited number of online fashion rental services exist.

NOTE: Insert list of competitors if they exist for your idea here. The market is far from saturated. Particularly when coming out of a down economy, women want to manage their resources more carefully without sacrificing their desire for strong fashion statements.

Auctions on eBay or other online sources that have a broader range of offerings including high-end fashion items would be considered competitors. In addition to online businesses, real world competitors exist with designer resale shops, thrift stores, or estate sales. These are more limited by geography.

A secondary competitive factor is designer knock offs. Women who are not committed to true designer goods may choose to purchase knock-offs. This shopper may not see the value in having time-limited access to an original designer item.

Operations Plan

The business will be based in low-overhead warehouse space. There will be no face-to-face contact with customers. Staffing will be bare bones to start. It is anticipated that heavy reliance on a subcontracted web consultant will eventually convert to in-house IT expertise being justified.

Initially the operation will work normal business hours with customer service calls being answered on two shifts from 7 A.M. to 10 P.M. daily.

Online merchant accounts will be established to take payments securely. Accounts will be negotiated with shippers for best rates and most reliable service.

Staff will be trained in aspects of their responsibility of business. All staff will be oriented to each other's responsibilities and the overall work flow of the business. Individuals will be cross-trained to cover for each other during illness or vacation absences.

Facilities will be kept secure. Appropriate risk management will be enforced including locking up inventory, limiting who has access to products, and carrying the relevant types of insurance.

Customer service calls will be handled on premise. As business grows this function may be outsourced. Bookkeeping will be contracted out initially.

Management Team

Faye Panthers and Hillary Chase are co-founders of the business. Ms. Panthers, a graduate of Fashion Institute of Technology, leaves a career in public relations for design houses including Versace, Calvin Klein, and Chanel. She brings more than fifteen years of design sensibility, understanding, and articulating fashion-forward trends for high net-worth individuals. Ms. Chase holds degrees from Parsons School of Design in fashion merchandising and an MBA from Columbia. She has held senior management positions for Diesel, Juicy Couture, and Burberry USA. She is a proven business executive with a strong knowledge base of fashion trends. Most recently she was responsible for launching Daily Candy Seattle and Chicago.

Both partners bring strong fashion industry experience. They have been researching business ideas for the past few years and have concluded that this model is ripe for explosion. It combines the booming interest in greening with preserving financial resources, while remaining engaged with high fashion. The fact that this is not the first business of its type out of the gate proves it is an idea with legs. Both Ms. Panthers and Ms. Chase have been studying the trend and have carefully thought through where improvements and profits can be made in the business model.

Conclusion

The sample in this appendix is a brief overview/guide to a simple business plan. Your business plan only needs to be as elaborate or as complex as the business you want to run. Information technology (IT) and business-to-business (B2B) plans have more technical terminology and explain in greater detail what their businesses are designed to accomplish. The more straightforward the business, the shorter the business plan. Most investors are looking for what the meat and potatoes of your business will entail, not superlatives as to why yours is the greatest business ever—they will make that determination for themselves. You will also need to furnish a financial analysis showing the funds needed to get the business started and running, projected sales, and when you expect to achieve profitability.

The business plan also needs to be a clear plan that you can follow. You know it's a great idea and therefore need not keep reminding yourself throughout the plan. Keep in mind who you are writing the business plan for: potential investors, yourself, or both.

The newer and more innovative the business, the shorter the competitive analysis. Conversely, if you're opening a familiar type of business in a crowded market, you'll need more time to define what makes your business different from those around you.

Studies show that business plans with charts and graphs are generally better received than those without. Therefore you should add a couple of colorful charts and graphs showing projected sales growth or your piece of the competitive pie. Don't overdo it—two or three may be quite sufficient.

APPENDIX B

Additional Resources

There are numerous organizations, websites, and associations that can help you research and gather information and locate answers to questions regarding any aspect of business. Make a list of key phone numbers and bookmark key websites so you will be able to access the resources you need. Business magazines are also very valuable, as well as trade publications in your industry.

Associations and Organizations

American Association of Franchisees and Dealers
Post Office Box 81887
San Diego, CA 92138-1887
800-733-9858
www.aafd.org

The D&B Corporation
103 JFK Parkway
Short Hills, NJ 07078
800-234-3867
www.dnb.com

Federal Trade Commission
600 Pennsylvania Avenue NW
Washington, DC 20580
General information: 202-326-2222
Anti-trust and competition issues: 202-326-3300
www.ftc.gov

Internal Revenue Service
Washington, DC 20224
800-829-1040
www.irs.gov

International Franchise Association
1350 New York Avenue NW
Suite 900
Washington, DC 20005-4709
202-628-8000
www.franchise.org

National Association of Home-Based Businesses
10451 Mill Run Circle
Suite 400
Owings Mills, MD 21117
410-363-3698
www.usahomebusiness.com

National Association for the Self-Employed
1023 15 Street NW
Suite 1200
Washington, DC 20005-2600
202-466-2100
www.nase.org

National Association of Women Business Owners
1411 K Street NW
Suite 1300
Washington, DC 20005
202-347-8686
Information service line: 800-556-2926
www.nawbo.org

National Institute for Occupational Safety and Health
Hubert Humphrey Building
200 Independence Ave., SW
Washington, DC 20201
800-35-NIOSH or 513-533-8328
www.cdc.gov/niosh

Occupational Safety and Health Administration (OSHA)
200 Constitution Avenue NW
Washington, DC 20210
www.osha.gov

U.S. Census Bureau
Washington, DC 20233
301-457-4608
www.census.gov

U.S. Department of Commerce
14th Street and Constitution Avenue NW
Room 5055
Washington, DC 20210
202-482-5061
www.commerce.gov

U.S. Department of Labor

200 Constitution Avenue NW
Washington, DC 20210
www.dol.gov

U.S. Patent and Trademark Office

General Information Services Division
Crystal Plaza 3, Room 2CO2
Washington, DC 20231
800-786-9199 or 703-308-4357
www.uspto.gov

U.S. Securities & Exchange Commission

Office of Investor Education and Assistance
450 Fifth Street NW
Washington, DC 20549
202-942-7040
www.sec.gov

U.S. Small Business Administration (SBA)

403 3rd Street SW
Washington, DC 2041
202-205-7701
www.sba.gov

U.S. Small Business Administration Regional Offices

Region 1, Boston: 617-565-8415
Region 2, New York: 212-264-1450
Region 3, King of Prussia, PA: 215-962-3700
Region 4, Atlanta: 404-347-4995
Region 5, Chicago: 310-353-5000
Region 6, Ft. Worth, TX: 817-885-6581
Region 7, Kansas City, MO: 816-374-6380
Region 8, Denver: 303-844-0500
Region 9, San Francisco: 415-744-2118
Region 10, Seattle: 206-553-7310

WebsitesAllBusiness

A comprehensive site with resources for small and medium-sized businesses.

www.allbusiness.com

BizLand

A web host for setting up your own website.

www.bizland.com

BizWeb

A guide to some 47,000 companies.

www.bizweb.com

Bplans.com

Numerous sample business plans for various industries.

www.bplans.com

The Business Start Page

Includes a short course on starting a business, tips, and reviews of top business books.

www.bspage.com

Business.gov

A one-stop shop for working with the many government agencies that impact business.

www.business.gov

BusinessFinance.com

A major online source for finding potential investors.

www.businessfinance.com

Business Nation

Business news, a library, discussions, opportunities, and resources.

www.businessnation.com

Business Owners' Idea Cafe

A good place for news, tips, expert advice, ideas, and schmoozing with other small business owners.

www.businessownersideacafe.com

BusinessTown.com

Information and articles covering topics from starting to selling your business.

www.businesstown.com

The Catalog Consultancy

Information and guidance for catalog and direct-mail businesses.

www.catalogconsultant.com

CFOC.gov

Sponsored by the U.S. Chief Financial Officers Council, this site has a wealth of information and resources available, specializing in public financial management.

www.cfoc.gov

Chamber of Commerce

Links to local chamber of commerce websites, and e-mail addresses.

www.chamber-of-commerce.com

Concept Marketing Group, Inc.

Find any association in any industry at this valuable resource site.

www.marketingsource.com/associations

Federal Citizen Information Center

Offers a small business information section with facts about getting started and more.

www.pueblo.gsa.gov

HomeBusiness.com

Detailed information and business solutions for the home-based business.

www.homebusiness.com

Hoovers

Provides detailed business and company information, industry reports, links, professional help, business news, and more.

www.hoovers.com

Inc.com

A wealth of articles and advice about starting and growing your business from the folks at Inc. magazine.

www.inc.com

Internet Corporation for Assigned Names and Numbers (ICANN)

Holder of domain names.

www.icann.org

MoreBusiness.com

Articles, tips, sample business and marketing plans, legal forms, contracts, a newsletter, and more are offered to entrepreneurs.

www.morebusiness.com

My Own Business

Free online course on how to start a business.

www.myownbusiness.org

National Association of Small Business Investment Companies (NASBIC)

Promotes growth in the business sector through numerous programs.

www.nasbic.org

Netfirms

Offers web hosting if you carry advertisements.

www.netfirms.com

Thomas Publishing Company, LLC

Publishers of numerous industry trade directories, which include listings of manufacturers and distributors.

www.thomaspublishing.com

Whois?

Site can be used to research ownership of domain names.

www.whois.com

Women's Business Development Center

Many valuable resources on writing a business plan and going after funding.

www.wbdc.org

MagazinesConsumer Goods Technology
Edgell Communications
4 Middlebury Boulevard
Randolph, NJ 07869

Entrepreneur magazine, Business Start-Ups magazine, and Entrepreneur's Home Office
Entrepreneur Media, Inc.
2392 Morse Avenue
Irvine, CA 92614
714-261-2325
www.entrepreneurmag.com

Forbes
60 Fifth Avenue
New York, NY 10011
212-620-2200
www.forbes.com

Inc.
38 Commercial Wharf
Boston, MA 02110
617-248-8000 or 800-234-0999
www.inc.com

MyBusiness
Hammock Publishing, Inc.
3322 West End Avenue
Suite 700
Nashville, TN 37203
615-385-9745

Minority Business Entrepreneur
3528 Torrance Boulevard
Suite 101
Torrance, CA 90503
310-540-9398
www.mbemag.com

Workforce Management
ACC Communications
245 Fischer Avenue
Suite B-2
Costa Mesa, CA 92626
714-751-4106
www.workforceonline.com

Index

Medicare tax, 222

Mentors, 14

Monitors, 129

Name, business, 50–52

Netsuite Business Suite
   Accounting, 236

Networking, 185–91, 261

Newsletters, 157, 181

Newspaper advertising, 178–79

Niche markets, 49–50

Occupational Safety and Health
   Administration (OSHA), 113

Office equipment. *See* Equipment

Offices, furnishing and equipment
   for, 117–34

Office space, 111–12, 116

Office supply stores, 130

Online advertising, 152

Online auctions, 153–54

Online directories, 150–51

Online marketing agencies, 150–51

Online presence, 135–47

Online selling, 149–58

Online shopping, for computers,
   129

Operating system (OS), 128

Opportunities, seeking new, 11

Outdoor advertising, 180

Outsourcing, 120, 238

Partnerships, 54–56, 61, 64, 90–92,
   218–19

Patents, 102–4

Payment options, for online selling,
   154–56

Payment terms, 89–90

PayPal, 155

Pay rates, 203

Payroll taxes, 222–24

Peachtree First Accounting, 235

Per diem rate, 211–12

Personal credit scores, 84

Personal service businesses, 62

Potential market, assessment of, 45

Preparation, 6–8

Press kits, 183

Press releases, 183, 261

Pressure vessels, 250–51

Pricing, 94–95, 165–68, 174–75,
   210–13

Primary research, 171

Processor types, 128

Productivity, 262–63

Product procurement, 161–65

Products
   bringing to market, 25–26
   pricing, 94–95, 165–67
   test marketing, 25

Professional associations, 98, 186–
   88, 275–83

Professional employee
   organization (PEO), 204

Professional image, 11

Professional networking groups,
   189–90

Professional services, hiring, 30

Profitability
   of business ideas, 17–18
   time frame for, 9–10, 92–95

Profit-and-loss statement, 234–35

Promotions, 175–76

Publicity, 41, 182–83, 261

Public relations, 184

Public speaking, 39–40

Quarterly taxes, 218

QuickBooks Pro, 235

Radio advertising, 179–80

Random access memory (RAM),
   127–28

Real property insurance, 245–46

SOFTWARE LICENSE AGREEMENT

YOU SHOULD CAREFULLY READ THE FOLLOWING TERMS AND CONDITIONS BEFORE USING THIS SOFTWARE PRODUCT. INSTALLING AND USING THIS PRODUCT INDICATES YOUR ACCEPTANCE OF THESE CONDITIONS. IF YOU DO NOT AGREE WITH THESE TERMS AND CONDITIONS, DO NOT INSTALL THE SOFTWARE AND RETURN THIS PACKAGE PROMPTLY FOR A FULL REFUND.

1. Grant of License
This software package is protected under United States copyright law and international treaty. You are hereby entitled to one copy of the enclosed software and are allowed by law to make one backup copy or to copy the contents of the disks onto a single hard disk and keep the originals as your backup or archival copy. United States copyright law prohibits you from making a copy of this software for use on any computer other than your own computer. United States copyright law also prohibits you from copying any written material included in this software package without first obtaining the permission of F+W Media, Inc.

2. Restrictions
You, the end-user, are hereby prohibited from the following: You may not rent or lease the Software or make copies to rent or lease for profit or for any other purpose. You may not disassemble or reverse compile for the purposes of reverse engineering the Software. You may not modify or adapt the Software or documentation in whole or in part, including, but not limited to, translating or creating derivative works.

3. Transfer
You may transfer the Software to another person, provided that (a) you transfer all of the Software and documentation to the same transferee; (b) you do not retain any copies; and (c) the transferee is informed of and agrees to the terms and conditions of this Agreement.

4. Termination
This Agreement and your license to use the Software can be terminated without notice if you fail to comply with any of the provisions set forth in this Agreement. Upon termination of this Agreement, you promise to destroy all copies of the software including backup or archival copies as well as any documentation associated with the Software. All disclaimers of warranties and limitation of liability set forth in this Agreement shall survive any termination of this Agreement.

5. Limited Warranty
F+W Media, Inc. warrants that the Software will perform according to the manual and other written materials accompanying the Software for a period of 30 days from the date of receipt. F+W Media, Inc. does not accept responsibility for any malfunctioning computer hardware or any incompatibilities with existing or new computer hardware technology.

6. Customer Remedies
F+W Media, Inc.'s entire liability and your exclusive remedy shall be, at the option of F+W Media, Inc., either refund of your purchase price or repair and/or replacement of Software that does not meet this Limited Warranty. Proof of purchase shall be required. This Limited Warranty will be voided if Software failure was caused by abuse, neglect, accident, or misapplication. All replacement Software will be warranted based on the remainder of the warranty or the full 30 days, whichever is shorter and will be subject to the terms of the Agreement.

7. No Other Warranties
F+W MEDIA, INC., TO THE FULLEST EXTENT OF THE LAW, DISCLAIMS ALL OTHER WARRANTIES, OTHER THAN THE LIMITED WARRANTY IN PARAGRAPH 5, EITHER EXPRESS OR IMPLIED, ASSOCIATED WITH ITS SOFTWARE, INCLUDING BUT NOT LIMITED TO IMPLIED WARRANTIES OF MERCHANTABILITY AND FITNESS FOR A PARTICULAR PURPOSE, WITH REGARD TO THE SOFTWARE AND ITS ACCOMPANYING WRITTEN MATERIALS. THIS LIMITED WARRANTY GIVES YOU SPECIFIC LEGAL RIGHTS. DEPENDING UPON WHERE THIS SOFTWARE WAS PURCHASED, YOU MAY HAVE OTHER RIGHTS.

8. Limitations on Remedies
TO THE MAXIMUM EXTENT PERMITTED BY LAW, F+W MEDIA, INC. SHALL NOT BE HELD LIABLE FOR ANY DAMAGES WHATSOEVER, INCLUDING WITHOUT LIMITATION, ANY LOSS FROM PERSONAL INJURY, LOSS OF BUSINESS PROFITS, BUSINESS INTERRUPTION, BUSINESS INFORMATION, OR ANY OTHER PECUNIARY LOSS ARISING OUT OF THE USE OF THIS SOFTWARE. This applies even if F+W Media, Inc. has been advised of the possibility of such damages. F+W Media, Inc.'s entire liability under any provision of this agreement shall be limited to the amount actually paid by you for the Software. Because some states may not allow for this type of limitation of liability, the above limitation may not apply to you. THE WARRANTY AND REMEDIES SET FORTH ABOVE ARE EXCLUSIVE AND IN LIEU OF ALL OTHERS, ORAL OR WRITTEN, EXPRESS OR IMPLIED. No F+W Media, Inc. dealer, distributor, agent, or employee is authorized to make any modification or addition to the warranty.

9. General
This Agreement shall be governed by the laws of the United States of America and the Commonwealth of Massachusetts. If you have any questions concerning this Agreement, contact F+W Media, Inc., via Adams Media at 508-427-7100. Or write to us at: Adams Media, a division of F+W Media, Inc., 57 Littlefield Street, Avon, MA 02322.